10,000
FRENCH
WORDS

William Rowlinson

Oxford   New York
OXFORD UNIVERSITY PRESS

Oxford University Press, Great Clarendon Street, Oxford OX2 6DP

Oxford New York

Athens Auckland Bangkok Bogota Bombay
Buenos Aires Calcutta Cape Town Dar es Salaam
Delhi Florence Hong Kong Istanbul Karachi
Kuala Lumpur Madras Madrid Melbourne
Mexico City Nairobi Paris Singapore
Taipei Tokyo Toronto Warsaw
and associated companies in
Berlin Ibadan

Oxford is a trade mark of Oxford University Press

British Library Cataloguing in Publication Data
10,000 French words. (Oxford minireference).
1. French language. Usage
I. Rowlinson, William 1931–
448
ISBN 0-19-864174-5

Library of Congress Cataloging in Publication Data
Rowlinson, W.
10,000 French words/William Rowlinson.
p. cm. (Oxford minireference)
1. French language—Glossaries, vocabularies, etc. 2. French
language—Conversation and phrase books—English. 3. French
language—Vocabulary. I. Title. II. Title: Ten thousand French
words. III. Series.
448.1—dc20 PC2680.R69 1991 90-22289
ISBN 0-19-864174-5

5 7 9 10 8 6

Printed in China

CONTENTS

INTRODUCTION

This book contains more than 10,000 French words, phrases, and structures arranged by topics and functions. They are collected under fifty-six headings arranged alphabetically, and are then further split into appropriate sub-areas.

The aim has been to make the vocabulary of a topic easily accessible and to provide the most comprehensive information possible about it. So most sub-areas are themselves divided into noun, verb, adjective, and structure sections, with items arranged alphabetically within each section. For many items, closely associated words are given in round brackets immediately after the headword.

- Genders of all head-nouns are indicated by **le/la**, or by *m/f* where the noun begins with a vowel or **h** 'mute'. In noun phrases the gender of each element is also shown, by *m* or *f*; the meaning of each element of a phrase is also given where it is not obvious.
- All irregular noun plurals are given, and all plurals of hyphenated nouns.
- Feminine forms of masculine nouns (e.g. professions, occupations) are always given where they exist.
- Irregular feminine and plural forms of adjectives are shown.
- Irregular verbs are marked with an asterisk.
- Main sections end with a comprehensive set of cross-references to related topics.

ABBREVIATIONS

abb	abbreviation
adj	adjective
colloq	colloquial
f	feminine
inf	infinitive
inv	invariable
m	masculine
®	proprietary term
pl	plural
qch.	**quelque chose**
qn.	**quelqu'un**
sb.	somebody
sing	singular
sth.	something

ACKNOWLEDGEMENTS

The author would like to thank Martine Pierquin
for her help and the editorial and
production staff of Oxford University Press
for their advice and support.

1. Accidents Les Accidents

un accident . . .

    dans la maison, accident in the home
    d'avion m / **d'aviation** f, aircraft accident
    de bateau / de navigation f, accident at sea (**le bateau**
    pl **-x,** boat)
    de montagne, mountaineering accident (**la montagne,**
    mountain)
    de voiture f / **de la circulation** / **de la route,** car /
    traffic / road accident
    du travail, industrial accident (**le travail,** work)

Les accidents de la route Road accidents

le choc, impact
la collision (de face f**),** (head-on) crash
le télescopage (en série f**) / le carambolage,** pile-up

LES CAUSES REASONS

l'alcool m, alcohol (**en état d'ébriété,** under the influence of
  alcohol; **l'état** m, state; **l'ébriété** f, intoxication)
le chauffard, road-hog
la crevaison, puncture (**un pneu a éclaté,** a tyre has burst)
l'état m **de la route,** the state of the road
l'excès m **de vitesse** f, speeding
le manque de visibilité f, poor visibility
le verglas, black ice
accélérer, to speed up
brûler un feu / un stop, to go through a red light / past a
  stop sign
déraper, to skid
doubler dans un virage, to overtake on a bend
ne pas observer la priorité, not to give priority

perdre le contrôle, to lose control
*prendre / *courir des risques *m*, to take / run risks
rouler trop vite, to drive too fast

LES CONSÉQUENCES RESULTS

l'amende *f*, fine
le / la blessé(e), injured person
la blessure, injury
la brûlure, burn
le choc, shock (**en état** *m* **de choc**, in a state of shock)
la commotion, concussion
les dégâts *m* / **les dommages** *m*, damage
le / la mort(e), dead person
le retrait du permis (de conduire), loss of driving-licence
le témoin (oculaire), (eye)witness

dresser un procès-verbal contre qn., to take sb.'s particulars
écraser qn., to run over sb.
s'écraser contre qch. / heurter qch., to run into sth.
s'évanouir, to faint
exploser, to explode
*faire un tonneau, to roll over (**le tonneau** *pl* **-x**, barrel)
indemniser, to compensate
perdre connaissance *f* / **du sang**, to lose consciousness / blood
subir un alcotest, to take a breath test
tuer, to kill

coincé, trapped
démoli, demolished
détruit, destroyed
endommagé, damaged
gravement blessé, seriously injured
indemne, unscathed
mort, dead
sain et sauf, safe and sound

Les accidents en mer Accidents at sea

le canot de sauvetage, lifeboat (**le sauvetage**, rescue)
la ceinture de sauvetage, lifebelt
l'équipage *m*, crew
le gilet de sauvetage, life-jacket
le/la naufragé(e), drowned man / woman
la navigation en collision *f*, collision course
la noyade, drowning

effectuer le sauvetage de, to rescue
***entrer en collision** *f* **avec qch.**, to run into sth.
***être troué sous la ligne de flottaison**, to be holed below
  the waterline
***faire naufrage** *m*, to be shipwrecked
heurter un rocher/une mine/un iceberg, to strike a
  rock/a mine/an iceberg
se noyer, to drown
***savoir nager**, to be able to swim
sombrer, to sink

Les accidents d'avion Aircraft accidents

l'accident *m* **d'avion** *m*, plane crash
l'amerrissage *m* **forcé**, ditching
l'atterrissage *m* **en catastrophe** *f*, crash landing
l'atterrissage forcé/sans visibilité *f*, forced/blind
  landing
l'erreur *f* **du pilote**, pilot error
l'explosion *f*, explosion
la fatigue des métaux, metal fatigue (**le métal** *pl* **-aux**
  metal)
la panne de moteur *m*, engine trouble
la sortie de secours, emergency exit (**le secours**, help)
l'hôtesse *f* **de l'air**, air hostess
le trou d'air *m* air pocket

amerrir, to ditch
atterrir, to land

Les accidents domestiques
Accidents in the home

la chute, fall
la commotion électrique, electric shock
l'échelle *f* **de sauvetage,** fire-escape (**le sauvetage,** rescue)
l'explosion *f* **de gaz** *m*, gas explosion
l'incendie *m*, fire

se brûler, to burn oneself
se casser / se fouler la cheville, to break / sprain one's ankle
se couper, to cut oneself
se couper le doigt, to cut one's finger
s'ébouillanter, to scald oneself
se *faire électrocuter, to electrocute oneself
*tomber de qch., to fall off sth.

Les services de secours
Emergency services

l'aide *f* / **le secours,** help
l'ambulancier *m*, ambulance man
l'assurance *f*, insurance
le bouche-à-bouche, kiss of life (**la bouche,** mouth)
le brancard, stretcher
la dépanneuse, towing truck
l'extincteur *m*, fire-extinguisher
le médecin, doctor
le pompier, fireman (**les pompiers** *m*, fire brigade)
les premiers secours, first aid
le service de dépannage *m*, roadside repair service
l'urgence *f*, emergency

appeler police *f* **secours** to ring the police emergency
  service (**appeler le 17** = ring 999)
dresser un constat, to make a report
*faire venir une ambulance, to call an ambulance
remorquer, to tow

SEE ALSO: **Birth, Marriage, and Death; Disasters;
  Health and Sickness; The Human Body**

2. Adornment La Parure

Le maquillage Make-up

le coupe-ongles *pl inv*, nail clippers
le crayon à sourcils *m*, eyebrow pencil (**le crayon à paupières**, eye-liner; **la paupière**, eyelid)
la crème de beauté *f*, face-cream
la crème hydratante, moisturizer
le démaquillant, make-up remover
le dissolvant, nail-varnish remover
le fard à paupières/l'ombre *f* **à paupières**, eye-shadow (**la paupière**, eyelid)
le fond de teint, foundation cream (**le teint**, complexion)
la houppette, powder-puff
la lime à ongles, nail-file (**l'ongle** *m*, nail)
le maquillage/le fard, make-up
le mascara/le rimmel, mascara
le miroir/la glace, mirror
le mouchoir en papier *m*/**le kleenex** ⑬, tissue (**le mouchoir**, handkerchief)
la pince à épiler, tweezers
la poudre, powder
le poudrier, compact
les produits *m* **de beauté** *f*, cosmetics
le rouge à joues, blusher
le rouge à lèvres, lipstick (**la lèvre**, lip)
le talc, talcum powder
le vernis à ongles *m pl*, nail varnish

se démaquiller, to take off one's make-up
se maquiller/se *faire une beauté, to put on one's make-up
*mettre (du rouge à lèvres etc.), to put on (lipstick etc.)
se vernir les ongles, to paint one's nails

La bijouterie Jewellery

l'alliance *f*, wedding ring
la bague, ring
les bijoux de fantaisie *f*/ **de pacotille**, costume jewellery
  (**le bijou** *pl* **-x**, jewel; **la pacotille**, gimcrack goods)
la boucle d'oreille *f*, ear-ring
les boutons *m* **de manchette** *f*, cuff-links
le bracelet (à breloques *f pl***)**, (charm) bracelet
la broche, brooch
la chaîne / **le collier**, necklace
la chaînette, chain
la chevalière, signet-ring
le clip, ear-clip
le coffret à bijoux, jewel box (**le bijou** *pl* **-x**, jewel)
la couronne, crown
la croix, cross
le diadème, tiara
l'épingle *f* **de cravate** *f*, tie-pin
la gourmette, chain bracelet
la montre (à quartz *m* / **digitale)**, (quartz / digital) watch
le pendant / **le pendantif**, pendant
le pendant d'oreille *f*, drop ear-ring
la pince à cravate *f*, tie-clip

Les pierres précieuses et les métaux
Jewels and metals

l'ambre *m* **jaune**, amber (**jaune**, yellow)
l'améthyste *f*, amethyst
l'argent *m*, silver (**en argent**, silver *adj*; **argenté** / **plaqué argent**, silver-plated)
le chrome, chromium (**chromé**, chrome-plated)
le corail, coral
le crystal (taillé), (cut) cristal
le cuivre, copper
le diamant / **le brillant**, diamond
l'émail *m*, enamel (*pl* **-s**; *alternative pl* **émaux** = *enamelled goods*)

l'émeraude *f*, emerald
l'étain *m*, pewter
le faux brillant, imitation diamond / paste
l'inox *m*, stainless steel
l'ivoire *m*, ivory
le jade, jade
l'onyx *m*, onyx
l'or *m*, gold (en or, gold *adj*; doré, gilt; plaqué or, gold-
  plated)
la perle, pearl
la pierre précieuse, precious stone (précieux *f* -euse,
  precious)
le platine, platinum
le rubis, ruby
le saphir, sapphire
la topaze, topaz
la turquoise, turquoise

Le parfum Perfume

l'atomiseur *m*, atomizer; spray
le déodorant, deodorant
l'eau *f* de Cologne, cologne
l'eau *f*; *pl* -x de toilette *f*, toilet water
le parfum, perfume
les sels *m* de bain *m*, bath salts

se parfumer / *mettre du parfum, to put on perfume
*sentir bon / mauvais, to smell nice / unpleasant

SEE ALSO: **Clothing; Describing People; Hair; The Human
Body**

3. **Animals** Les Animaux

Les mammifères Mammals

l'âne *m* **/ l'ânesse** *f*, donkey
l'antilope *f*, antelope
la baleine, whale
la belette, weasel
le bélier / la brebis, ram / ewe
le bétail *sing*, cattle
le blaireau *pl* **-x**, badger
le bœuf, ox
le buffle, buffalo
le caniche, poodle
le castor, beaver
le cerf / la biche, stag / doe
le chameau *pl* **-x / la chamelle**, camel
le chamois, chamois
le chat / la chatte, cat (**le chaton**, kitten)
la chauve-souris *pl* **-s-**, bat
le cheval *pl* **-aux / la jument**, horse / mare (**le poulain**, colt / foal)
la chèvre / le bouc, goat / billy-goat (**le chevreau** *pl* **-x**, kid)
le chien / la chienne, dog / bitch (**le chiot**, puppy; **le bâtard**, mongrel)
le cochon / la truie, pig / sow
le cochon d'Inde / le cobaye, guinea-pig (**l'Inde** *f*, India)
le dauphin, dolphin
le dromadaire, dromedary
l'écureuil *m*, squirrel
l'éléphant *m*, elephant
la fouine, polecat
le furet, ferret
la gazelle, gazelle
la girafe, giraffe
le hamster, hamster
le hérisson, hedgehog

l'hippopotame *m*, hippopotamus
l'hyène *f*, hyena
le lapin, rabbit
le léopard, leopard
le lévrier, greyhound
le lièvre, hare
le lion / la lionne, lion / lioness (**le lionceau** *pl* **-x**, lion cub)
le loir, dormouse
le loup / la louve, wolf / she-wolf
la loutre, otter
le lynx, lynx
le marsouin, porpoise
le mouton, sheep (**l'agneau** *m*; *pl* **-x**, lamb)
le mulet / la mule, mule / she-mule
le mulot, field-mouse
l'ours *m* (**blanc**), (polar) bear (**blanc** *f* **-nche**, white)
la panthère, panther
le phoque, seal
le poney, pony
le porc-épic *pl* **-s -s**, porcupine
le rat, rat
le renard / la renarde, fox / vixen
le renne, reindeer
le rhinocéros, rhinoceros
le sanglier, wild boar
le singe, monkey
la souris, mouse
la taupe, mole
le tigre / la tigresse, tiger / tigress
la vache / le taureau *pl* **-x**, cow / bull (**le veau** *pl* **-x**, calf)
le zèbre, zebra

Les oiseaux Birds

l'aigle *m*, eagle (**l'aiglon** *m*, eaglet)
l'alouette *f*, lark
l'autruche *f*, ostrich
la bécasse, woodcock

la bécassine, snipe
le bouvreuil, bullfinch
la buse, buzzard
le cacatoès, cockatoo
la caille, quail
le canard, duck / drake (**la cane**, duck [to differentiate from *drake*]; **le caneton**, duckling)
le canari / le serin, canary
le chardonneret, goldfinch
la colombe, dove
la chouette, barn-owl
la cigogne, stork
le coq de bruyère, grouse (**la bruyère**, heath / heather)
le corbeau *pl* **-x**, crow
le cormoran, cormorant
la corneille, rook
le coucou, cuckoo
le cygne, swan
le dindon / la dinde, turkey
l'épervier *m*, hawk
le faisan / la (poule) faisane, cock / hen pheasant
le faucon, falcon
le flamant (rose), flamingo
la grive, thrush
le héron, heron
le hibou *pl* **-x**, owl
l'hirondelle *f*, swallow
l'ibis *m*, ibis
le martinet, swift
le martin-pêcheur *pl* **-s -s**, kingfisher
le merle, blackbird
la mésange, tit
le moineau *pl* **-x**, sparrow
la mouette, seagull
l'oie *f* / **le jars**, goose / gander
l'oiseau *m*; *pl* **-x (de proie** *f*)**, bird (of prey)
le paon / la paonne, peacock / peahen
le pélican, pelican
la perdrix, partridge

le **perroquet**, parrot
la **perruche**, hen parrot / parakeet / budgerigar
la **pie**, magpie
le **pigeon (voyageur)**, (homing) pigeon
le **pingouin**, auk (le **manchot**, penguin)
le **pinson**, chaffinch
la **pintade**, guinea-fowl
la **poule** / le **coq**, hen / cock
la **poule d'eau**, moorhen (l'**eau** *f*; *pl* **-x**, water)
le **poulet**, chicken
le **poussin**, chick
le **puffin**, puffin
le **ramier**, wood-pigeon
le **rossignol**, nightingale
le **rouge-gorge** *pl* **-s -s**, robin
le **sansonnet**, starling
la **tourterelle**, (turtle-)dove
le **vanneau** *pl* **-x**, lapwing
le **vautour**, vulture

Les poissons et les mollusques
Fish and molluscs

le **cheval** (*pl* **-aux**) **marin**, sea-horse
la **méduse**, jellyfish
l'**oursin** *m*, sea-urchin
la **pieuvre**, octopus
le **poisson rouge**, goldfish
le **requin**, shark

FOR EDIBLE FISH SEE **Food**

Les insectes Insects

l'**abeille** *f*, bee
l'**araignée** *f*, spider
le **bourdon**, bumble-bee

le **cafard,** cockroach
la **chenille,** caterpillar (la **chrysalide,** chrysalis; le **papillon,**
  butterfly; le **papillon de nuit,** moth; la **nuit,** night)
la **cigale,** cicada
la **coccinelle,** ladybird
le **cousin,** gnat
la **fourmi,** ant
le **frelon,** hornet
le **grillon,** cricket
la **guêpe,** wasp
le **hanneton,** cockchafer
la **larve,** grub
la **libellule,** dragonfly
la **mouche,** fly
la **mouche bleue,** bluebottle
le **moustique,** mosquito
le **pou** *pl* **-x,** louse
la **puce,** flea
la **punaise,** bug
la **sauterelle,** grasshopper
la **sauterelle d'Afrique** *f,* locust
le **scarabée,** beetle
le **taon,** horse-fly

Les reptiles, les amphibiens, et les vers
Reptiles, amphibians, and worms

l'**alligator** *m,* alligator
le **boa,** boa
le **cobra,** cobra
la **couleuvre,** grass snake
le **crapaud,** toad
le **crocodile,** crocodile
la **grenouille,** frog
le **lézard,** lizard
la **sangsue,** leech
le **serpent (à sonnettes),** (rattle)snake (la **sonnette,** bell /
  rattle)

la tortue, tortoise (**la tortue de mer,** turtle; **la mer,** sea)
le ver (de terre *f*)**,** (earth)worm (**le ver à soie** *f*, silkworm;
  le ver luisant, glow-worm)
la vipère, adder / viper

Les marsupiaux Marsupials

le kangourou, kangaroo
le koala, koala bear
le marsupial *pl* **-aux,** marsupial *also adj*

Leurs corps Their bodies

l'aile *f*, wing
les bois *m* **/ la ramure,** antlers
la bosse, hump
la bouche, mouth [of cow, horse, sheep]
le bec, beak
la carapace, shell
la corne, horn
la crinière, mane
la défense, tusk
l'écaille *f*, scale
la fourrure, fur
la griffe, claw
la gueule, mouth
le museau *pl* **-x,** snout / muzzle
la nageoire, fin
la patte, paw
le piquant, quill / bristle
la plume, feather
la poche, pouch
le poil, hair
la queue, tail
la rayure, stripe
la robe, coat
le sabot, hoof
les serres *f*, talons

la tache, spot
la toison, fleece
la trompe, trunk

Leurs cris Their calls

aboyer, to bark
barrir, to trumpet
bêler, to bleat
beugler, to bellow
bourdonner, to buzz
***braire,** to bray
cancaner, to quack
caqueter, to cackle
chanter, to sing / crow
croasser, to caw / croak
gazouiller, to twitter
glouglouter, to gobble
glousser, to cluck
grogner, to grunt / growl
hennir, to neigh
hurler, to howl
jacasser, to chatter
meugler / mugir, to moo
miauler, to mew
pépier, to chirp
ronronner, to purr
roucouler, to coo
rugir, to roar
siffler, to hiss
ululer, to hoot

Ce qu'ils font, ce qu'on leur fait faire
What they do, what we make them do

la chasse au cerf / au renard, stag / fox hunting
le chien d'aveugle *m / f,* guide-dog
le chien de garde *f,* guard dog

la course de taureaux / de chevaux, bullfight / horse-race
  (**le taureau** *pl* **-x**, bull; **le cheval** *pl* **-aux**, horse)
l'équitation *f*, horse-riding
le fer à cheval, horseshoe
la piqûre, sting
la promenade à cheval *m*, (horse-)ride
les rênes *f*, reins
la selle, saddle
la toile d'araignée *f*, spider's web
une vie de chien *m*, a dog's life

agiter / remuer la queue, to wag its tail
*aller à dos de . . ., to ride on a . . . (**le dos**, back)
butiner, to gather honey
donner la patte, to put out a paw
dresser les oreilles *f*, to prick up one's ears
essaimer, to swarm
*faire le beau, to sit up and beg (**le beau** *pl* **-x**, dandy /
  swaggerer)
*faire le gros dos, to arch one's back (**gros**, big)
*monter à cheval / *faire du cheval, to go riding (**le cheval**
  pl **-x**, horse)
montrer / *sortir / rentrer les griffes, to show / put out /
  draw in one's claws
muer, to cast one's skin
nager, to swim
piquer, to sting
planer, to soar / hover
pondre des œufs *m*, to lay eggs
ramper, to crawl
tondre, to shear
se tortiller, to wriggle
*traire, to milk
se transformer en, to change into
voler, to fly
voleter, to flutter

bas les pattes!, down! (**la patte**, paw)
chien méchant!, beware of the dog! (**méchant**, bad)

SEE ALSO: **Food; Nature**

4. Arguing For and Against
Les Arguments pour et contre

Les arguments pour Arguing for

. . . a fait de grands progrès, . . . has made great strides
à l'heure actuelle, at this moment in time
à première vue, at first sight
à titre d'exemple *m*, to quote an example
c'est pareil avec, it's just the same with
c'est tellement plus facile de, it's so much easier to
c'est une question de, it's a question of
ce qui est sûr, c'est que . . ., what's certain is that . . .
ce qui frappe, c'est . . ., what strikes one is . . .
cela est dû surtout à, that is due above all to
comme beaucoup d'autres choses *f* **du reste,** like many other things, incidentally
d'abord et avant tout, first and foremost
d'après les sondages *m*, according to the polls
d'autant plus que, all the more so because
de mon côté, as for me
en ce cas-là, in that case
en ce qui concerne . . ., as far as . . . is concerned
en conséquence *f*, as a result
en plus, c'est un grand avantage de, moreover, it's a great help to
en premier lieu/tout d'abord, in the first place
. . . est à la fois . . . et . . ., . . . is both . . . and . . .
. . . est nettement supérieur à, . . . is clearly superior to
et pour cause *f*, and with good reason
il faut compter aussi avec . . ., you must also take . . . into account
il ne faut pas oublier que, it must not be forgotten that
il s'agit de, it's a question of
il y va de, it concerns
je ne pourrais pas m'en passer, I couldn't do without it
le fait est que, the fact is that

on distingue des différences importantes entre,
   important differences can be seen between

on ferait beaucoup mieux de, one would do much better to

pour ainsi dire, so to speak

pour ma part, as far as I'm concerned

pour répondre aux besoins *m* **de,** in order to respond to
   the needs of

qui peut douter que (+ SUBJUNCTIVE), who can doubt that

sans parler de . . ., not to mention . . .

si besoin *m* **est,** if necessary

sur le plan . . ., as far as . . . is concerned

tout cela est la conséquence de, all that is a result of

tout dépend de, it all depends on

tout prêt à concéder que, quite ready to concede that

tout un chacun, each and every one

. . . va de mieux en mieux, . . . gets better and better

vous savez parfaitement que, you know perfectly well that

Les arguments contre   Arguing against

autant dire que . . ., that's as good as saying that . . .

avoir tort, be wrong

bien entendu, mais . . ., certainly, but . . .

ce sont les aspects négatifs, those are the negative points

ça, c'est quand même autre chose, that's something
   else again

cela a l'air d'être . . ., mais . . ., that appears to be . . .,
   but . . .

cela dépend de toutes sortes d'autres choses, that
   depends on all sorts of other things

cela dit, that said

cela n'a aucun rapport avec / cela n'a rien à voir avec,
   that has nothing to do with

cela ne sera certainement pas suffisant, that certainly
   won't be enough

cela ne sert pas à grand-chose, that's not very useful

cela ne veut pas dire que, that doesn't mean that

ce n'est pas ça, that's not it

ce qu'il y a de plus extraordinaire encore, c'est que . . .,
what's even more extraordinary is that . . .

certes, . . ., mais, it's true that . . ., but

c'est totalement faux, it's absolutely wrong

c'est plutôt le contraire, it's rather the reverse

d'autre part, on the other hand

en dépit du bon sens, with no regard for common sense

en fin de liste *f*, at the bottom of the list

en réalité *f*, in reality

en revanche *f*, on the other hand

étant donné que, given that

il faut également préciser que, equally it must be said
that

il ne reste qu'à . . ., the only thing left to do is to . . .

il paraît difficile de croire que, it seems difficult to
believe that

je me demande si, I wonder if

même dans ce cas, je ne pourrais pas me passer de . . .,
even so I couldn't do without . . .

je ne suis pas tout à fait d'accord, I'm not entirely in
agreement

je trouve que c'est un peu dommage, parce que, I
think it's rather a pity, because

la pire des solutions, the worst possible solution

le plus gros problème n'est pas là, that's not where the
greatest problem lies

loin de là, far from it

nous devons faire autre chose, we should do something
else

. . . n'y est pour rien, . . . is not a factor in this

on a trop tendance *f* **à penser que**, we tend too much to
think that

on ferait mieux de, we would do better to

on ne se contente pas de, we're not satisfied to

pas question *f* **de**, there's no question of

pas tant que cela, not as much as all that

sans compter . . ., not counting . . .

tout de même, all the same

Tirer une conclusion Drawing a conclusion

à condition *f* que, on condition that

alors (que), **par contre**, whereas on the other hand

à mi-chemin entre . . . et . . ., half-way between . . . and . . .

à une exception près, with one exception

bref, in short

ça ne pose pas de problèmes *m*, that doesn't present any problems

ce qui est clair c'est . . ., what's clear is . . .

c'est ainsi que . . ., that's why . . .

comment faire?, what is to be done?

dans la mesure où, to the extent that

démentir l'accusation *f* d'avoir . . ., refute the charge of having . . .

de toute façon, at all events

. . . d'un côté, . . . de l'autre, . . . on the one hand, . . . on the other

d'une manière générale, in general terms

en fin de compte, in the end

en somme *f*, to sum up

en tout cas, at all events

en un mot, in a word

et tout cela grâce à, and all that thanks to

faute de mieux, for want of something better

il faut faire en sorte que, we should arrange it so that

il faut le faire, soit avec . . ., soit à l'aide de . . ., it has to be done, either with . . ., or with the help of . . .

je terminerai en citant . . ., I will end by quoting . . .

moins à cause de . . . qu'à cause de . . ., more because of . . . than . . .

sans plus de façons *f*, without more ado

si c'est . . . ou si ça ne l'est pas, whether it's . . . or whether it isn't

surtout que, above all because

une fois pour toutes, once and for all

SEE ALSO: **Liking, Disliking, Comparing**

5. Art and Architecture
L'Art et l'architecture

Les beaux-arts Fine arts

l'**aquarelle**, water-colour [painting] (**les couleurs** f **à l'eau** f, water-colours [paints])

l'**argile** f, clay

l'**art** m, art (**les arts décoratifs**, decorative arts; **les beaux-arts**, fine arts; l'**œuvre** f **d'art**, work of art)

l'**artiste** m/f (**peintre**), artist

l'**atelier** m, studio

le **buste**, bust

le **cadre**, frame

la **caricature**, caricature

le **catalogue**, catalogue

le **chevalet**, easel

le **ciseau** pl **-x**, chisel

la **collection**, collection

la **couleur**, colour / paint (**les couleurs à l'huile** f, oils)

le **dessin**, drawing

l'**esquisse** f, sketch

l'**exposition** f, exhibition

la **fresque**, fresco

le **fusain**, charcoal

la **gravure**, engraving

l'**image** f, picture

la **miniature**, miniature

le **modèle**, model

la **mosaïque**, mosaic

le **moulage**, cast

le **musée**, museum / gallery (**le musée d'art** / **la galerie d'art**, art gallery)

la **nature morte**, still-life

la **palette**, palette

le **pastel**, pastel [drawing]

le **paysage**, landscape

le paysagiste, landscape artist
le peintre, painter
la peinture, painting / paint
le pinceau *pl* **-x**, brush
la plinthe, plinth
le portrait, portrait
la poterie, pottery
le sculpteur, sculptor
la sculpture, sculpture (**la sculpture sur bois** *m*, wood carving)
la statue, statue
le tableau *pl* **-x**, painting
la tapisserie, tapestry
le vernis, varnish
le vitrail *pl* **-aux**, stained-glass window

créer, to create
dessiner (d'après nature *f*), to draw (from life)
esquisser, to sketch
façonner, to shape
*faire du / de la . . ., to do . . .
graver, to engrave
mouler, to mould
*peindre (à l'huile *f* **/ à l'aquarelle** *f*), to paint (in oils / in water-colour)
poser (pour), to pose / sit (for)
tailler / sculpter (dans), to carve (from)

L'architecture Architecture

l'arc *m*, arch (**une arche**, arch [of bridge])
l'architecte *m*, architect
le bâtiment, building
la cathédrale, cathedral
la céramique, ceramics
le chapiteau *pl* **-x**, capital
la colonne, column
le contrefort, buttress
la coupole, cupola

la décoration, decoration
le dôme, dome
le portique, portico
le style roman / gothique / baroque / classique,
  romanesque / gothic / baroque / classical style
la voûte, vault

bâtir / *construire, to build

SEE ALSO: **Cinema and Photography; Colours; Materials**

6. Birth, Marriage, and Death
La Naissance, le mariage, et la mort

La naissance Birth

l'accouchement *m*, childbirth
les aliments *m* **pour bébé** *m*, baby food
l'anniversaire *m*, birthday (**célébrer / fêter son anniversaire**, to celebrate one's birthday)
le / la baby-sitter, baby-sitter (***faire du baby-sitting**, to baby-sit)
le baptême, christening
le bébé (de deux jours / de cinq mois), (two-day-old / five-month-old) baby
le biberon, feeding bottle
la chaise de bébé *m*, high chair
la conception, conception
la couche (à jeter), (disposable) nappy
la date de naissance *f*, date of birth
le / la filleul(e), godson / god-daughter
le fœtus, foetus
la mère, mother
la naissance, birth
le parrain / la marraine, godfather / godmother
le père, father
la poussette, pushchair
la voiture d'enfant *m / f*, pram

accoucher (de), to give birth (to)
changer, to change
*faire manger, to feed
*naître, to be born
sevrer, to wean
téter, to suckle

Le mariage Marriage

l'alliance *f*, wedding-ring
l'anniversaire *m* / **le cadeau** *pl* **-x de mariage** *m*,
  wedding anniversary / present
la bague de fiançailles *f*, engagement ring
le / la célibataire, single man / woman
les confettis *m*, confetti
le contrat / l'acte *m* **de mariage**, marriage
  contract / certificate
le couple, couple
la demande en mariage, proposal
la demoiselle d'honneur *m*, bridesmaid
le divorce, divorce
la dot, dowry
l'époux *m*; *f* **-ouse**, spouse / husband / wife
l'état *m* **civil**, marital status
l'ex-femme *f* / **l'ex-mari** *m* (*both pls* **- -s**), ex-wife /
  ex-husband
le faire-part *pl inv* **de mariage**, wedding invitation
la femme, wife
les fiançailles *f*, engagement
le / la fiancé(e), fiancé(e)
le vieux garçon, confirmed bachelor
le garçon d'honneur *m*, best man
les jeunes mariés / les nouveaux mariés *m pl*, newly-weds
le jour du mariage, wedding-day
la lune de miel, honeymoon (**le miel**, honey)
le mari, husband
le mariage civil / religieux, registry-office / church wedding
le mariage d'amour *m* / **de convenance** *f*, love-match /
  marriage of convenience
le / la marié(e), groom / bride
la noce [often used in plural: **les noces**], wedding
les noces d'argent *m* / **de vermeil** / **d'or** *m* / **de diamant**
  m, silver / ruby / golden / diamond wedding (**le vermeil**,
  silver-gilt)
la nuit de noces *f*, wedding-night
le / la petit(e) ami(e), boy-friend / girl-friend
la séparation, separation

le témoin, witness
la vieille fille, spinster
le voyage de noces *f*, honeymoon trip

demander qn. en mariage / *offrir le mariage à qn.,
  to propose (**accepter / refuser**, to accept / refuse)
divorcer, to get divorced (**divorcer d'avec qn.**, to
  divorce sb.; **elle *veut divorcer**, she wants a divorce)
épouser, to marry (**elle l'a épousé en secondes noces**,
  he was her second husband)
féliciter (de), to congratulate (on)
se fiancer (à / avec), to become engaged (to)
marier [of priest], to marry / join in wedlock
se marier avec qn., to marry sb.
rompre les fiançailles *f*, to break off the engagement
se séparer, to separate

célibataire, single
divorcé, divorced
fiancé, engaged
marié, married
séparé, separated

La mort Death

l'acte *m* **de décès** *m*, death certificate
le cadavre, corpse
les cendres *f*, ashes
le cercueil, coffin
le cimetière, cemetery / churchyard
le corbillard, hearse
le cortège, procession
la couronne (mortuaire), wreath
le crématorium, crematorium
le / la décédé(e) / le / la défunt(e), the deceased
les droits *m* **de succession** *f*, death duties
l'entrepreneur *m* **de pompes** *f* **funèbres**, undertaker
l'épitaphe *f*, epitaph
le fossoyeur, grave-digger

les funérailles *f*, funeral
l'héritage *m*, inheritance
l'héritier *m*; *f* **-ière (de)**, heir / heiress (to)
le legs, bequest (***faire un legs**, make a bequest / leave a legacy)
le linceul, shroud
le lit de mort *f*, deathbed
la mort / le décès, death
le / la mort(e), dead man / woman
l'orphelin *m*; *f* **-e**, orphan
la succession, estate
le testament, will
la tombe, grave
le tombeau *pl* **-x**, tomb (**la pierre tombale**, tombstone)
l'urne *f*, urn
le veuf / la veuve, widower / widow

déshériter, to disinherit
(s')empoisonner, to poison (oneself)
enterrer / ensevelir, to bury
*être en deuil *m*, to be in mourning
*être sur le point de mourir, to be about to die
hériter (de), to inherit (from)
incinérer, to cremate
laisser, to leave [in will]
léguer, to bequeath
*mourir (de mort naturelle / violente), to die (a natural / violent death)
se noyer, to drown
(se) pendre, to hang (oneself)
périr, to perish
*rester veuve, to be left a widow
se suicider, to commit suicide
tuer, to kill

SEE ALSO: **Accidents; Disasters; Health and Sickness; Identity; Relationships; War, Peace, and the Armed Services**

7. Cinema and Photography
Le Cinéma et la photographie

Le cinéma Cinema

l'acteur *m* / l'actrice *f* de cinéma *m*, film actor / actress
le balcon, circle
la caisse, box-office
la caméra, cine camera
la caméra vidéo, video camera / camcorder
le cinéaste, film-maker
le court métrage, short (**le métrage**, footage)
le dessin animé, cartoon
l'écran *m*, screen
l'entracte *m*, interval
le film documentaire / historique / d'épouvante *f* / de
science-fiction *f*, documentary / historical / horror /
science-fiction film
le film en couleurs *f* / en noir *m* et blanc *m* / muet, colour /
black and white / silent film
le film policier, thriller
le film sous-titré / en VO, subtitled / original-language film
(**VO = version originelle**, original version)
le film synchronisé / en VF, film dubbed into French (**VF
= version française**)
le long métrage, feature film (**le métrage**, footage)
le metteur en scène, *f*, director
l'ouvreuse *f*, usherette
le parterre, stalls
la place, seat
le programme, programme
le projecteur, projector
la publicité, adverts
le ralenti, slow-motion
la salle (de cinéma), cinema [the building]
le scénario, script / screenplay
la séance, performance / showing

le spectacle permanent, continuous performance
les spectateurs *m*, audience
le ticket, ticket
la vedette *always f*, star
la vidéocassette, video cassette
le western, western

*aller voir, to go and see
durer, to last
filmer, to film
jouer, to be showing
réserver / louer, to book
tourner un film, to make a film

La photographie Photography

l'agrandissement *m*, enlargement
l'album *m*, album
l'ampoule flash *f* / **le cube flash**, flash-bulb / -cube
l'appareil *m* (-photo) *pl* **-s -s**, camera
la bobine, roll film
le cadre, frame
le capuchon, lens cap
la cellule (photoélectrique) / le posemètre, light / exposure
  metre
la chambre noire, dark-room
le chargeur, film cartridge / cassette
le compte-poses *pl inv*, exposure counter
le développement, developing
la diapositive, slide / transparency
l'épreuve *f* / **la copie**, print
l'étui *m* **à appareil** *m*, camera case
l'exposition *f*, exposure [time]
le film (ultra-rapide), (high-speed / fast) film
le filtre, filter
le flash, flash
l'instantané *m*, snapshot
le levier d'avancement *m* / **l'enrouleur** *m*, film-wind
le négatif / le cliché, negative

l'objectif *m* **(grand-angulaire)**, (wide-angle) lens
l'obturateur *m*, shutter
sur papier mat / brillant, matt / glossy
la pellicule / le rouleau *pl* **-x**, roll film
le photographe, photographer
la photo(graphie), photo(graph)
la photo en couleurs *f* **/ en noir** *m* **et blanc** *m* **/ d'identité** *f*,
  colour / black and white / passport photo
le pied, tripod
la pile, battery
la pose, exposure / shot
la sous-exposition, under-exposure
le télémètre, range-finder
le téléobjectif, telephoto lens
le viseur, viewfinder

agrandir, to enlarge
bloquer, to jam
charger l'appareil *m*, to load the camera
développer, to develop
encadrer, to frame
exposer, to expose
*faire / *prendre une photo / un cliché, to take a photo
*mettre au point, to focus
retoucher, to retouch
tirer, to print

automatique, automatic
flou, hazy / out of focus

SEE ALSO: **Art and Architecture; Leisure and Hobbies; The Media; Theatre**

8. Clothing Les Vêtements

Ce qu'on porte sur la tête
What you wear on your head

le béret, beret
le bonnet, bonnet
le bonnet de bain *m* / **de ski** *m*, bathing / ski cap
la casquette, cap
le chapeau *pl* -x (**melon** *m* / **de paille** *f* / **de soleil** *m* / **à larges bords** *m*), (bowler / straw / sun / broad-brimmed) hat
le foulard, headscarf
le képi, [French military] cap
le voile, veil

. . . aux pieds . . . on your feet

le bas, stocking
les baskets *f*, training shoes
la botte (en caoutchouc) / **la bottine**, (Wellington) boot (**le caoutchouc**, rubber)
la chaussette, sock
la chaussure / **le soulier (en toile** *f* / **de marche** *f*), (canvas / walking) shoe
les chaussures *f* **de ski** *m*, ski boots
le collant, tights
l'espadrille *f*, beach shoe / espadrille
la jambière, leg-warmer
le mocassin, moccasin
la pantoufle / **le chausson**, slipper
le sabot, clog
la sandale, sandal
les tennis *f*, tennis shoes

. . . sur le corps . . . on your body

l'anorak *m*, anorak
le bikini, bikini
le bleu de travail, overalls
le blouson, blouson / bomber jacket
le (blue-)jean, (pair of) jeans
les bretelles *f*, braces
le cache-col / cache-cou *both pls* -s -s, [man's] scarf / muffler
le caleçon *sing*, (under)pants
la canne, cane / walking-stick
le cardigan, cardigan
le châle, shawl
le chandail, heavy jumper
la chemise (de sport *m*), (sports) shirt
la chemise de nuit *f*, nightdress / nightshirt
le chemisier, blouse
le col-roulé *pl inv*, polo-neck sweater
la combinaison, underskirt
le complet (veston), [man's] (lounge) suit (**le veston**, jacket)
la confection, ready-made dress / ready-made clothes
le costume (sur mesure *f* / **de bain** *m*), (made-to-measure / bathing) suit
le costume national *pl* -aux, national dress
la cravate, tie
la culotte courte; le short, [child's] shorts
les dessous *m*, [women's] underwear
l'écharpe *f*, scarf
l'ensemble *m* (**pantalon** *m*), (trouser-)suit
l'étole *f*, stole
le gant, glove
le gilet, waistcoat
le gilet de corps / le maillot de corps, vest (**le corps**, body)
l'habit *m* (**de soirée**), (tail)coat (**la soirée**, evening)
l'imper(méable) *m*, mac / raincoat
la jaquette, [woman's] jacket / [man's] morning-coat
la jarretelle, suspender

la jupe, skirt (**la mini-jupe** *pl* **- -s**, mini-skirt)
la jupe-culotte *pl* **-s -s**, culottes
le jupon, petticoat
le linge, underwear / linen
la lingerie, lingerie
le maillot de bain *m*, swim-suit / trunks
le manchon, muff
le manteau *pl* **-x (de fourrure** *f*), (fur) coat
le mouchoir, handkerchief
la moufle, mitten
le nœud papillon, bow-tie
l'ombrelle *f*, parasol
une paire de . . ., a pair of . . .
le pantalon, (pair of) trousers
le pantalon de ski *m*, ski pants
le parapluie, umbrella
le pardessus, overcoat
le peignoir (de bain *m*), dressing-gown (bathrobe)
le porte-jarretelles *pl inv*, suspender belt
le pull(-over) *pl* **les pulls / les pull-overs (à col** *m* **rond / à
   col en V)**, (round necked / V-necked) pullover / sweater
le pyjama, pyjamas
la redingote, frock-coat
la robe (du soir / montante / décolletée / de mariée),
   (evening / high-necked / low-necked / wedding) dress (**la
   mariée**, bride)
la robe de chambre *f*, dressing-gown
le sac à main *f* **/ à bandoulière**, handbag / shoulder-bag
   (**la bandoulière**, shoulder-strap)
la salopette, dungarees / overalls
le short, shorts
le slip, (under)pants / swimming-trunks
le smoking, dinner-jacket
le sous-vêtement *pl* **- -s**, (article of) underwear
le soutien-gorge *pl* **-s -**, bra
le sweatshirt, sweatshirt
le tablier, apron
le tailleur, [woman's] tailored suit
la tenue de soirée *f*, evening dress

le training / le survêtement, tracksuit
le tricot, jumper / vest
le T-shirt / le teeshirt, T-shirt
l'uniforme *m,* uniform
la veste (de sport *m),* [man's or woman's] (sports) jacket
le veston, [man's] jacket

Les parties d'un vêtement
Parts of a piece of clothing

la boucle, buckle
le bouton, button
la boutonnière, buttonhole
le bouton pression *f* **/ de col** *m* **/ de manchette** *f,* press-stud / collar stud / cuff-link
la ceinture, belt
le col, collar
la couture, seam
le crochet, hook
la doublure, lining
la fermeture éclair, zip (**l'éclair** *m,* flash of lightning)
la garniture, trimming
le lacet, shoe-lace
la manche, sleeve
la manchette, cuff
l'ourlet *m* **/ le bord,** hem
le pli, pleat
la poche, pocket
le revers, lapel; turn-up
le ruban, ribbon
la semelle (de cuir *m* **/ de caoutchouc** *m* **/ de crêpe** *m* **/ compensée),** (leather / rubber / crepe / platform) sole
le talon (aiguille / plat / haut), (stiletto / low / high) heel (**l'aiguille** *f,* needle)
la voilette, hat-veil

Comment sont les vêtements
What clothes are like

à carreaux / quadrillé, check (**le carreau** *pl* **-x**, square)
à fleurs *f*, flowered
à la mode, fashionable
à manches courtes / longues, short- / long-sleeved
à pois, spotted (**le pois**, pea)
ample, loose-fitting
assorti, matching
bouffant, bouffant / puffed
brodé, embroidered
chic *sing inv; pl* **-s**, smart
chiffonné, crumpled
collant, close-fitting
criard, flashy
croisé, double-breasted
de bon / mauvais goût, in good / bad taste
déchiré, torn
décontracté, casual
démodé, old-fashioned
dernier cri *inv*, in
droit, single-breasted
en haillons *m*, in rags
en prêt-à-porter *m*, off the peg
étroit, tight-fitting
grand teint *m*, colour-fast
imprimé, printed
habillé, formal
moulant, figure-hugging
négligé, sloppy
neuf *f* **neuve**, brand new
pimpant, trim
plissé, pleated
raide, stiff
râpé, threadbare
rayé / à rayures *f*, striped
rêche, rough

sans repassage *m*, non-iron
sobre, sober
souple, soft
trop juste, too tight
uni, plain
usé, worn out
voyant / criard, loud

Ce que vous en pensez, ce que vous en faites
What you think about them, what you do with them

*aller à qn., to suit sb.
attacher, to fasten
boutonner, to button (up)
se changer, to get changed
*coudre qch., to sew sth. (on)
déboutonner, to unbutton
déchirer, to tear
*défaire, to undo
dénouer, to untie
se déshabiller, to undress
détacher, to unfasten
essayer, to try on
*être (très) bien ajusté, to fit
*faire faire, to have made
se froisser, to get creased
garnir de, to trim with
s'habiller (de), to dress (in)
laver (à la main / à la machine), to (hand- / machine-)wash
*mettre, to put on
nettoyer, to clean
nouer, to tie
ôter / enlever, to take off
passer / enfiler, to slip on / into
porter, to wear
raccommoder, to mend

raccourcir, to shorten
rallonger, to lengthen
rapiécer, to patch
réparer, to repair
repasser (à la vapeur), to (steam-)iron
repriser, to darn
ressemeler, to (re)sole
retoucher, to alter
rétrécir, to shrink
se rhabiller, to get dressed again
tricoter / *faire du tricot, to knit
user (complètement), to wear out

Les étoffes Materials

la robe en (coton etc.), (cotton etc.) dress
l'acrylique *m*, acrylic
la batiste, cambric
le cachemire, cashmere
le caoutchouc, rubber
le chamois, suede [of jacket]
le coton, cotton
le cuir, leather
le daim, suede [of shoes]
la dentelle, lace
le drap, cloth
le feutre, felt
la flanelle, flannel
la fourrure, fur
la gabardine, gabardine
le jean, denim
le jersey, jersey
la laine (vierge), (new) wool (**vierge**, virgin)
la laine peignée, worsted (**peigner**, to comb)
le lin / la toile, linen
la mousseline, chiffon
le nylon, nylon
le poil de chameau *m*; *pl* **-x**, camel-hair

le polyester, polyester
la popeline, poplin
le satin, satin
la soie (naturelle / artificielle), (real / artificial) silk
le tissu (synthétique), (man-made) material
le tissu-éponge *pl* **-s -s**, terrycloth
la toile (de coton *m***)**, (cotton) cloth
la toile cirée, oilcloth
le tweed, tweed
le velours, velvet
le velours côtelé, corduroy (**côtelé**, ribbed)
le velours de coton *m*, velveteen

SEE ALSO: **Adornment; Colours; The Human Body; Numbers and Quantities**

9. Colours Les Couleurs

de quelle couleur est . . .?, what colour is . . .?
il / elle est . . ., it is . . .

   argenté, silver
   beige, beige
   blanc *f* **-nche**, white
   bleu, blue
   bleu marine *f* **l roi** *m* **l ciel** *m* [both parts of *adj inv*],
     navy / royal / sky blue
   blond, blond [hair]
   brun, brown [hair, etc.]
   chair *inv*, flesh-coloured
   châtain *f usually inv*, light brown / chestnut
   doré, gold
   écarlate, scarlet
   fauve, fawn / buff / tawny [hair]
   gris, grey
   indigo *inv*, indigo (blue)
   infra-rouge, infra-red
   jaune, yellow
   lavande *inv*, lavender
   marron *inv*, brown
   mauve, mauve
   multicolore, multicoloured
   noir, black
   noisette *inv*, hazel
   or *inv*, gold
   orange *inv* **l orangé**, orange
   pourpre / pourpré, crimson
   rose, pink
   rouge, red
   roux *f* **rousse**, red [hair]
   turquoise *inv*, turquoise
   ultra-violet *f* **ultra-violette**, ultra-violet
   vert, green
   violet *f* **-ette**, purple / violet

clair†, light
foncé† / sombre†, dark
pâle†, pale
vif *f* vive, vivid / bright (**d'un bleu vif**, bright blue)

blanchâtre, whitish
bleuâtre, bluish
brunâtre, brownish
grisâtre, greyish
jaunâtre, yellowish
noirâtre, blackish
rosâtre, pinkish
rougeâtre, reddish
verdâtre, greenish

argenter, to silver
blanchir, to turn white / bleach
bleuir, to turn blue / make blue
brunir, to turn brown / tan / darken
*devenir . . ., to become . . .
dorer, to gild / make golden
grisonner, to go grey
jaunir, to colour yellow / turn yellow / fade
noircir, to blacken / darken / become black
rendre . . ., to make . . .
rougir, to turn red / blush
verdir, to make green / turn green

SEE ALSO: **Adornment; Clothing; Hair; Materials; The Senses**

---

† Colour adjectives qualified by this word are invariable: **des costumes** *m* **vert clair / vert foncé / vert sombre / vert pâle**, light / dark / pale green suits

10. Cooking and Eating
La Cuisine et le manger

La batterie de cuisine Kitchen equipment

l'allumette *f*, match
l'assiette *f*, plate (**l'assiette creuse**, soup-plate; **creux**, hollow)
la balance *sing*, scales
le beurrier, butter dish
le bocal *pl* **-aux**, storage jar
la boîte, box / can (**en boîte**, canned)
le bol, bowl
la bouilloire (électrique), (electric) kettle
la bouteille, bottle (**le bouchon**, cork)
la cafetière, coffee-pot
la carafe, carafe / jug
la casserole, saucepan
les ciseaux *m*, scissors
la cocotte-minute *pl inv*, pressure-cooker
le coquetier, egg-cup
la corbeille à pain *m*, bread-basket
la coupe à fruits *m*, fruit bowl
le couteau *pl* **-x** (**à éplucher / à pain** *m*), (vegetable / bread) knife (**éplucher**, to peel)
le couvert, place-setting at table (**mettre le couvert**, to lay the table; **la nappe**, table-cloth)
la cruche, jug
la cuillère [sometimes **cuiller**] (**à café / à soupe** *f* **/ à dessert** *m* **/ de service** *m*), (tea / soup / dessert/ table) spoon (**le café**, coffee)
la cuvette, bowl / food container
le décapsul(at)eur, bottle-opener
le dessous de plat, table-mat (**le plat**, dish)
la ficelle, string
le film étirable, cling-film (**étirer**, to stretch)

le filtre, [coffee] filter / percolator
le fouet, whisk
la fourchette, fork
la friteuse, chip pan
le gant isolant, oven glove
le légumier, vegetable dish
le livre de cuisine *f*, cookery book
la louche, ladle
la marmite, stew-pan
le mixer, mixer
le moulin à café *m*, coffee-mill
l'ouvre-boîte(s) *m*; *pl* --s, can-opener
le panier, basket
la passoire, colander
le plat, dish
le plateau *pl* -x, tray
la poêle, frying-pan
le poêle, stove
le poivrier, pepper-pot
le pot (à lait *m* / **de confiture** *f*), (milk) jug / jar (of jam)
le presse-ail / **-fruits** *both pl inv*, garlic-press / juice-extractor
la râpe, grater
la recette, recipe
le rouleau *pl* -x **(à pâtisserie** *f*), rolling-pin
le saladier, salad bowl
la salière, salt-cellar
la saucière, sauce-boat
la soucoupe, saucer
la soupière, soup tureen
le sucrier, sugar-bowl
le tamis, sieve
la tasse (à thé *m* / **à café** *m*), (tea / coffee-)cup
la théière, teapot **(le couvre-théière** *pl* --s, tea-cosy)
le thermos®, flask
le tire-bouchon *pl* --s, corkscrew
la vaisselle *sing*, dishes
le verre, glass
le verre à vin *m* / **à eau** *f*, wineglass / water tumbler

Les assaisonnements Flavourings

l'ail *m*, garlic (**la tête / la gousse d'ail**, head / clove of garlic)
l'aneth *m*, dill
l'anis *m*, aniseed
l'assaisonnement *m*, flavouring
le basilic, basil
la cannelle, cinnamon
les câpres *f*, capers
le cerfeuil, chervil
la ciboulette *usually sing*, chive(s)
le clou de girofle, clove
les conserves *f* **au vinaigre**, pickles
le cumin, cumin (**le cumin des prés**, caraway; **le pré**, meadow)
l'édulcorant *m* **/ la sucrette**, artificial sweetener
l'épice *f*, spice
l'estragon *m*, tarragon
la feuille de laurier, bay-leaf (**le laurier**, laurel)
les fines herbes, herbs
le gingembre, ginger
la marjolaine, marjoram
la menthe, mint
le miel, honey
la moutarde, mustard
la noix (de) muscade *f*, nutmeg (**la fleur de muscade**, mace)
l'origan *m*, oregano
le persil, parsley (**le bouquet de persil**, bunch of parsley)
le piment, pimento
le poivre, pepper
le romarin, rosemary
le safran, saffron
la sauge, sage
le sel, salt
le sucre (en poudre *f* **/ en morceaux** *m***)**, (granulated / lump) sugar
le thym, thyme
la vanille, vanilla
le vinaigre (de vin *m***)**, (wine) vinegar

Les huiles   Oils

le beurre, butter
l'huile *f* (**d'olive** *f* / **d'arachide** *f* / **de tournesol** *m*),
  (olive / peanut / sunflower) oil
la margarine, margarine
le saindoux, lard

La préparation   Preparation

arroser, to baste
assaisonner (de), to flavour (with)
*battre, to beat
*bouillir, to be boiling
*bouillir / *cuire (à feux doux / vif), to boil / cook (on a
  low / high heat)
braiser, to braise
concasser, to crush
couper (finement / grossièrement), to cut
  (thinly / thickly)
***cuire (or *faire cuire) au four / à la vapeur / à la
  broche**, to bake / steam / barbecue (**le four**, oven; **la
  broche**, skewer)
décongeler, to thaw
délayer / diluer, to dilute
désosser, to bone
écosser, to shell
égoutter, to drain
éplucher, to peel
*faire à manger, to get a meal
farcir, to stuff
fondre, to melt
fouetter, to whisk
*frire, to fry
garnir, to garnish
glacer, to ice
griller, to grill/toast
hacher, to mince/chop

mariner, to marinate
mélanger, to mix
mijoter, to simmer
pétrir, to knead
pocher, to poach
porter à ébullition *f*, to bring to the boil
préparer, to prepare
râper, to grate
remuer, to stir
rôtir, to roast
sauter, to sauté
tremper, to soak

Les repas Meals

le banquet, banquet
le casse-croûte *pl inv*, snack
le déjeuner, lunch
le dîner, dinner
le festin, feast
le goûter, [children's] tea
le petit déjeuner, breakfast
le pique-nique *pl - -s*, picnic
le repas, meal
le souper, supper

A table Eating

l'appétit *m*, appetite (**bon appétit!**, enjoy your meal!)
le goût, taste
la portion, helping

avaler, to swallow
*avoir faim, to be hungry (**la faim**, hunger)
couper l'appétit *m*, to spoil one's appetite
découper, to carve
déjeuner, to (have) lunch
dévorer, to devour
dîner, to have dinner / dine

entamer qch., to start on sth. / cut into sth.
*faire circuler, to pass round
goûter, to taste / appreciate / have a snack (**goûter à qch.**,
  to try sth.; **goûter de qch.**, to take just a little of sth.)
manger, to eat (**manger du bout des dents**, to pick at
  one's food; **le bout**, end; **la dent**, tooth)
se nourrir de, to live on
*offrir (un plat), to offer (a dish) round
passer, to pass
*prendre le petit déjeuner / le goûter, to have
  breakfast / tea
*reprendre de, to have a second helping of
se *servir de, to help oneself to
*servir qch. à qn., to help sb. to sth.
souper, to have supper
c'est . . .

  acide / acidulé, sour / tart
  amer _f_ **amère**, bitter
  appétissant, appetizing
  copieux _f_ **-euse**, ample / large [helping]
  coriace, tough
  croustillant, crisp
  cru, raw
  difficile / facile à digérer, indigestible / digestible
  épicé, spicy
  fade, tasteless / insipid
  faisandé, high [meat, game]
  fort, strong
  fumé, smoked
  immangeable, uneatable
  nourrissant, nourishing / substantial
  rassis, stale
  salé, salted / salty
  séché, dried
  sucré, sweet
  tendre, tender

Au restaurant Eating out

l'addition *f*, bill
l'auberge *f*, inn
la brasserie, large café [serving food]
le café / le bistro(t), café/ bar pub
la carte, menu [i.e., the list of dishes] (**la carte des vins** *m* / **des boissons** *f*, wine / drinks list)
le cendrier, ashtray
le couvert, cover charge
le cure-dent *pl* - -**s**, toothpick
le garçon / le serveur, waiter
la garniture, accompanying vegetables
le maître d'hôtel, head waiter
le menu, fixed-price menu
le montant, amount / total
la pizzeria, pizzeria
un plat à emporter, a take-away [dish]
le pourboire, tip
la restauration, catering (**la restauration rapide**, fast food)
le self, self-service restaurant
la serveuse, waitress
le service, service (**service compris / prix** *m* **nets**, service included)
la serviette, napkin
le snack, snack-bar
le sommelier, wine waiter
la spécialité de la maison, house / chef's speciality
le supplément, supplement / extra charge

gardez la monnaie, keep the change
on paye chacun sa part, we're paying separately

SEE ALSO: **Drinks; Food; The Senses; Tobacco and Drugs**

11. Crimes and Criminals
Les Crimes et les criminels

Les crimes Crimes

l'agression *f*, assault
l'arme *f*, weapon
l'attaque *f* (**à main armée**), (armed) attack (**la main**, hand)
l'attentat *m* (**sur la vie de qn.**), outrage / attempt (on sb.'s life)
la bagarre, scuffle / punch-up
le butin, loot
le cambriolage, burglary
le chantage, blackmail
la contrebande, smuggling
la contrefaction, forgery / counterfeiting
le coup (**de fusil / de revolver** *m*), shot (**le fusil**, rifle / gun)
le coup de pied / de poing, kick / punch (**le pied**, foot; **le poing**, fist)
le couteau *pl* **-x**, knife
le crime, crime
la drogue *usually sing*, drugs
le détournement, hijacking / embezzlement
l'effraction *f*, break-in
l'enlèvement *m*, kidnapping
l'escroquerie *f*, fraud
l'espionnage *m*, spying
le / un faux, forgery / a forgery
le fusil, gun / rifle
le hold-up *pl inv*, hold-up
l'homicide *m*, homicide
l'incendie *m* volontaire, arson
le larcin, (petty) larceny
le meurtre / l'assassinat *m*, murder
l'otage *m*, hostage
le parjure, perjury
le pistolet (**mitrailleur**), (automatic) pistol

le **poignard**, dagger
le **poison**, poison
le **pot de vin** *m*, bribe [literally pot of wine]
le **proxénétisme**, procuring
la **rançon**, ransom
le **revolver**, revolver
les **stupéfiants** *m*, narcotics
le **système d'alarme** *f*, burglar alarm
le **trafic de drogue** *f*, drug trafficking
la **trahison**, treason
le **vagabondage**, vagrancy
le **viol**, rape
le **vol (avec agression** *f*), robbery (with violence)
le **vol à l'américaine**, confidence trick
le **vol à l'arraché** *m*, snatch-theft
le **vol à la tire**, pocket-picking
le **vol à l'étalage**, shop-lifting (**l'étalage** *m*, display)
le **vol à main armée**, armed robbery (**la main**, hand)
le **vol avec effraction** *f* / **violence** *f*, housebreaking /
  robbery with violence

Les criminels et les criminelles
Criminals

l'**assassin(e)** / le **meurtrier** *f* -**ière**, murderer
la **bande**, gang
le **bandit**, bandit
le **braconnier**, poacher
le **cambrioleur** *f* -**euse**, burglar
le **maître-chanteur** *pl* -**s**-**s**, blackmailer
le / la **complice**, accomplice
le **contrebandier** *f* -**ière**, smuggler
le **criminel** *f* -**elle**, criminal
l'**escroc** *m*, crook
l'**espion** *f* -**nne**, spy
le **gangster**, gangster
le **malfaiteur** *f* -**trice**, wrong-doer / offender

le / la parjure, perjurer
le pirate de l'air, hijacker
le / la pyromane, arsonist
le recéleur f **-euse,** receiver
le / la récidiviste, old / persistent offender
le / la terroriste, terrorist
le / la trafiquant(e), drug dealer
le traître f **-tresse,** traitor / traitress
le / la vagabond(e), vagrant
le voleur f **-euse,** thief
le voyou f **-oute,** hooligan / yob

Ce qu'ils font What they do

*abattre, to bring down / kill
agresser, to mug
assassiner, to murder
attaquer, to attack
se bagarrer, to fight
se *battre avec, to fight with
cambrioler, to burgle
*commettre, to commit
dérober, to steal
dévaliser une banque / une maison, to rob a bank / rifle a house
se droguer, to take drugs
empoisonner, to poison
enlever, to abduct
escroquer qch. à qn., to cheat sb. of sth. / swindle sb. out of sth.
espionner, to spy
étrangler, to strangle
*être impliqué dans, to be implicated in
*faire sauter, to blow up
forcer, to force
fouiller, to search
importuner, to pester / importune
incendier / *mettre le feu à, to set fire to

kidnapper, to kidnap
menacer, to threaten
poignarder, to stab
*prendre qn. en otage *m*, to take sb. hostage
se prostituer, to prostitute oneself
sauver, to rescue
soudoyer, to bribe
tirer sur, to shoot at
tromper, to deceive
tuer, to kill
en *venir aux coups *m*, to come to blows
violer, to rape
voler, to steal

Les cris Cries

à l'aide *f*!, help! / get help!
à l'assassin *m*!, murder!
allez-vous-en!, clear off!
arrêtez cet homme!, stop that man!
attention *f*!, look out!
au feu!, fire!
au secours!, help!
au voleur!, stop thief!
circulez!, move along!
haut les mains *f*!, hands up!
laissez-moi tranquille!, leave me alone!
rendez-vous!, surrender! / give yourself up!

SEE ALSO: **Describing People; Justice and Law**

12. Describing People
La Description des gens

l'âge *m*, age
l'apparence *f*, appearance
le caractère, character / personality (**de bon / mauvais caractère**, good- / ill-natured)
le comportement, behaviour
la conduite, conduct
le défaut / la faute, fault
la description, description
l'habitude *f*, habit
le mérite, merit
les mœurs *f*, morals / customs
la (bonne / mauvaise) qualité, (good / bad) quality
la vertu, virtue
le vice, vice

*avoir, to have
se comporter / se *conduire, to behave
*décrire, to describe
*être, to be
montrer, to show
sembler / *paraître, to seem / appear

L'apparence extérieure External appearance

l'allure *f*, looks
le bouton, spot
la cicatrice, scar
le double menton, double chin
l'expression *f*, expression
la fossette, dimple
le geste, gesture
le grain de beauté *f*, beauty spot / mole
la malpropreté, dirtiness
le poids, weight

la propreté, cleanliness
la ressemblance (à / avec), resemblance (to)
la ride, wrinkle
la tache de rousseur, freckle
la taille, height [also *size* and *waist*]
le teint, complexion
le trait, feature

*avoir l'air *m,* to look
mesurer/*faire, to be . . . tall
peser, to weigh
porter, to have [beard, scar, etc.]
ressembler à, to look like

aux yeux *m* **enfoncés,** with deep-set eyes
aveugle, blind
beau *pl* **-x;** *m sing. before vowel* **bel;** *f* **belle,** beautiful / handsome
boiteux *f* **-euse,** lame
bossu, hunch-backed
boutonneux *f* **-euse,** spotty
bronzé / basané, tanned
chétif *f* **-ive,** weedy
clair, fair [of complexion]
couperosé, blotchy
de petite / grande taille, short / tall (**le nain,** dwarf; **le géant,** giant)
de taille moyenne, of medium height
droitier *f* **-ière,** right-handed
faible, weak
fort, strong
gaucher *f* **-chère,** left-handed
grand, tall
gros *f* **-sse/gras** *f* **-sse,** fat / stout
jeune, young
joli, pretty / good-looking
laid, ugly
long *f* **-ngue,** long
maigre, thin
malpropre, dirty
mat, sallow

mignon *f* **-onne**, cute / sweet
mince, slim
muet *f* **-ette**, dumb
musclé, muscular
obèse, obese
ovale, oval
pâle, pale
petit, small
pointu, pointed
propre, clean
raide, straight [hair]
ridé, wrinkled
rond, round
sensuel *f* **-elle**, sensual / sensuous
soigné, well-groomed / trim
sourd, deaf
svelte, slender
trapu, stocky
vieux *m sing before vowel* **vieil**; *f* **vieille**, old

Les qualités et leurs conséquences
Good qualities and their effects

l'affabilité *f*, affability
l'amabilité *f*, kindness / amiability
l'ambition *f*, ambition
l'amitié *f*, friendship
l'amour *m*, love
l'amour-propre *m*, self-respect [can also mean *egotism*]
la bienveillance, benevolence
la bonté, goodness / kindness
la bravoure, bravery
la candeur, candour / artlessness
la charité, charity
le charme, charm
la chasteté, chastity
la compassion, compassion
la confiance, trust

la conscience, conscience
la considération, consideration
la cordialité, cordiality
le courage, courage
la courtoisie, courtesy
le cran, guts
la délicatesse, delicacy / refinement
la discrétion, discretion
la douceur, gentleness
la droiture, uprightness
l'égard *m*, regard / respect (**par égard pour**, out of respect for)
l'estime *f*, esteem
l'exactitude *f*, exactness
la fidélité, fidelity
la fierté, pride
la franchise, openness / frankness
la gaieté, cheerfulness
la générosité, generosity
la gentillesse, kindness
l'habileté *f*, skill
l'honnêteté *f*, honesty
l'honneur *m*, honour (**la parole d'honneur**, word of honour)
l'humanité *f*, humanity
l'humilité *f*, humility
l'humour *m*, humour (**le sens de l'humour**, sense of humour)
l'innocence *f*, innocence
l'intelligence *f*, intelligence
l'intrépidité *f*, fearlessness
la joie, joy
la justice, justice
la libéralité, liberality
la magnanimité, magnanimity
la miséricorde, mercy
la modération, moderation
la modestie, modesty
la moralité, morality
la noblesse, nobility

l'**obéissance** *f*, obedience
le **pardon**, forgiveness
la **patience**, patience
la **permission**, permission
la **pitié**, pity (***avoir pitié de qn.** / ***plaindre qn.**, to pity sb.)
la **politesse**, politeness
la **prévoyance**, foresight
la **probité**, probity
la **prudence**, caution
la **pureté**, purity
la **récompense**, reward
la **reconnaissance** / la **gratitude**, gratitude
la **réserve**, reserve
le **respect**, respect
la **retenue**, restraint
la **sagesse**, wisdom / prudence
la **simplicité**, simplicity
la **sincérité**, sincerity
le **tact**, tact
la **timidité**, timidity / shyness
la **tolérance**, tolerance
la **vaillance**, gallantry
le **zèle**, zeal

actif *f* **-ive**, active
affectueux *f* **-euse**, affectionate
agréable, pleasant
aimable, nice / kind
ambitieux *f* **-euse**, ambitious
amical *pl* **-aux**, friendly
amusant, amusing
appliqué, hard-working
avisé, shrewd / cautious
bon *f* **-nne**, good
brave, decent / worthy
calme, quiet
candide, artless
charitable, charitable
charmant, charming
chaste, chaste

compatissant, compassionate
content / **heureux** *f* **-euse**, happy
courageux *f* **-euse**, brave
décent, decent
digne (de), worthy (of)
discret *f* **-crète**, discreet
doux *f* **-ouce**, gentle
droit, just
drôle, funny
gai, cheerful
généreux *f* **-euse**, generous
gentil *f* **-ille**, kind
habile, skilful
honnête, honest
humble, humble
indulgent, indulgent
intelligent, intelligent
joyeux *f* **-euse**, cheerful
magnanime, magnanimous
modéré, moderate
modeste, modest
moral *pl* **-aux**, moral
naturel *f* **-elle**, natural
noble, noble
obéissant, obedient
optimiste, optimistic
paisible, peaceable
patient, patient
poli, polite
prudent, cautious
pur, pure
raisonnable, reasonable
réservé, reserved
respectable, respectable
respectueux *f* **-euse**, respectful
sage, wise / well-behaved
sensible, sensitive
sérieux *f* **-euse**, serious
serviable, helpful

simple / **sans façons** f, simple
sincère, sincere
spirituel f **-elle**, witty
sympathique / colloq **sympa** inv, nice
tolérant, tolerant
vertueux, virtuous

approuver, to approve
se dominer / **se modérer** / **se maîtriser**, to control oneself
s'entendre, to get on (together)
garder son sang-froid, to keep cool
laisser, to let
obéir (à), to obey
***permettre**, to allow
persévérer, to persevere
récompenser, to reward

Les défauts et leurs conséquences
Faults and their consequences

l'affectation f, affectation
l'arrogance f, arrogance
la bêtise, stupidity
la colère, anger (**se *mettre en colère contre**, to get angry with)
la cruauté, cruelty
la cupidité, greed
la curiosité, inquisitiveness
le dédain, disdain
la déloyauté, disloyalty
le désordre, disorder
l'effronterie f, effrontery
l'égoïsme m, egotism
l'envie f, envy
l'embarras m, embarrassment
l'étourderie f, thoughtlessness
l'excuse f, excuse (***faire ses excuses**, to apologize)
la flatterie, flattery
la folie, madness / silliness

la fourberie, cheating
la fraude, fraud
la gourmandise, greediness
la grossièreté, coarseness
l'habitude *f* **du mensonge,** lying / mendacity (**le mensonge,** lie; **le menteur** *f* **-euse,** liar)
la honte, shame (***avoir honte,** to be ashamed)
l'humeur *f,* mood (**de bonne / mauvaise humeur,** in a good / bad mood)
l'hypocrisie *f,* hypocrisy
l'immoralité *f,* immorality
l'impatience *f,* impatience
l'impertinence *f,* impertinence / cheek
l'impolitesse *f,* rudeness
l'imprudence *f* **/ la négligence,** carelessness
l'impudence *f,* impudence
l'indifférence *f,* indifference
l'indiscrétion *f,* indiscretion
l'ingratitude *f,* ingratitude
l'inimitié *f,* enmity
l'insolence *f,* insolence
l'intolérance *f,* intolerance
la jalousie, jealousy
la lâcheté, cowardice
le laisser-aller, slovenliness
la malhonnêteté, dishonesty
la malice, malice / spite
la méchanceté, viciousness
la méfiance, mistrust / distrust
le mépris, scorn / contempt
la mesquinerie, meanness
la moquerie, mockery
la nonchalance, indolence
l'orgueil *m,* pride
la paresse, laziness
la punition, punishment
la rancune, rancour / resentment
la réprimande, reprimand
la rudesse, roughness
la ruse, cunning

le sans-gêne, offhandedness
le soupçon, suspicion
la suffisance, complacency / conceit
la taquinerie, teasing
la témérité, recklessness
la tromperie, deceit
le toupet, cheek
la vanité, vanity
la vantardise, boastfulness
la vulgarité / la grossièreté, vulgarity

arrogant, arrogant
astucieux *f* **-euse**, cunning / artful
avare, miserly
bavard, talkative
bête, silly / stupid
bizarre, strange
calomnieux *f* **-euse**, libellous / slanderous
capricieux *f* **-euse**, capricious
coupable, guilty
cruel *f* **-elle**, cruel
curieux *f* **-euse**, odd
désobéissant, disobedient
désolé, sorry
désordonné, untidy
détestable, hateful
distrait, absent-minded
effronté, cheeky
égoïste, selfish
embarrassé / gêné, embarrassed
ennuyeux *f* **-euse**, boring / troublesome
entêté, stubborn
envieux *f* **-euse**, envious
espiègle, mischievous
étourdi, irresponsible
étrange, strange
fâché, angry
fier *f* **fière**, proud
fou *m sing.* before vowel **fol**; *f* **folle**, foolish / mad
frivole, frivolous

gauche / maladroit, clumsy
grossier *f* **-ière**, coarse
hautain, haughty
hostile, hostile
hypocrite, hypocritical
idiot, stupid
indécent, indecent
indifférent, unconcerned
indiscret *f* **-crète**, indiscreet / tactless
ingrat, ungrateful
immoral *pl* **-aux**, immoral
impatient, impatient
impitoyable, ruthless
impoli, rude
importun, tiresome
impulsif *f* **-ive**, impulsive
inadmissible, inadmissible / objectionable
incorrigible, incorrigible
indifférent, indifferent
indigne (**de**), unworthy (of)
injurieux *f* **-euse**, insulting
insolent, insolent
intolérant, intolerant
jaloux *f* **-ouse**, jealous
lâche, cowardly
maladroit, clumsy
malheureux *f* **-euse**, unhappy
malicieux *f* **-euse**, mischievous
mauvais, bad
méchant, malicious / naughty
méfiant, distrustful
menteur *f* **-euse**, lying
méprisant, contemptuous
mesquin, mean
meurtrier *f* **-ière**, murderous
moqueur *f* **-euse**, mocking
naïf *f* **-ïve**, naive
négligé, slovenly
négligent, careless

obséquieux *f* **-euse**, obsequious
obstiné, obstinate
perfide, treacherous
pessimiste, pessimistic
possessif *f* **-ive**, possessive
prétentieux *f* **-euse**, pretentious
querelleur *f* **-euse**, quarrelsome
rancunier *f* **-ière**, spiteful
rusé, wily
sauvage, unsociable
soupçonneux *f* **-euse**, suspicious
stupide, stupid
suspect, doubtful / suspect
téméraire, foolhardy
timide, shy
triste, sad
trompeur *f* **-euse**, deceitful
vaniteux *f* **-euse**, vain
vantard, boastful
vicieux *f* **-euse**, vicious
vilain, nasty
vindicatif *f* **-ive**, vindictive
violent, violent
volage, fickle
vulgaire, vulgar

s'adonner à, to indulge in
calomnier, to slander
*commettre, to commit
contrarier, to vex
désapprouver, to disapprove
désobéir (à), to disobey
empêcher, to prevent
ennuyer / fâcher, to annoy
s'excuser, to apologize
se fâcher, to get annoyed
*faire semblant de, to pretend to
gronder, to tell off (**se *faire gronder**, to be told off)
injurier / insulter, to insult
*interdire, to forbid

*mentir, to lie
offenser, to offend
pardonner, to forgive
punir, to punish
regretter, to regret
se *repentir, to repent
rougir, to blush
tromper, to deceive
trouver à redire à, to find fault with (***redire**, to say again /
  criticize)
en *vouloir à, to have a grudge against

SEE ALSO: **Clothing; Education; Hair; Health and
Sickness; The Human Body; Identity; Jobs; Places and
Languages; Relationships**

13. Directions Les Directions

Ce qu'on demande What you ask

à combien d'ici est . . . ?, how far is . . . from here?
où se trouve le/la . . . ?, where is the . . . ?
pour aller au/à la . . . ?, how do I get to the . . . ?
suis-je bien sur la route pour . . . ?, am I on the right road
  for . . . ?

Où il se trouve Where it is

à (environ) [+ time/distance] **d'ici**, (about) [time/distance]
  from here
à côté *m* **de**, next (door) to
à droite (de), on the right (of)
à gauche (de), on the left (of)
à l'autre bout *m* **de**, at the other end of
à l'extérieur *m*/**l'intérieur** *m* **de**, outside/inside
à peu près, approximately/about
après (les feux *m***)**, after (the traffic lights)
à proximité *f* **de**, near to
à travers, across/through
au bord de, beside
au bout de, at the end of
au carrefour/croisement, at the crossroads
au coin de la rue, at the corner
au-delà de, beyond
au-dessous de, below
au-dessus de, above
au fond de, at the bottom of
au milieu de, in the middle of
au nord/au sud/à l'est *m*/**à l'ouest** *m* **(de)**, to the north/
  south/east/west (of) (**au nord-ouest**, to the north-west)
au premier *etc.* **étage**, on the first *etc.* floor
auprès de, beside
au rond-point, at the roundabout

autour de, around
avant, before
chez, at / to the house / shop of
contre, against
dans, in
de, from
de ce / l'autre côté (de), on this / the other side (of)
de ce côté-là, that way
dedans, inside
dehors, outside
depuis . . . jusqu'à . . ., from . . . to . . .
derrière, behind
dessous, underneath
dessus, on top
devant, in front of
en bas *m* **de**, at the bottom of
en face *f* **de**, opposite
en haut *m* **de**, at the top of
en route *f* **pour**, on the way to
entre . . . et, between . . . and
face à, facing
juste . . ., just . . .
là, there
là-bas, over there
là en bas, down there
là-haut, up there
le long de, along
loin de, far from
n'importe où, anywhere
nulle part, nowhere
par là, that way
parmi, among
partout, everywhere
pas loin de, not far from
pendant [+ distance], for
près de / tout près de, near
presque, almost
quelque part, somewhere
sous, under

sur, on (**sur** [+ distance], for)
vers, towards

Ce qu'on fait What you do

*aller tout droit, to go straight on
avancer, to go forwards
chercher, to look for
continuer (jusqu'à), to keep on (up to/as far as)
demander, to ask
*descendre, to go down
*faire demi-tour *m*, to turn round
indiquer, to point to
*monter, to go up
montrer, to show
passer devant/par/sous, to go past/through/under
*prendre, to take
reculer, to reverse
*retourner, to go back
*revenir sur vos pas, to go back the way you came (**le pas**, footstep)
*suivre, to follow
tourner, to turn
trouver, to find
*voir, to see

SEE ALSO: **Holidays; Places and Languages; Shops and Shopping; Towns; Transport**

14. Disasters Les Catastrophes

Ce qu'elles sont What they are

l'avalanche *f*, avalanche
le coup de foudre *f*, thunderbolt
le cyclone, cyclone
l'éboulement *m*, landslide
l'épidémie *f*, epidemic
l'éruption *f* **volcanique**, volcanic eruption (**le volcan**, volcano)
la famine, famine
l'incendie *m*, fire
l'inondation *f*, flood
l'orage *m*, storm (**par forte mer**, in rough seas)
l'ouragan *m*, hurricane
la peste, plague
le raz-de-marée *pl inv*, tidal wave
la sécheresse, drought
la tempête, storm / tempest
la tornade, tornado
le tremblement de terre *f*, earthquake
le typhon, typhoon

Ce qu'elles font What they do

arracher, to uproot
être bloqué par les neiges *f*, to be cut off by snow
brûler, to burn
casser, to break
couler / sombrer, to sink
déborder, to overflow
démolir, to demolish
*détruire, to destroy
dévaler, to flow down [lava]
éclater, to burst / splinter / explode
s'écrouler, to collapse

s'effondrer, to cave in
endommager, to damage
***entrer en éruption** f, to erupt
étouffer, to suffocate
exploser, to explode
frapper de la foudre, to strike by lightning
glisser, to slide
inonder, to flood
***réduire en cendres** f, to reduce to ashes
***tomber**, to fall
trembler, to shake / quake
tuer, to kill

Leurs effets Their results

l'asphyxié m; f **-ée**, suffocated person
le / la blessé(e), injured person
la blessure, wound
la brûlure, burn
le choc, shock
la chute, fall
le coma, coma
les dégâts m, damage
la destruction, destruction
la disette, famine / lack of food (**la disette d'eau** f, drought / lack of water)
l'éruption f, eruption
l'explosion f, explosion
la lave, lava
la malnutrition, malnutrition
le manque (de), lack (of)
le / la mort(e), dead person
le / la noyé(e), drowned person
la panique, panic
le / la survivant(e), survivor
la victime *always* f, victim

se casser le / la / les . . ., to break one's . . .
***disparaître**, to disappear

*être coincé (**par/entre**), to be trapped (by/between)
*être gravement/grièvement blessé, to be seriously
  injured
s'évanouir, to faint
*mourir de faim f/de soif f/de froid m/de ses blessures
  f, to die of hunger/thirst/cold/one's wounds
*mourir d'une mort violente, to die a violent death
se noyer, to drown
perdre/*reprendre connaissance f, to lose/regain
  consciousness
perdre du sang, to lose blood
saigner, to bleed
suffoquer, to choke/suffocate
vomir, to be sick

Au secours! Help!

l'ambulance f, ambulance
le bouche-à-bouche, kiss of life (**la bouche**, mouth)
le brancard, stretcher
la ceinture/le gilet de sauvetage m, life-belt/jacket
la Croix-Rouge, Red Cross
le docteur/le médecin, doctor
l'échelle f, ladder
l'hélicoptère m, helicopter
l'hôpital m, hospital
l'infirmière f; m -ier, nurse
le pompier, fireman (**les pompiers**, fire-brigade)
les premiers soins, first aid
la respiration artificielle, artificial respiration
le sauvetage (**aérien en mer** f), (air-sea) rescue
le secouriste, relief-worker/first-aid worker
le secours m, help/assistance
les secours m d'urgence f, emergency relief
les secours m en montagne f, mountain rescue
la sortie de secours m, emergency exit
l'SOS m, SOS
le tuyau (**d'incendie** m), (fire) hose

l'urgence *f*, emergency (**. . . d'urgence**, emergency . . .)
la voiture des pompiers *m* / **la pompe à incendie** *m*,
  fire-engine
le volontaire, volunteer

donner l'alarme *f*, to raise the alarm
*éteindre, to put out [fire]
héliporter, to transport by helicopter
sauver, to save / rescue
*secourir qn., to come to the aid of sb.

SEE ALSO: **Accidents; Crimes and Criminals; Health
  and Sickness; War, Peace, and the Armed Services;
  The Weather**

15. Drinks Les Boissons

Les boissons non-alcoolisées
Non-alcoholic drinks

le café / le café nature / le café noir, black coffee

le café complet, coffee and continental breakfast

le café crème / le crème / le café au lait, white coffee **(la crème,** cream: **le lait,** milk)

le café décaféiné, decaffeinated coffee

le café en poudre, instant coffee **(la poudre,** powder)

le café express, espresso coffee

le café filtre, filter coffee

le café glacé, iced coffee

la camomille, camomile tea

le chocolat chaud, chocolate

le citron pressé, fresh lemon juice [with sugar and water]

la citronnade, lemon squash

le coca®, coke®

le diabolo-menthe *pl* **-s -,** lemonade with mint cordial

l'eau *f*; *pl* **-x,** water

l'eau gazeuse, soda-water

l'eau minérale (gazeuse), (carbonated) mineral water

l'eau *f* **tonique, le schweppes®,** tonic water

l'infusion *f*, herbal tea

le jus de fruit *m* **/ d'orange** *f* **/ de pommes** *f* **/ de pamplemousse** *m* **/ de raisin** *m* **/ de tomate** *f*, fruit / orange / apple / grapefruit / grape / tomato juice

le jus d'orange pressée, fresh orange-juice

le lait (écrémé / demi-écrémé), (skimmed / semi-skimmed) milk

le lait grenadine *f*, milk with grenadine cordial

la limonade, lemonade

l'orangeade *f*, orangeade

le sirop, cordial / concentrated fruit-juice [served diluted]

le thé (nature / au citron / au lait), tea (with nothing / with lemon / with milk)

le thé à la menthe, mint tea
le tilleul, lime tea
la verveine, verbena tea

Les boissons alcoolisées Alcoholic drinks

l'apéritif *m*, aperitif
l'armagnac *m*, Armagnac brandy
la bière (blonde), (lager) beer
la bière (à la) pression / en bouteille *f*, draught / bottled beer
la (bière) brune, brown ale
le (vin) blanc cassis *m*, white wine with blackcurrant cordial
le bordeaux, claret
le bourgogne, burgundy
le calvados, apple brandy
le champagne, champagne
le cidre, cider
le cognac, Cognac brandy
le digestif, after-dinner liqueur
l'eau-de-vie *f*, *pl* **-x - -,** brandy / spirits
la fine, (quality) brandy
le gin-tonic *pl* **-s -,** gin and tonic
le kir, white wine with blackcurrant liqueur
le kirsch, cherry brandy
la liqueur, liqueur
le marc, rough brandy [made from fruit or wine lees]
le muscat, muscatel [sweet wine]
le panaché, shandy
le pastis, aniseed aperitif [served diluted]
le porto, port
le rhum, rum
le sherry / le (vin de) Xérès, sherry
le vermouth, vermouth
le vin (rouge / blanc / rosé), (red / white / rosé) wine
la vodka, vodka
le whisky *pl* **-ys,** whisky

Leurs récipients Their containers

une canette de bière *f*, a can of beer
un bol de chocolat *m*, a bowl of chocolate
une bouteille de vin *m*, a bottle of wine
une carafe / une cruche / un pichet d'eau *f*, a jug of water
un carton de lait *m*, a carton of milk
un pot de thé *m*, a pot of tea
une tasse de café *m*, a cup of coffee
un verre de limonade *f*, a glass of lemonade

Comment vous les préférez
How you prefer them

le demi, small [⅓ litre] beer
la demi-bouteille *pl* **- -s**, half bottle
le quart, quarter-litre

à l'eau *f*, with water
avec de la glace / avec des glaçons *m*, with ice / ice-cubes
bouché, bottled / in bottle
brut, dry [champagne]
capiteux *f* **-euse**, heady [wine]
chambré, at room temperature
corsé, full-bodied [wine]
doux *f* **douce**, sweet [wine]
léger *f* **-gère**, light
mousseux *f* **-euse**, sparkling; fizzy
pétillant, gently sparkling
pur, neat
sec *f* **sèche**, neat [drink] / dry [wine]

Ce qu'on fait What you do

arroser, to lace [a drink]
avaler, to swallow
*boire (à), to drink (to)
*boire à la bouteille, to drink from the bottle

*boire d'un seul coup, to swig down (le coup, blow/gulp)
*boire un coup, to have a drink
consulter le tarif des consommations, to look at the
  (drinks) price-list (la consommation, drink)
demander la carte des vins m, to ask for the wine list
se désaltérer to quench one's thirst
s'enivrer, to get drunk
*être ivre/soûl, to be drunk (un ivrogne, a drunk)
*être sobre, to be sober
*offrir à boire à qn., to buy sb. a drink
siroter, to sip

Ce qu'on dit What you say

à votre santé!, good health! (la santé, health)
buvable/potable, drinkable (imbuvable, undrinkable)
cela a bon/mauvais goût, that tastes nice/unpleasant (le
  goût, taste)
cela (vous) fait du bien, that does you good
délicieux f -euse, delicious
j'ai (très) soif, I'm (very) thirsty (la soif, thirst)
je paye la tournée, I'm standing a round
qu'est-ce que vous prenez?, what will you have?

SEE ALSO: Cooking and Eating; Food; The Senses;
  Tobacco and Drugs

16. Education L'Éducation

Les institutions The institutions

le Collège d'Enseignement Secondaire (CES), 11–16 comprehensive school (**l'enseignement** *m*, education)
l'école *f* (**maternelle / de commerce** *m* **/ libre**), (nursery / business / private) school
l'école mixte / de filles *f* **/ de garçons** *m*, mixed / girls' / boys' school
l'école normale, teacher-training college (**normal** *pl* **-aux**, standard)
l'école primaire / communale, primary school
l'école secondaire / le collège, secondary school
la Grande École, higher technical institute / specialist college
l'Institut *m* **Universitaire de Technologie** *f* **(IUT)**, technical institute [= polytechnic]
l'internat *m*, boarding-school
le lycée, sixth-form college
le lycée technique, technical college
l'université *f* **/ la faculté**, university

Les personnes Who people are

le cancre, dunce
le collégien *f* **-enne**, (secondary) pupil
le directeur *f* **-trice**, head teacher [comprehensive school]
l'écolier *f* **-ière**, schoolboy / girl
l'élève *m* / *f*, pupil
l'enseignant *m*; *f* **-te**, teacher
l'étudiant *m*; *f* **-te** (**en médecine**), (medical) student
l'externe *m* / *f*, day-boy / girl
l'inspecteur *f* **-trice**, inspector
l'instituteur *f* **-trice, le maître / la maîtresse d'école** *f*, teacher [nursery, primary education]
l'interne *m* / *f*; **le / la pensionnaire**, boarder

le lycéen *f* **-enne,** (sixth-form) student
le maître de conférences, lecturer (**la conférence,** lecture)
le moniteur *f* **-trice (de natation** *f* **/ d'éducation** *f*
physique), (swimming / gym) instructor
le pion *f* **-nne,** supervisor
le professeur *always m,* teacher [secondary, higher
education] (**le / la prof** [colloquial], teacher)
le professeur de faculté *f* **/ de français** *m,*
university / French teacher
le proviseur, head [sixth-form college]
le recteur, principal/vice-chancellor [university]

Ce qu'on fait What they do

*aller à / quitter l'école *f,* to go to / leave school
*apprendre à + INF, to learn to
*apprendre à qn. à + INF, to teach sb. to
*apprendre par cœur *m,* to learn by heart
*apprendre qch., to learn sth.
*apprendre qch. à qn., to teach sb. sth.
se *conduire (bien / mal), to behave (well / badly)
copier (sur), to copy (from)
corriger, to correct
*écrire, to write
enseigner, to teach
épeler, to spell
*être fort en, to be good at
*être présent / absent / renvoyé, to be present / absent /
expelled
étudier, to study
examiner (sur), to examine (on)
*faire l'école buissonnière, to truant (**buissonnier** *f*
-ière, bush / hedge *adj*)
interroger (sur), to question (on)
*lire, to read
louer, to praise
paresser, to idle
poser des questions *f,* to ask questions

punir, to punish
ramasser, to collect in
recopier, to copy out
redoubler une classe, to repeat a year
repasser, to look over / go over [lesson / work]
répondre, to answer
réviser, to revise
travailler (dur), to work (hard)

Ce qu'on apprend What they learn

l'algèbre *f*, algebra
l'allemand *m*, German
l'anglais *m*, English
l'arithmétique *f*, arithmetic
les arts *m* **ménagers**, domestic science
la biologie, biology
le chant, singing
la chimie, chemistry
les cours *m* **commerciaux**, business studies
la couture, needlework
le dessin, drawing / art [as school subject]
le droit, law
l'écriture *f*, writing
l'électronique *f*, electronics
l'espagnol *m*, Spanish
le français, French
la géographie, geography
la géométrie, geometry
la gymnastique / l'éducation *f* **physique**, physical education / PE
l'histoire *f*, history
l'informatique *f*, computer science
l'instruction religieuse, religious education
les langues (vivantes / classiques) *f*, (modern / classical) languages
le latin, Latin
la lecture, reading

la littérature, literature
les math(s) *f* / **les mathématiques** *f*, maths / mathematics
la médecine, medicine
la musique, music
l'orthographe *f*, spelling (**la faute d'orthographe**, spelling mistake)
la pharmacie, pharmacy
la philosophie, philosophy
la physique, physics
la psychologie, psychology
les sciences (appliquées / naturelles / physiques / pures / sociales) *f*, (applied / natural / physical / pure / social) science
la technique, technology
les travaux manuels, handicraft (**le travail** *pl* **-aux**, work)

Le milieu Things around them

la bibliothèque, library
le bloc, pad
le brouillon, rough version
le bulletin / le livret scolaire, report
le bureau *pl* **-x du directeur / de la directrice**, head's study
le bureau *pl* **-x du professeur** *m*, teacher's desk
le cahier, exercise book
la calculette / la calculatrice, calculator
la cantine / le réfectoire, dining-hall
le carnet, notebook
le cartable / la sacoche, school-bag / satchel
le casier, locker
le châtiment corporel, corporal punishment
le chiffon / le torchon, (board) duster
la classe, class (**la classe de sixième**, first form; **la classe de première**, sixth form)
la cloche, bell
la conférence, lecture
la copie au propre, fair copy

le couloir, corridor
la cour (de récréation *f*), playground
le cours, class / course
la craie, chalk
le crayon, pencil
les devoirs *m*, homework (**un devoir,** a piece of homework)
la distribution des prix *m*, prize-giving
l'emploi *m* **du temps,** timetable
l'enseignement *m* **/ l'éducation** *f*, education
l'étude *f*, study
l'exercice *m*, exercise
le feutre, felt-tip (pen)
la gomme, rubber
le gymnase, gym
le laboratoire, laboratory
la leçon, lesson
le livre *I (more colloq)* **le bouquin,** book
la matière, (school) subject
l'ordinateur *m*, computer
le placard, cupboard
la punition, punishment
le pupitre, desk
la récréation, break
la règle, ruler
la retenue, detention (***avoir une heure de retenue,**
  have an hour's detention)
la salle de classe *f* **/ de conférence** *f*, classroom / lecture room
la serviette, briefcase
le stylo (à) bille *f*, ball-point
le stylo (à plume *f*), (fountain) pen
le tableau *pl* **-x noir,** blackboard (***écrire au / essuyer le tableau noir,** write on / clean the blackboard)
le taille-crayon(s) *pl inv*, pencil sharpener
la (classe) terminale, final year
la trousse, pencil-case
le vestiaire, cloakroom

Les examens Examinations

l'admis(e), successful candidate

l'agrégation *f*, university / lycée teachers' competitive examination (**un(e) agrégé(e)**, (top) university / lycée teacher)

le bac(calauréat) / le bachot, college-leaving certificate (= A levels)

le brevet (de technicien), (technical) certificate

le CAPES, (secondary) teacher's certificate

le certificat, certificate

le certificat d'aptitude professionnelle (CAP), vocational training certificate

le concours, competitive examination

le diplôme, diploma

le doctorat, doctor's degree (= PhD)

l'épreuve *f*, test / paper [in examination]

l'examen *m*, examination

l'examinateur *m*; *f* **-trice**, examiner

la faute / l'erreur *f*, mistake

le grade, degree

l'interrogation *f* (**orale / écrite**) / **le test**, (oral / written) test

la licence, first degree (= BA / BSc)

la maîtrise, master's degree (= MA / MSc)

la moyenne, pass mark

la note, mark

le problème, problem

la question, question

la réponse, answer

le résultat, result

échouer à / rater un examen, to fail an examination

*faire passer / passer un test, to give / have a test

*obtenir sa licence, to graduate

*obtenir une bonne / mauvaise note, to get a good / bad mark

préparer / passer un examen, to be working for / sit an examination

réussir à / *être reçu à un examen, to pass an examination

L'année scolaire The academic year

les grandes vacances *f*, summer holidays
le jour de congé, day off (**le congé**, leave)
la rentrée (des classes *f*), new school year [beginning of September]
le trimestre, term
les vacances *f* (**scolaires / de Noël** *m or f* **/ de Pâques** *f pl*), (school / Christmas / Easter) holidays
les vacances *f* **de neige**, winter skiing holidays (**la neige**, snow)

SEE ALSO: **Identity; Reading and Writing; Science**

17. **Feelings** Les Émotions

la disposition, mood
l'émotion *f*, emotion
l'état *m* **d'esprit** *m*, state of mind
l'humeur *f*, humour [= mood]
la passion, passion
la sensation, sensation
la sensibilité, sensitivity
la sensiblerie, sentimentality
un sentiment, a feeling

Le bonheur Happiness

l'allégresse *f*, cheerfulness
le bonheur, happiness
le calme, calm
la chance, luck
le contentement, content
le désir, desire
l'enthousiasme *m*, enthusiasm
l'entrain *m*, high spirits
l'espoir *m*, hope
l'exaltation *f*, rapture
l'extase *f*, ecstasy
la félicité, bliss
la gaieté, cheerfulness
l'humour *m*, humour
l'insouciance *f*, freedom from care
la joie, joy
l'optimisme *m*, optimism
la passion, passion
le plaisir, pleasure
le ravissement / un délice, delight / a delight
un régal, a treat
le rire, laugh(ter)
la satisfaction, satisfaction

la sérénité, serenity
le sourire, smile

s'amuser, to enjoy oneself
*avoir le fou rire, to get the giggles (**le fou rire**, mad laughter)
se *complaire à, to delight in
se délecter à [*sometimes* **de**], to revel in
éclater de rire, to burst out laughing
égayer, to cheer (up) / gladden
enchanter / ravir, to delight
s'enthousiasmer pour, to be enthusiastic about
*être de bonne humeur, to be in a good mood
*être en veine *f*, to be in luck
plaisanter, to joke
porter bonheur *m* (**à**), to bring good luck (to)
*prendre plaisir *m* **à**, to take pleasure in
se réjouir de, to be delighted at
remonter le moral à qn., to cheer sb. up
*rire (de), to laugh (at)
*sourire (de), to smile (at)

bien aise (de), very pleased (to)
bienheureux *f* **-euse**, blissful
chanceux *f* **-euse**, lucky
charmé / enchanté / ravi (de), delighted (to)
content, pleased
fortuné, fortunate
gai, bright / cheerful
heureux *f* **-euse**, happy
insouciant, happy-go-lucky
jovial *pl* **-aux**, jovial
optimiste (à l'égard de), optimistic (about)
radieux *f* **-euse / rayonnnant**, radiant
sans souci, carefree
satisfait, satisfied
transporté de joie *f*, overjoyed
veinard, lucky

Le malheur Unhappiness

l'abattement *m*, dejection
l'affliction *f*, affliction
l'agitation *f*, restlessness
l'angoisse *f*, anguish
le chagrin, grief
la déception / le désappointement, disappointment
la dépression, depression
le désespoir, despair
le désillusionnement, disillusionment
la détresse, distress
la douleur, sorrow
l'émoi *m*, agitation / excitement
l'inquiétude *f* / l'anxiété *f*, anxiety
la larme, tear
le mal du pays / la nostalgie, homesickness
la malchance, bad luck
le malheur, misfortune / unhappiness
le mécontentement (de), dissatisfaction (with)
la mélancolie, melancholy
la préoccupation, preoccupation
le regret, regret
le sanglot, sob
la souffrance, suffering
le soupir, sigh
la torture, torture
le tourment, torment
le tracas, worry
la tristesse, sadness
le trouble, uneasiness

affliger, to pain
blesser / offenser qn., to hurt sb.'s feelings
bouleverser, to shatter
choquer, to shock
consoler, to comfort
consterner, to dismay
*décevoir, to disappoint
déconcerter, to disconcert

déprimer, to depress
désespérer (de), to despair (of)
désoler, to distress
*émouvoir, to affect
fondre en larmes *f*, to burst into tears
gémir, to groan
perdre courage *m*, to lose heart
se *plaindre (de), to complain (about)
pleurer, to cry / weep
pousser (un soupir / un sanglot), to give (a sigh / a sob)
sangloter, to sob
*souffrir, to suffer / put up with
soupirer, to sigh
supporter, to put up with
se tourmenter / se tracasser, to worry
troubler, to disturb

abattu, dejected
accablé, overwhelmed
affligé, distressed
blessé / offensé, hurt
bouleversé, shattered
consterné, appalled
contrarié (de), upset (at)
découragé, despondent
déçu, disappointed
de mauvaise humeur, in a bad mood
déprimé, depressed
désabusé, disenchanted
désappointé, let down
désespéré, desperate / despairing
désolé, sorry
ému, touched / moved
ennuyé, worried [also *annoyed* and *bored*]
inconsolable, disconsolate
inquiet *f* **-iète**, anxious / uneasy
malheureux *f* **-euse**, unhappy
maussade / grognon *f inv or* **-onne / renfrogné**, grumpy
mécontent (de), dissatisfied (with)
mélancolique, gloomy

misérable, miserable
morose, morose
navré, heartbroken
peiné (de), pained / upset (at)
pénible, painful
préoccupé, preoccupied
soucieux f **-euse (de)**, anxious (about)
triste, sad

La surprise Surprise

l'ahurissement m, bewilderment
l'ébahissement m, astonishment
l'étonnement m, surprise / wonder
la stupéfaction, stupefaction
la stupeur, amazement
la surprise, surprise

abasourdir, to bewilder
ahurir, to daze
bouleverser, to throw into confusion
ébahir, to astonish
éberluer colloq, to flabbergast
effarer, to startle
émerveiller, to amaze / fill with wonder
épater colloq, to astound
étonner / *surprendre, to surprise
s'étonner de, to be surprised at
*faire impression f **(sur qn.)**, to make an impression (on sb.)
*faire sensation f, to make a sensation
impressionner, to impress
renverser, to stagger
*revenir de sa surprise, to recover from one's surprise
stupéfier, to dumbfound

abasourdi, bewildered
baba colloq inv, open-mouthed
confondu (de), disconcerted (by) / dumbfounded (at)
étonnant / surprenant, surprising
étonné / surpris, surprised

foudroyé, thunderstruck
soufflé *colloq*, taken aback
stupéfait, astounded
stupéfiant, astounding

La peur Fear

l'alarme *f*, alarm
l'angoisse *f*, agony
l'appréhension *f* **(de)**, dread (of)
la consternation, consternation
l'effroi *m* **/ l'épouvante** *f* **/ la terreur**, terror
l'ennui *m* **/ l'inquiétude** *f* **/ l'anxiété** *f*, anxiety
la frayeur, fright
le frisson, shiver
l'horreur *f*, horror
l'inquiétude *f*, uneasiness
la peur / la crainte, fear
le souci, worry

*avoir des ennuis** *m*, to be worried
*avoir grand-peur que** [+ SUBJUNCTIVE], to be very
  much afraid that
*avoir peur** *f* **(que** [+ SUBJUNCTIVE] **/ de)**, to be afraid
  (that / of)
*craindre**, to fear
épouvanter, to scare
se *faire du souci, to worry
*faire mourir de frayeur** *f*, to frighten to death
*faire peur** *f* **à / effrayer**, to frighten
frémir, to shudder
frissonner, to shiver
s'inquiéter de, to worry about
intimider, intimidate
menacer, threaten
*mourir de peur** *f*, to die of fright
redouter, to dread
trembler, to tremble
affolé, panic-stricken

apeuré, frightened
craintif *f* **-ive**, fearful
effaré, scared
effrayant, frightening
effrayé, afraid
frappé de terreur *f*, terror-stricken
inquiet *f* **-iète**, anxious
intrépide, fearless
menaçant, menacing
mort de peur *f*, petrified
nerveux *f* **-euse**, nervous

La colère Anger

la colère / **l'emportement** *m*, anger (**en colère** / **de mauvaise humeur**, in a bad temper)
la contrariété, vexation
le cri, cry
l'exaspération *f*, exasperation
la fureur / **la furie**, fury
l'hostilité *f*, hostility
l'indignation *f*, indignation
l'irascibilité *f*, hot temper
l'irritation *f*, annoyance
la rage, rage
la rancune, grudge
le ressentiment, resentment
la rogne *colloq*, bad temper
le stress, stress
la susceptibilité, irritability
la tension, tension

agacer, to irritate
crier, to shout
énerver qn., to get on sb.'s nerves
***être en colère** *f* / **fou de rage** *f*, to be angry / fuming (**fou** [*m sing before vowel* **fol**; *f* **folle**], mad)
exaspérer, to incense
s'exciter, to get excited

se fâcher / se *mettre en colère f, to get angry
*faire qch. par dépit m, to do sth. out of spite
bouillir de colère f, to fume with rage
s'indigner, to become indignant
s'irriter (de qch. / contre qn.), to get annoyed (at sth. / with sb.)
laisser éclater sa colère, to give vent to one's anger
rager, to be in a rage
râler, to be hopping mad / gripe
rogner, to grouse

ennuyé, annoyed [also *bored* and *worried*]
ennuyeux f **-euse**, annoying
fâché, angry / annoyed
furieux f **-euse**, furious
haineux f **-euse**, full of hatred
hostile (à / envers), hostile (to)
indigné (de / contre), indignant (at / with)
rancunier f **-ière**, resentful
vindicatif f **-ive**, malicious

SEE ALSO: **Describing People; Liking, Disliking, Comparing**

18. Food Les Aliments

le dessert / l'entremets *m*, dessert
l'entrée *f* / **le plat principal** *pl* -**aux**, main course [**l'entrée**
  was originally a dish between the soup and roast]
le fromage, cheese
le hors-d'œuvre *pl inv*, hors d'œuvre / starter
la nourriture, food (**un aliment,** a food)
le plat (végétarien), (vegerarian) dish (**le plat du jour,**
  today's special)
le potage, soup (**la soupe,** thick soup; **le consommé,**
  clear soup)

Les plats Dishes

la blanquette, white stew
le bœuf bourguignon / mode, beef stew in red wine / with
  carrots
la bouchée à la reine, vol-au-vent (**la reine,** queen)
le bouillon, broth
la brandade (de morue *f***),** salt cod in cream
la brochette, kebab [also means *skewer*]
la carbonnade, beef in beer
le cari, curry
le cassoulet, bean casserole with pork etc.
le civet, game stew
le coq au vin, chicken in red wine
le couscous, couscous [semolina with meat and vegetables
  in a spicy sauce]
la crépinette, small flat spicy sausage
la daube, beef stew in red wine
l'estouffade *f*, braised meat
la fondue, fondue [melted cheese in white wine]
la galantine, cold meat in aspic
la garbure, cabbage soup

le gratin dauphinois, potatoes baked with cheese (**au gratin**, with a cheese and breadcrumb crust)
la gratinée, French onion soup with grated cheese
le haricot de mouton, vegetable and lamb stew (**le mouton**, mutton)
la julienne, soup with chopped vegetables
la macédoine de fruits *m* / **de légumes** *m*, fruit salad / mixed vegetables
le navarin, lamb and vegetable stew
le pâté, pie / pâté (**le pâté de foie** *m*, liver pâté; **le pâté de campagne**, coarse-chopped pâté; **la campagne**, country)
la piperade, Basque omelette with peppers and tomatoes
la pissaladière, Provençal pizza
le potage Parmentier / **Crécy**, thick potato / carrot soup
le pot-au-feu *pl inv*, beef and vegetable stew
la poule au pot, chicken stewed with vegetables
le poulet chasseur, chicken in mushrooms and white wine (**le chasseur**, huntsman)
la quiche lorraine, egg-and-bacon quiche
la raclette, melted Alpine cheese with potatoes and pickles
le ragoût, stew
la ratatouille, mixed Provençal vegetables
les rillettes *f*, fat potted pork
le salmis, game stew
le soufflé (au fromage), (cheese) soufflé
la terrine, pâté [also the pot it's made in]
la vichyssoise, cold leek and potato soup

Les sauces Sauces

l'aïoli *m*, garlic mayonnaise
la béchamel, white sauce
le coulis, poured sauce [usually sweet]
la gelée / **le chaud-froid** *pl* -s -s, jelly
la mayonnaise, mayonnaise
la rouille, mayonnaise with pimento
la sauce, sauce / gravy (**la sauce tomate** *f* / **à la menthe**, tomato / mint sauce)

le suprême, thickened chicken broth
le velouté, thick cream sauce
la vinaigrette, French dressing

LES NOMS DES SAUCES NAMES OF SAUCES

la sauce . . .
    béarnaise, egg yolk, butter, lemon juice
    bordelaise, red wine, mushrooms, shallots
    financière, Madeira, olives, mushrooms
    forestière, mushrooms
    gribiche / ravigote, French dressing with chopped
      hard-boiled egg
    lyonnaise, onion
    maître d'hôtel, butter, parsley, lemon juice (**le maître
      d'hôtel** m, head waiter)
    marchand de vin, red wine and shallots (**le marchand
      de vin** m, wine merchant)
    meunière, brown butter, parsley, lemon juice (**la
      meunière**, miller's wife)
    Mornay, cream and cheese
    normande, cream and mushrooms
    provençale, tomatoes and garlic
    rémoulade, mustard mayonnaise with shallot
    tartare, mustard mayonnaise with capers

La viande Meat

les abats m, offal
l'andouille(tte) f, tripe sausage
le bacon, bacon
les basses-côtes f, spare ribs
le blanc, breast [of chicken etc.]
le boudin (noir), black pudding
la boulette, meatball
le carré (d'agneau m**)**, rack (of lamb)
la cervelle, brains

la charcuterie, assorted pork products
le châteaubriand, porterhouse steak
la côte / la côtelette, rib / chop / cutlet
la cuisse, leg [of chicken etc.]
l'épaule *f*, shoulder
l'escalope *f* **(panée)**, (breaded) escalope
le foie, liver (**le foie gras**, goose-liver pâté)
le gigot (d'agneau *m***)**, leg of lamb
la grillade, grilled meat
la (viande) hachée / le hachis, mince (**le hachis parmentier**, cottage pie; **parmentier**, with potatoes)
le hamburger, hamburger
le jambon (de pays), (uncooked cured) ham (**le pays**, country)
le jambonneau *pl* **-x**, knuckle of pork
la langue (de bœuf *m***)**, (ox-)tongue
le lard, (fat) bacon
le médaillon, tenderloin steak
le pied de porc *m*, (pig's) trotter
le ris, sweetbread
le rognon, kidney
le rosbif, roast beef (**la tranche**, slice; **les rosbifs**, the Brits)
le rôti, joint / roast
la saucisse / la merguez, sausage (**la saucisse de Francfort / de Strasbourg**, frankfurter)
le saucisson, (cold) salami-sausage
la selle (d'agneau *m***)**, saddle (of lamb)
le steak / le bifteck, steak (**le steak tartare**, tartare steak [raw mince]; **bleu**, very rare; **saignant**, rare; **à point**, medium rare; **bien / trop cuit**, well done/overdone)
le tournedos, fillet steak
les tripes *f*, tripe

LES NOMS DES VIANDES NAMES OF MEATS

l'agneau *m*, lamb
le bœuf, beef

le canard / le caneton, duck(ling) (**le magret de canard**, duck breast)
la cuisse de grenouille *f*, frog's leg (**la cuisse**, thigh)
la dinde, turkey
l'escargot *m*, snail
le mouton, mutton
l'oie *f*, goose
le porc, pork
la poularde, (fattened) pullet
la poule, hen / stewing-fowl
le poulet, chicken
le poussin, spring chicken
le veau, veal
la viande de cheval, horsemeat
la volaille, poultry / chicken

Le gibier Game

la bécasse, woodcock
la bécassine, snipe
la caille, quail
le canard sauvage, wild duck
le chevreuil, venison
le coq de bruyère, grouse (**la bruyère**, heather / heath)
le faisan, pheasant
la grive, thrush
le lapin / le lapereau *pl* **-x**, (young) rabbit
le lièvre, hare (**le civet de lièvre**, jugged hare)
la perdrix / le perdreau *pl* **-x**, (young) partridge
le pigeon, pigeon
la pintade, guinea-fowl
le sanglier, wild boar

Les poissons Fish

la bisque, seafood soup
la bouillabaisse, very substantial Provençal fish soup
les crustacés *m*, shellfish

la darne, (fish) steak
les fruits *m* **de mer** *f*, seafood
la matelote / la bourride, fish stew
le poisson, fish
la quenelle (de poisson), light (fish) dumpling

LES NOMS DES POISSONS NAMES OF FISH

l'aiglefin *m*, haddock
l'anchois *m*, anchovy
l'anguille *f*, eel
la barbue, brill
la belon, oyster [from river Belon]
le brochet, pike
le calmar, quid
la carpe, carp
le colin, hake
la coquille Saint-Jacques, scallop
le crabe, crab
la crevette (rose), prawn (**la crevette grise,** shrimp)
la daurade, sea-bream
l'écrevisse *f* **/ la langouste,** crayfish
le flétan, halibut
la (petite) friture, whitebait
le goujon, gudgeon
le hareng (mariné), (marinated) herring
le homard, lobster
l'huître *f*, oyster
la langoustine, scampi / king prawn
la limande, lemon sole
la lotte (de mer *f*), monkfish
le loup (de mer *f*) **/ le bar,** sea bass (**le loup,** wolf)
le maquereau *pl* **-x,** mackerel
le merlan, whiting
la merluche, hake
la morue / le cabillaud, cod
la moule, mussel (**les moules marinière,** mussels
  cooked in their shells in white wine)
la palourde, clam

la perche, perch
la plie / le carrelet, plaice
le poulpe, octopus
la praire, clam
la raie, skate
le rouget, (red) mullet
la sardine, sardine
le saumon (fumé), (smoked) salmon
la sole, sole
le thon, tuna
la truite (au bleu), (poached) trout
le turbot, turbot

Les œufs Eggs

le jaune / le blanc d'œuf *m*, yolk / white of egg
l'œuf *m* **à la coque / dur / mollet / poché / sur le plat**,
  boiled / hard-boiled / soft-boiled / poached / fried egg (**la coque**, shell)
les œufs brouillés / au jambon / au bacon, scrambled
  eggs / ham and eggs / eggs and bacon
l'omelette *f* **(nature / au fromage)**, (plain / cheese) omelette

Les légumes, les noix, et la salade
Vegetables, nuts, and salad

les crudités *f*, mixed raw vegetables
le légume (en conserve / surgelé), (canned / frozen)
  vegetable
la noix, nut / walnut
la salade, green salad (**la salade panachée / composée**,
  mixed salad; **la salade niçoise**, mixed salad with eggs,
  olives, and anchovies; **la salade russe**, Russian salad)

LES NOMS DES LÉGUMES
NAMES OF VEGETABLES

l'artichaut *m*, artichoke (**le fond d'artichaut**, artichoke
  heart)
les asperges *f*, asparagus
l'aubergine *f*, aubergine
l'avocat *m*, avocado
la betterave, beetroot
la blette, spinach beet / Swiss chard
le bolet, boletus [mushroom]
le brocoli, broccoli
la carotte, carrot
le céléri, celery (**la branche / le pied de céléri**, stick / head
  of celery; **le pied**, foot)
le céléri-rave *pl* **-s -s**, celeriac
le cèpe, cepe [mushroom]
le champignon (de Paris), (button) mushroom
la chanterelle, chanterelle [mushroom]
les (pommes) chips *f*, crisps
le chou *pl* **-x (rouge)**, (red) cabbage (**les choux de
  Bruxelles**, sprouts)
la choucroute, sauerkraut
le chou-fleur *pl* **-x -s**, cauliflower
le concombre, cucumber
le cornichon, gherkin
la courgette, courgette (**la courge**, marrow)
le cresson, watercress
l'échalote *f*, shallot
l'endive *f*, chicory (**la chicorée (frisée)**, endive)
les épinards *m*, spinach
le fenouil, fennel
la fève, broad bean
le flageolet, kidney bean
les (pommes) frites *f*, chips
le haricot, bean
les lentilles *f*, lentils
le maïs, sweetcorn
la morille, morel [mushroom]

le navet, turnip

l'oignon *m*, onion

l'olive *f*, olive

les petits pois *m*, peas (**la gousse de pois**, pea-pod; **les pois gourmands / les mange-tout** *m*, mange-tout peas)

le poireau *pl* -**x**, leek

le poivron, pepper

la pomme de terre *f*, potato [literally, apple of earth] (**en robe des champs**, in its jacket; **le champ**, field)

les pommes de terre sautées, fried potatoes

les pommes *f* **vapeur / mousseline / allumettes / dauphine,** boiled / mashed / matchstick / croquette potatoes (**la vapeur**, steam; **la mousseline**, muslin; **l'allumette** *f*, match)

le potiron, pumpkin

la purée (de pommes *f* **de terre)**, mashed potato

le radis, radish (**la botte**, bunch)

le riz (pilaf), (pilao) rice

la salade / la laitue, lettuce

la tomate, tomato

le topinambour, Jerusalem artichoke

la truffe, truffle

LES NOMS DES NOIX† NAMES OF NUTS

l'amande *f*, almond

la cacahouète, peanut

le marron / la châtaigne, chestnut

la noisette, hazel-nut

la noix, walnut

la noix d'acajou, cashew nut (**l'acajou** *m*, mahogany)

la noix de coco *m*, coconut

la noix du Brésil, Brazil-nut

la pistache, pistachio

† **Amande, cacahouète** and **pistache** are technically **graines** *f*, seeds, in French.

Le pain et les pâtes Bread and pasta

la biscotte, rusk
les céréales *f*, cereals
les corn-flakes *m*, cornflakes
la crêpe (de sarrasin *m* **/ de froment** *m*), (buckwheat / wheatflour) pancake
le croque-monsieur *pl inv*, toasted cheese and ham sandwich
la croûte, crust
la farine, flour
la galette, round biscuit / buckwheat pancake (**la galette aux pommes** *f* **/ des Rois**, apple tart / Twelfth Night cake; **le roi**, king)
la gaufrette, wafer
la miette / la mie, crumb
le pain (complet), (wholemeal) bread
le pain grillé, toast (**un toast**, a piece of toast)
les pâtes *f*, pasta (**la pâte**, dough)
le sandwich *pl* -s (**jambon / au jambon**), (ham) sandwich
la tartine (à la confiture), slice / piece of bread and butter (with jam)

LES NOMS DES PAINS NAMES OF BREADS

la baguette, French stick / baguette
la brioche, bun
le chausson (aux pommes *f*), puff-pastry apple turnover
le croissant, croissant
la ficelle, thin French stick
le gros pain, large loaf
le pain au chocolat, puff-pastry bun with chocolate in it
le pain bis / complet / de seigle *m*, brown / wholemeal / rye bread (**bis**, brownish-grey)
le pain d'épice, gingerbread (**l'épice** *f*, spice)
le petit pain (au cumin / aux pavots *m*), roll (with caraway seeds / with poppy seeds)

LES NOMS DES PÂTES NAMES OF PASTA

les macaroni *m*, macaroni
les nouilles *f*, noodles
les spaghetti *m*, spaghetti
le vermicelle *m*, vermicelli [fine pasta for soup]

Les fromages Cheeses

le bleu d'Auvergne, Auvergne blue-veined cheese
le brie / le camembert, soft white round cheeses
le cantal, hard yellow mountain-cheese
le chester, Cheshire
le chèvre, goat's cheese (**la chèvre**, goat)
l'emmenthal *m* / **le gruyère**, hard Swiss cheeses with holes
le fromage à tartiner, cheese spread
le petit suisse, small cream cheese eaten with sugar
le port-salut, mild medium-soft cheese
le roquefort, medium-soft blue-veined sheep's cheese

Les fruits Fruits

la compote de fruits *m*, stewed fruit
un fruit, a (piece of) fruit
les fruits secs, dried fruit
la salade de fruits (frais), (fresh) fruit cocktail

LES NOMS DES FRUITS NAMES OF FRUITS

l'abricot *m*, apricot
l'airelle *f*, cranberry
l'ananas *m*, pineapple
la banane, banana
le brugnon / la nectarine, nectarine
le cassis, blackcurrant
la cerise, cherry
le citron, lemon

le coing, quince
la datte, date
la figue, fig
la fraise (des bois), wild strawberry (**le bois**, wood)
la framboise, raspberry
la grenade, pomegranate
la groseille (à maquereau), gooseberry (**le maquereau**
  pl **-x**, mackerel)
la groseille (rouge), redcurrant
la mandarine, tangerine / mandarin
la mangue, mango
le melon, melo
la mûre (sauvage), blackberry (**sauvage**, wild) (**la mûre**
  is also *mulberry*)
la myrtille, bilberry
l'orange *f*, orange
le pamplemousse, grapefruit
la pastèque, watermelon
la pêche, peach
la poire, pear
la pomme, apple
la prune, plum
le pruneau *pl* **-x**, prune
le raisin (blanc / noir) *sing*, (white / black) grape / grapes
  (**je prendrai du raisin**, I'll have some grapes)
le raisin sec *pl* **-s -s**, raisin (**sec** *f* **sèche**, dry; **le raisin de**
  Corinthe, currant; **le raisin de Smyrne**, sultana)
le reine-claude *pl* **-s -s**, greengage
la rhubarbe, rhubarb

Les desserts et les douceurs
Puddings and sweets

le baba au rhum, rum baba
la bavaroise, flavoured mixture of custard and whipped
  cream
le beignet (aux pommes *f***)**, (apple) fritter
le biscuit / le petit gâteau *pl* **-x**, biscuit

le biscuit salé, cracker (**salé,** salted)
le bonbon, sweet (**un bonbon à la menthe,** a mint)
le chewing-gum, chewing-gum
le chocolat (au lait / à croquer / à *cuire), (milk / plain / cooking) chocolate (**une plaque / une tablette de chocolat,** a block of chocolate; **un chocolat,** a chocolate; **croquer,** to munch)
le chou *pl* **-x à la crème,** cream puff
le clafoutis, cherries baked in batter
la confiture, jam (**la confiture d'oranges** *f*, marmalade)
la coupe glacée, ice-cream sundae
la crème, cream (**la (crème) chantilly,** whipped cream; **à la crème,** with cream)
la crème anglaise, (egg) custard (**la crème pâtissière,** thick custard filling)
la crème caramel, caramelized egg-custard
la crêpe (suzette), (flambé orange) pancake
le diplomate, cold custard pudding with sponge fingers
l'éclair *m*, eclair
l'esquimau ℗ *m; pl* **-x,** choc-ice / ice-lolly
le flan, custard tart
le gâteau *pl* **-x / la pâtisserie,** cake / pastry
la glace (à la vanille / aux fraises, etc.), (vanilla / strawberry, etc.) ice-cream (**le cornet,** cornet / cone)
le massepain, marzipan
le mille-feuille *pl* **- -s,** custard slice
la mousse au chocolat, chocolate mousse
le parfait, dairy ice
le petit four, small fancy pastry (**le four,** oven)
la religieuse, (nun-shaped!) éclair (**la religieuse,** nun)
le sabayon, zabaglione [whipped egg yolks, sugar, and Marsala]
le sablé, shortbread
le savarin, large rum baba
le sorbet, water-ice / sorbet
le soufflé, soufflé
la tarte (aux pommes *f* **/ aux cerises** *f*, **etc.),** apple / cherry, etc. tart

la tarte à la frangipane, almond tart
la tartelette, small tart
la tarte tatin, caramelized apple tart
la tourte, layer cake
le vacherin glacé, ice-cream cake
le yaourt, yogurt

SEE ALSO: **Cooking and Eating; Drinks; The Home;
The Senses; Tobacco and Drugs**

19. **Furniture** Les Meubles

le meuble, piece of furniture
les meubles / le mobilier / l'ameublement *m*, furniture
meubler, to furnish

Le vestibule The hall

la boîte aux lettres *f*, letter-box
le coffre, chest
le paillasson, doormat
le portemanteau *pl* **-x,** coat-rack (**le crochet,** hook)
le porte-parapluie *pl inv*, umbrella stand
la sonnette, doorbell
le téléphone, telephone

Le séjour The living-room

l'abat-jour *m*; *pl inv*, lampshade
l'applique *f*, wall-light
l'amplificateur *m*, amplifier
le bibelot, ornament
la bibliothèque, bookcase
le bureau *pl* **-x / le secrétaire,** desk
le canapé, couch
le cendrier, ashtray (**fumer,** to smoke)
la chaîne (stéréo), hi-fi / stereo
la chaise longue, chaise longue
le coussin, cushion
le disque, record (**passer un disque,** to put on a record)
le disque compact / le CD / le compact disc *pl inv*,
  compact disc / CD
l'étagère *f*, set of shelves
le fauteuil, armchair

le fauteuil à bascule, rocking-chair (**la bascule**, rocker)

le haut-parleur *pl* **- -s**, (loud)speaker

le lampadaire, standard lamp

la lampe, lamp (**l'ampoule** *f*, bulb)

le magnétophone (à cassette), cassette recorder (**la cassette**, cassette)

le magnétoscope, video recorder (**la vidéocassette**, video cassette; **le film vidéo** *pl* **-s -**, video film)

le mobilier de salon *m*, (drawing-room) suite

la moquette, (fitted) carpet

le paravent, (folding) screen

la pendule, clock

la photo(graphie), photograph

le piano (à queue), (grand) piano (**le tabouret**, piano-stool)

le porte-revues *pl inv*, magazine rack / canterbury

le radiateur, radiator

le radiateur à accumulation *f*, storage heater

la radio / le poste (de radio), radio

le radiocassette, radio cassette player

le rayon, shelf

le rayonnage, shelving

le rideau *pl* **-x**, curtain

le seau à charbon *m*, coal-scuttle (**le seau** *pl* **-x**, bucket)

le sofa, sofa

la table roulante / basse, trolley / coffee-table

le tableau *pl* **-x**, picture / painting

le tabouret, stool

le tapis, carpet / rug (**le tapis de foyer** *m*, hearth-rug)

la télévision / le téléviseur, television (set) (**à la télévision**, on television)

le tisonnier, poker

le tourne-disque(s) *pl* **- -s / l'électrophone** *m*, record-player

le vase, vase

la vitrine, (glass-fronted) cabinet

allumer / *éteindre, to switch on / off

allumer le feu, to light the fire

écouter, to listen to

*écrire, to write

*lire, to read
regarder, to look at
se relaxer, to relax
tirer les rideaux, to draw the curtains (**le rideau** *pl* **-x**,
  curtain)

La salle à manger The dining-room

le buffet / la desserte, sideboard
la chaise, chair
le chandelier, candlestick (**la bougie**, candle)
la nappe, tablecloth
la serviette, table napkin
la table, table (**la rallonge**, leaf / extension; **à table!**, let's
  eat!)
le vaisselier, dresser

approcher une chaise (de la table), to draw up a chair (to
  the table)
se *mettre à table, to sit down to eat
*mettre / dresser la table, to lay the table

La terrasse The terrace

le banc, bench
le barbecue, barbecue (**le charbon de bois**, charcoal; **le
  bois**, wood)
la chaise longue / le transat, deck-chair
la chaise pliante, folding chair
le guéridon, pedestal table
le parasol, sunshade / garden umbrella

La cuisine The kitchen

la chaise de bébé *m*, high chair
le chauffage central, central heating
la climatisation, air-conditioning
le congélateur, freezer

la **cuisinière** (**électrique** / **à gaz** *m*), (electric / gas) cooker
l'**évier** *m*, sink
le **four**, oven (**au four**, in the oven)
le **four à micro-ondes** *f*, microwave
le **fourneau** *pl* -x, (heating) stove
le **frigo** / le **réfrigérateur**, fridge / refrigerator (**le bac à glaçons**, ice-tray)
le **gril**, grill
le **grille-pain** *pl inv*, toaster
le **robinet**, tap
le **tabouret**, stool
le **tuyau** *pl* -x, drain
le **ventilateur**, fan

La chambre à coucher The bedroom

l'**armoire**(-**penderie** *pl* -s -s) / la **penderie**, wardrobe
le **berceau** *pl* -x, cradle
la **bouillotte**, hot-water bottle
le **cintre**, (clothes-)hanger
la **coiffeuse** / la **table de toilette**, dressing-table
la **commode**, chest of drawers (**le tiroir**, drawer)
la **corbeille à papiers** *m*, waste-paper basket
la **couette**, duvet
la **couverture** (**chauffante**), (electric) blanket (**chauffer**, to heat)
le **couvre-lit** *pl* -s / le **couvre-pied(s)** *pl* -s, bedspread
la **descente de lit** *m*, bedside rug
le **drap**, sheet
l'**édredon** *m*, eiderdown
la **glace**, mirror
la **lampe de chevet** *m*, bedside lamp
le **lit**, bed
le **lit d'enfant**, cot (l'**enfant** *m* / *f*, child)
la **literie**, bedclothes
le **matelas**, mattress
l'**oreiller** *m*, pillow
le **placard**, cupboard

le poster / l'affiche *f*, poster
le réveil(-radio *pl* **-s -)**, (radio) alarm
la table de nuit / de chevet *m*, bedside table (**la nuit**, night)
la taie (d'oreiller *m*), pillowcase
le transistor, transistor
le traversin, bolster
la veilleuse, night-light
le walkman *pl* **-s**, walkman (**le casque d'écoute**, headset)

*****aller / *****être au lit**, to go to / be in bed
*****faire le lit**, to make the bed
*****mettre en ordre** *m*, to tidy up
ranger ses affaires *f*, to put one's things away

La salle de bains   The bathroom

l'armoire *f* **de toilette** *f*, bathroom cabinet
la baignoire, bath
le bain moussant, bubble bath
le bidet, bidet
le blaireau *pl* **-x**, shaving-brush
la bonde / le tampon, plug
la brosse à dents *f*, toothbrush
la chasse d'eau, (lavatory) flush (**l'eau** *f*; *pl* **-x**, water; **tirer la chasse d'eau**, to pull the chain)
le chauffe-bain *pl* **- -s / le chauffe-eau** *pl inv*, immersion heater (**la veilleuse**, pilot-light)
le dentifrice / la pâte dentifrice, toothpaste
le déodorant, deodorant
la douche, shower
le drap de bain *m*, bath towel
l'éponge *f*, sponge
l'essuie-main(s) *m*; *pl inv*, hand-towel
le gant de toilette *f*, glove flannel
le lavabo, wash-basin
le miroir de salle de bains, bathroom mirror
le papier hygiénique, toilet paper

le peigne, comb
le pèse-personne *pl* - -**s**, bathroom scales
le porte-serviette(s) *pl inv*, towel-rail
le rasoir (électrique), (electric) razor (**la lame**, blade)
le savon, soap
le sèche-cheveux *pl inv*, hairdrier
la serviette (de toilette *f*), towel
le shampooing, shampoo
le store (vénitien), (Venetian) blind
le tapis de bain *m*, bath mat
les toilettes *f* / **les WC** (pronounced [dublvese] or
  [vese]) / **les waters**, lavatory

se brosser les dents *f* / **les cheveux** *m*, to brush one's
  teeth / hair
se coiffer, to do one's hair
se doucher, to shower
s'essuyer, to dry oneself
se laver, to wash
monter / baisser le store, to pull up / down the blind
*prendre un bain, to have a bath
se raser, to shave

SEE ALSO: **The Home; Materials**

20. Greetings and Replies
Les Salutations et les réponses

L'arrivée Arrival

allô!, hello [on phone]
attention!, look out!
avez-vous fait bon voyage?, did you have a good trip?
(soyez le / la) bienvenu(e)!, welcome!
bonjour, hello / good morning / good afternoon
bonsoir, hello / good evening
(comment) ça va?, how are things? (**ça va (bien) merci**, fine; **comme ci comme ça**, so-so)
comment allez-vous? / **comment tu vas?**, how are you? (**très bien, merci**, very well, thank you)
entrez!, come in
pardon, Monsieur / **pardon, Madame** / **excusez-moi**, excuse me
salut!, hi!
s'il vous plaît, . . ., excuse me, can you tell me . . .? [literally, *please*, . . .]
très heureux (*f* -euse) **de te** / **vous voir**, delighted to see you
vous désirez?, can I help you?

Le départ Departure

à bientôt, see you soon
à demain, see you tomorrow
adieu, farewell
à lundi prochain, see you next Monday
amusez-vous / **amuse-toi bien**, have a good time
à tout à l'heure / **à plus tard**, see you later (**tout à l'heure**, in a moment)
au plaisir de vous revoir, look forward to seeing you again
au revoir, goodbye
bonne après-midi, have a nice afternoon

bonne nuit, good night, sleep well
bonne route, safe journey (**la route**, road)
bonne soirée, have a good evening
bonsoir, good evening / good night
bon voyage, have a good trip
dors / dormez bien, sleep well
salue(z) X de ma part, all the best to X
salut!, bye then!

Les rencontres Meetings

connaissez-vous . . . ?, have you met . . . ? / do you know
. . . ?
heureux (*f* **-euse**) **de faire votre connaissance** *f***!** /
  enchanté(e)!, pleased to meet you
je vous présente . . ., may I introduce . . . ?
puis-je me présenter?, may I introduce myself? (**je
  m'appelle . . .**, my name is . . .)
voudriez-vous + INF, would you like to?
vous vous connaissez?, do you know each other? (**on se
  connaît déjà de vue** *f*, we already know each other by sight)
X, voici Y, X, this is Y

Les excuses Apologies

(je suis) désolé(e), I'm awfully sorry
excusez-moi de vous avoir dérangé(e)(s), sorry to have
  troubled you
je regrette infiniment, I'm extremely sorry
je vous dérange, Monsieur / Madame?, am I disturbing
  you?
ne m'en veux / voulez pas, . . ., please don't be angry with
  me, but . . . [note the special imperative forms of **vouloir**
  used in this expression]
pardon / je m'excuse, sorry / I beg your pardon
pardonnez-moi, please forgive me

Les invitations Invitations

allons-y, let's go [= get going]

ne vous dérangez pas, don't go to a lot of trouble

on s'en va?, shall we go? [= leave]

on se revoit?, shall we see each other again?

puis-je vous raccompagner / inviter à . . .?, may I see you home / invite you to . . .?

qu'est-ce que je vous offre?, what will you have?

servez-vous, help yourself

vas-y / allez-y, go ahead (and do it)

vous permettez?, may I?

Les circonstances spéciales
Special occasions

à vos souhaits! / santé! *f colloq*, bless you [after a sneeze] (**le souhait**, desire)

à votre santé! / à ta santé! / à la vôtre! / à la tienne! / santé!, cheers!

bon anniversaire!, happy birthday!

bon appétit!, enjoy it / your meal

bon courage!, all the best

bon rétablissement!, get well soon

bonne année!, happy New Year!

bonne chance!, good luck!

bonne fête!, many happy returns (of your name day) (**la fête**, name / saint's day)

bonne journée!, have a good day

bravo!, bravo ! / well done!

félicitations *f* **(pour)**, congratulations (on) (**toutes mes félicitations!**, all the best)

joyeuses Pâques, happy Easter!

joyeux Noël, merry Christmas!

meilleurs vœux, best wishes

nos sincères condoléances *f*, our sincerest sympathy

X vous rappelle à son bon souvenir / vous transmet son bon souvenir, X sends best wishes (**le souvenir**, remembrance)

Les réponses Replies

ah bon, ah well, in that case . . .

au contraire, quite the reverse

à votre service *m*, glad to help

bien entendu, certainly

bien sûr (que non), of course (not)

ça dépend, that depends

ça m'est égal, it's all the same to me

ça ne fait rien / cela n'a aucune importance, it doesn't matter

ça, par exemple / ça alors, well, really

ça va sans dire, that goes without saying

ce n'est pas la peine, it's not worth it

ce n'est rien / il n'y a pas de mal, that's all right [in reply to apology] (**le mal** *pl* maux, harm / hurt)

c'en est trop, it's too much

c'est exact, that's right

c'est très aimable, that's very kind of you

comment? / quoi? [*ruder*] **/ hein?** [*rudest*], (I beg your) pardon / what?

d'accord/d'ac *colloq*, OK

de rien / je vous en prie / (il n'y a) pas de quoi, don't mention it

doucement!, calm down! / go easy!

entendu!, agreed!

et alors?, so what?

super, terrific

flûte! / mince! / zut (alors)!, bother!

formidable, great

jamais de la vie, not on your life

j'arrive, I'm coming

je regrette / suis désolé(e), no, I'm sorry

je serais ravi(e), I'd be delighted

justement, exactly

laissez-moi tranquille, leave me alone

mais non [contradicting positive statement], no, you're wrong, it isn't

mais oui [agreeing with positive statement], you're right, it is

mais si [contradicting negative statement], you're wrong, it is

merci / non merci, no thank you (**oui merci / oui, s'il vous plaît**, yes thank you)

merci de l'invitation *f*, thanks for asking (me)

merci mille fois, thanks a million (**la fois**, time)

merci pour votre aide *f*, thanks for your help

ne t'en fais pas / ne vous en faites pas, don't worry

ne t'inquiète pas / ne vous inquiétez pas, don't worry

oh là là, oh dear

oui, ça va, yes, that's all right

(oui) s'il vous plaît, (yes) please

parfait, great

pas du tout, not at all

pas question *f*, out of the question

quand même, all the same

que faire? / quoi faire?, what shall we do?

quel dommage!, what a pity!

quelle barbe!, what a bore! (**la barbe**, beard)

quelle horreur!, how dreadful!

quel toupet!, what a nerve! (**le toupet**, cheek)

sans blague, you don't say (**la blague**, joke)

sensas(s)!, great!

tant mieux, all the better

tant pis, so much the worse / too bad

tiens, well, well

vaut mieux pas, better not

volontiers / avec plaisir *m*, with pleasure

vraiment?, really?

SEE ALSO: **Directions; Identity; Post and Telephone; Reading and Writing; Shops and Shopping**

21. **Hair** Les Cheveux

la barbe, beard
les cheveux *m*, hair
les favoris *m*, sideboards
la moustache, moustache
le poil, body hair

Comment les décrire How to describe it

*être chauve, to be bald

aux cheveux . . ., with . . . hair
*avoir les cheveux . . ., to have . . . hair

  argentés, silver
  blancs, white
  blond roux, sandy
  blonds, fair / blonde
  bruns, dark / brown
  châtain clair, light brown
  châtain roux, auburn
  châtains, brown / chestnut
  gris, grey
  gris argent, silver grey
  grisonnants, greying
  noirs, black
  poivre et sel, salt-and-pepper
  roux, red
  bouclés / frisés, curly
  brillants, glossy
  courts, short
  crépus, frizzy
  drus / épais, thick
  fins, fine
  gras, greasy
  longs, long
  mi-longs, medium length

nattés, plaited
ondulés, wavy
plaqués, plastered down
plats/raides, straight
rares, thin
ras/en brosse, cropped
secs, dry
sur le dos, down one's back
teints, dyed
ternes, dull

Ce qu'on en fait What you do with it

la boucle, curl
le chignon, bun (**en chignon**, in a bun)
la frange, fringe
la mèche, lock/strand of hair (also *streak*)
la natte, braid/plait/pigtail
la perruque, wig
le postiche, hair-piece
la queue de cheval, pony-tail (**le cheval** *pl* **-aux**, horse)
la raie, parting
la tresse, braid/plait

se brosser les cheveux *m*, to brush one's hair
se coiffer, to do one's hair
se peigner, to comb one's hair
se raser, to shave
se *teindre les cheveux *m*, to dye one's hair

Ce qu'on met dessus What you use on it

le baume, conditioner
le bigoudi/le rouleau *pl* **-x**, roller
la brosse à cheveux *m*, hairbrush
les ciseaux *m*, scissors
la coloration, tint
l'épingle *f* **à cheveux** *m*, hairpin
le fixatif/le fixateur, setting-lotion

le gel, gel
la lame (de rasoir *m*), (razor) blade
la laque, hair-spray
la lotion après-rasage / l'after-shave *m*; *pl inv*, aftershave
la mousse à raser / la crème à raser, shaving-foam / -cream
le peigne, comb
le rasage, shave
le rasoir (électrique), (electric) razor
le sèche-cheveux *pl inv*, hairdrier
le shampooing, shampoo

Chez le coiffeur At the hairdresser's

le brushing, blow-dry
le coiffeur / la coiffeuse, hairdresser
la coiffure, hair-do
la coupe (de cheveux *m*), (hair)cut
la mise en plis, set (**le pli**, fold / curl)
la permanente, perm
le reflet, highlight
le rinçage, rinse
le salon de coiffure *f*, hairdresser's
le séchoir, [hairdresser's] hairdrier

coiffer qn., to do sb.'s hair
couper, to cut
égaliser / raccourcir / rafraîchir, to trim
se *faire couper les cheveux *m*, to have a haircut
se *faire faire un brushing, to have a blow-dry
se *faire friser les cheveux *m* / ***teindre les cheveux**, to
  have one's hair curled / dyed
*prendre un rendez-vous, to make an appointment
sur les côtés *m* / **sur le haut**, at the sides / on top

SEE ALSO: **Adornment; Colours; Describing People; The
Human Body**

22. Health and Sickness
La Santé et les maladies

Les symptômes Symptoms

l'accès *m* (de faiblesse *f* / de fièvre *f*), (fainting-)
  fit / attack (of fever)
l'agonie *f*, agony; death throes
l'ampoule *f*, blister
la blessure / la plaie, wound
le bleu *pl* -s / la meurtrissure / la contusion, bruise
la bosse / la grosseur, lump
le bouton, spot
la brûlure, burn
le catarrhe, catarrh
la cécité, blindness
le choc, shock
la cicatrice, scar
la claudication, lameness
le clou / le furoncle, boil
le coma, coma
la commotion cérébrale, concussion
la contagion, contagion
le cor, corn
la coupure, cut
les crampes *f*, cramp
la crise (de), attack (of)
la démangeaison, itch
la démence, insanity
la douleur (aiguë / irritante / lacinante / sourde), (sharp /
  nagging / throbbing / dull) pain
l'écharde *f*, splinter
l'égratignure *f*, scratch
l'enflure *f*, swelling
l'engelure *f*, chilblain
l'entorse *f*, sprain
l'épidémie *f*, epidemic

l'épuisement *m*, exhaustion
l'éraflure *f*, graze
l'éruption *f*, rash
l'évanouissement *m*, faint
la faiblesse, weakness
la fièvre, fever
la folie, madness
la foulure, fracture
les frissons *m*, shivers
le hoquet, hiccup (***avoir le hoquet**, to have hiccups)
l'indigestion *f*, indigestion
l'indisposition *f*, illness / upset
l'infection *f*, infection
l'infirmité *f*, infirmity
l'inflammation *f* (**de**), inflammation (of)
l'intoxication *f* (**alimentaire**), (food) poisoning
le mal *pl* **maux**, ache / complaint
une maladie grave / douloureuse / contagieuse, a
  serious / painful / contagious illness
le microbe, microbe
la morsure, bite
la nausée, nausea / vomiting
l'œil (*m*; *pl* **les yeux**) **poché**, black eye (**pocher**, to poach)
la paralysie, paralysis
la piqûre (d'insecte *m*), (insect) bite
la plaie, wound
le point (de côté *m*), stitch (in the side)
le poison, poison
le renvoi, belch
le saignement / l'hémorragie *f*, bleeding (**les
  saignements de nez** *m*, nosebleed)
la sueur, sweat
la suppuration, suppuration
le symptôme, symptom
la tension basse / l'hypotension *f*, low blood-pressure
la tension élevée / l'hypertension *f*, high blood-pressure
  (***faire de l'hypertension**, have high blood-pressure)
la toux, cough

la tumeur, tumour
la verrue, wart
le vertige, dizziness
le virus, virus
les vomissements *m*, vomiting

Les maladies Diseases

l'acné *m*, acne
les aigreurs *f* **d'estomac** *m*, heartburn
l'anémie *f*, anemia
l'angine *f*, tonsillitis (**les amygdales** *f*, tonsils; **une angine de poitrine** *f*, angina)
l'appendicite *f*, appendicitis
l'arthrite *f*, arthritis
l'asthme *m*, asthma
une attaque, a stroke (**une attaque de . . .**, an attack of . . .)
les ballonnements *m*, flatulence
la bronchite, bronchitis
les calculs *m* **biliaires / rénaux**, gallstones / kidney stones
le cancer, cancer
le choléra, cholera
la colique, colic
la conjonctivite, conjunctivitis
la constipation, constipation
la coqueluche, whooping cough
le coup de soleil *m*, sunburn
la crise cardiaque / d'épilepsie *f*, heart attack / epileptic fit
la crise de foie *m*, liver attack [= stomach upset]
la cystite, cystitis
la dépression nerveuse, nervous breakdown
le diabète, diabetes
la diarrhée, diarrhoea
la diphthérie, diphtheria
la dysenterie, dysentery
l'engelure *f*, frost-bite
l'épilepsie *f*, epilepsy
la fièvre typhoïde / écarlate, typhoid / scarlet fever

la gastrite, gastritis
la goutte, gout
la grippe, flu
les hémorroïdes *f*, hemorrhoids
la hernie, hernia
une indigestion, indigestion
l'infarctus *m* **(du myocarde)**, coronary (thrombosis)
l'insolation *f*, sunstroke
l'insomnie *f*, insomnia
la jaunisse, jaundice
la lèpre, leprosy (**le lépreux** *f* **-euse**, leper)
la leucémie, leukemia
le lumbago, lumbago
le mal *pl* **maux (de tête etc.)**, (head etc.)ache
le mal de mer *f* **/ de l'air** *m* **/ des transports** *m*, sea / air /
   travel sickness
la maladie vénérienne, venereal disease
la migraine, migraine
la névralgie, neuralgia
les oreillons *m*, mumps
la peste, plague
la pleurésie, pleurisy
la pneumonie, pneumonia
la rage, rabies
le refroidissement, chill
les rhumatismes, rheumatism
le rhume (de cerveau / de poitrine *f*), (head / chest)
   cold (**le cerveau** *pl* **-x**, brain; **le gros rhume**, heavy cold)
le rhume des foins *m*, hay fever
la rougeole, measles
la rubéole, German measles
la salmonellose, salmonella poisoning
la scarlatine, scarlet fever
la septicémie, septicemia / blood-poisoning
le SIDA, AIDS
le tétanos, tetanus
la tuberculose, tuberculosis
le typhus, typhus

l'ulcère *m*, ulcer
la varice, varicose vein
la varicelle, chicken-pox
la variole, smallpox
la verrue (plantaire), verruca (**la plante du pied**, sole)

Comment on est How are you

abattu, depressed
allergique (à), allergic (to)
anémique, anaemic
asthmatique, asthmatic
aveugle, blind (**la canne blanche**, white stick)
bien portant / sain, healthy
boiteux *f* **-euse**, lame
borgne, one-eyed
bossu, hump-backed
cardiaque, with a heart condition
cassé, broken
constipé, constipated
débile, mentally deficient
diabétique, diabetic
en bonne / mauvaise santé, in good / bad health
enceinte, pregnant
enflé, swollen
en forme *f*, fit (**en pleine forme**, on top form)
enroué, hoarse
épileptique, epileptic
épuisé, exhausted
estropié, crippled / lame
évanoui / sans connaissance *f*, unconscious
faible, weak (**affaibli par la maladie**, weakened by illness)
fiévreux *f* **-euse**, feverish
fou, *m sing* before vowel **fol**; *f* **folle**, mad (**devenir fou**, to go mad)
foulé, sprained
guéri, cured
handicapé, disabled

hors d'haleine *f*, short of breath
indemne, unscathed
indisposé, unwell
infecté, infected
infirme, disabled
malade, ill (**malade comme un chien**, sick as a parrot; **le chien**, dog)
maladif *f* **-ive**, sickly
mal portant, in poor health
mutilé, disabled (by wounds)
paralysé (de), paralysed (in)
pénible, painful
piqué (par), stung (by)
souffrant, unwell
sourd, deaf (**un appareil acoustique**, hearing-aid)
sourd-muet (*f* **sourde-muette**), deaf and dumb

Ce qu'on fait What you do

s'affaiblir, to grow weaker
*aller bien / mal / mieux, to be well / ill / better
appeler / *faire venir le médecin, to send for the doctor
attraper, to catch
*avoir chaud / froid, to be hot / cold
*avoir de la fièvre, to be feverish
*avoir / *faire de la température, to have a (high) temperature (***avoir quarante de fièvre**, to have a temperature of 40°C)
*avoir la tête qui tourne, to feel dizzy (**la tête**, head)
*avoir mal à (la tête etc.), to have (head etc.)ache
*avoir mal au cœur, to feel sick (**le cœur**, heart)
se casser (la jambe etc.), to break (one's leg etc.)
se *démettre / se déboîter (l'épaule *f* **etc.)**, to dislocate (one's shoulder etc.)
s'écouter, to coddle oneself
empirer, to get worse
enfler / gonfler, to swell
s'enrouer, to become hoarse

éprouver / *ressentir (une douleur), to feel (a pain)

éternuer, to sneeze

*être en convalescence, to convalesce

*être enrhumé, to have a cold

s'évanouir, to faint

se *faire du mal, to hurt oneself

*faire mal, to hurt (**cela me fait mal**, that hurts; **le mal**, hurt)

se *faire mal à (la jambe etc.), to hurt (one's leg etc.)

se *faire opérer (de), to have an operation (on)

*faire une cure, to take a cure / take the waters

*faire une rechute, to have a relapse

se fouler (la cheville etc.), to sprain (one's ankle etc.)

frissonner, to shiver

garder le lit, to stay in bed

grossir, to put on weight

s'infecter, to become infected

maigrir, to lose weight

perdre / *reprendre connaissance *f*, to lose / regain consciousness

se porter bien / mal, to be in good / poor health

*prendre (des médicaments), to take (medicines)

*prendre froid / se refroidir, to catch a chill

se refermer, to heal [wound]

se *remettre / se rétablir / guérir (de), to recover (from)

se reposer, to rest

*rester au chaud, to keep warm

saigner, to bleed

se *sentir (bien / malade / mieux), to feel (well / ill / better)

*souffrir (de), to suffer (from)

supporter, to bear / put up with

*tomber malade, to fall ill

se tordre (le poignet etc.), to twist (one's wrist etc.)

tousser, to cough

transpirer / suer, to sweat

vomir, to be sick

Les médecins Doctors

le / la charlatan(e), quack
le chirurgien, surgeon
le / la dermatologue, dermatologist
le (médecin) généraliste, general practitioner
le / la gynécologue, gynaecologist
le médecin / le docteur, doctor
le médecin consultant, consultant
le / la neurologue, neurologist
l'oculiste *m / f,* eye specialist
l'orthopédiste *m / f,* orthopedist
l'ostéopathe *m / f,* osteopath
l'oto-rhino-laryngologiste *m / f; pl - - -s,* ear, nose, and
  throat specialist
le / la pédiatre, children's doctor / pediatrician
le / la pédicure, chiropodist
le / la psychiatre, psychiatrist
le / la psychologue, psychologist
le / la spécialiste, specialist

Ce qu'ils font What they do

ausculter, to sound the chest
conseiller, to advise
diagnostiquer, to diagnose
*envoyer à l'hôpital *m,* to send to hospital
examiner, to examine
guérir, to cure
*mettre au régime, to put on a diet (**maigrir,** to lose
  weight)
*prendre rendez-vous *m,* to make an appointment
*prescrire, to prescribe

Chez le médecin At the doctor's

le cabinet (médical *pl* **-aux),** surgery
le certificat médical *pl* **-aux,** medical certificate
la consultation, consultation

la contraception, contraception
le diagnostic, diagnosis
l'examen *m* **/ l'analyse** *f*, examination
la feuille de maladie, health-insurance form
les heures *f* **de consultation** *f* **/ de visite** *f*, surgery /
  visiting hours
le / la malade, patient
la médecine, medicine
le nerf, nerve
l'ordonnance *f*, prescription (**rédiger / exécuter une**
  ordonnance, to write out / make up a prescription)
la piqûre / l'injection *f*, injection
le pouls, pulse (**tâter / *prendre le pouls,** to feel the pulse)
le prélèvement (de sang *m* **/ d'urine** *f*), (blood / urine)
  sample
les premiers soins *m*, first aid
la pression, blood pressure (**contrôler la pression,** to
  check blood pressure)
les règles *f*, menstruation (***avoir ses règles,** to have
  one's period)
le remède, cure
le rendez-vous *pl inv*, appointment
la respiration, breathing
le sang, blood (**le groupe sanguin,** blood group; **le**
  système sanguin, circulatory system)
la santé, health
le stéthoscope, stethoscope
la température, temperature (***prendre la**
  température, to take one's temperature)
le thermomètre, thermometer
le vaccin, vaccine / vaccination

A l'hôpital At the hospital

l'ambulance *f*, ambulance
l'amélioration *f*, improvement
l'anesthésie *f* (**générale / locale**), (general / local)
  anaesthetic

l'assurance maladie *f*, health insurance

l'avortement *m*, abortion

le bain de boue *f* / **de vapeur** *f* / **thermal**, mud / steam / mineral bath

le bilan (de santé *f*), (health) check-up

la béquille, crutch

le brancard, stretcher

la clinique, clinic

la convalescence, convalescence

la courbe de température *f*, temperature chart

l'écharpe *f*, sling

l'échographie *f*, ultrasound / ultrasonics

la fausse couche, miscarriage [literally, *false confinement*]

le fauteuil roulant, wheelchair

la guérison / **le rétablissement**, recovery

l'hémogramme *m*, blood count

les heures *f* **de visite** *f*, visiting hours

l'hôpital *m*; *pl* **-aux**, hospital

l'hydrothérapie *f*, hydrotherapy

l'hygiène *f*, hygiene

l'infirmière *f* (*m* **-ier**) (**de nuit**), (night) nurse

le masseur *f* **-euse**, masseur / masseuse

le médecin de service *m*, duty doctor

l'opération *f* / **l'intervention** *f*, operation

le plâtre, plaster cast

la prise de sang *m*, blood test

la radio(graphie), X-ray

le régime, diet

le repos, rest

la salle d'opération *f*, operating-theatre

le SAMU (Service d'aide médicale urgente), emergency medical service

le sanatorium, sanatorium

le service / **la salle d'hôpital**, ward

le service de réanimation, intensive-care unit

les soins *m* (**pré-nataux** / **post-opératoires**), (antenatal / post-operative) care

la sortie (de clinique *f*), discharge

le traitement, course of treatment

la transfusion sanguine, blood transfusion
l'urgence *f,* emergency (**la salle d'urgence,** emergency
ward; **un(e) accidenté(e) de première urgence,**
emergency case)

masser, to massage
s'occuper de, to look after
opérer (un(e) malade), to operate (on a patient)
panser, to dress [wound]
radiographier, to X-ray
soigner, to treat / look after
traiter par les ultrasons *m,* to give ultrasound treatment

Chez le pharmacien   At the chemist's

l'analgésique *m* **/ l'antalgique** *m,* pain-killer
l'antibiotique *m,* antibiotic
l'antiseptique *m* **/ le désinfectant,** antiseptic
l'aspirine *f,* aspirin
la bande / le bandage, bandage (**la bande adhésive,**
adhesive tape; **la bande élastique,** elastic bandage)
le calmant / le sédatif, tranquillizer
le comprimé / le cachet, tablet
le coton hydrophile, cotton wool
l'eau *f* **dentifrice,** mouthwash
le fortifiant, tonic
le gargarisme, gargle
les gouttes *f* **(nasales / pour les oreilles** *f* **/ pour les yeux**
m), (nasal / ear / eye) drops
le laxatif / le purgatif, laxative
le liniment / la friction, liniment
le médicament / le remède, medicine
le pansement, dressing / bandage
la pastille, lozenge
la pénicilline, penicillin
la pharmacie (de garde / de service *m),* (duty) chemist's
(**la garde,** care)
la pilule (contraceptive), (contraceptive) pill

la pommade / la crème, ointment
le préservatif, condom
le remontant, tonic
la serviette hygiénique, sanitary towel
le sirop (pour la toux), cough mixture
le somnifère, sleeping-tablet
le sparadrap, sticking-plaster
le suppositoire, suppository
le tampon, tampon
la trousse de secours, first-aid kit (**le secours**, help)
la vitamine, vitamin
la vaseline ⓟ, vaseline ⓟ

avaler, to swallow
diluer, to dissolve
mâcher, to chew

à *prendre à jeun / avant les repas *m* **/ après les repas /**
trois fois *f* **par jour** *m* **/ en cas de douleurs** *f*, to be taken
on an empty stomach / before meals / after meals / three
times a day / in case of pain (**jeûner**, to fast)
usage externe / interne, for external / internal use

Chez le dentiste At the dentist's

l'abcès *m*, abscess
l'appareil *m* **(dentaire)**, brace
le bridge, bridge
le cabinet dentaire, dentist's surgery
la carie (dentaire), dental decay / caries
la couronne, crown
la dent (du devant / du fond / du bas / du haut),
(front / back / bottom / top) tooth
la dent de lait *m* **/ de sagesse** *f* **/ cassée / branlante**,
milk / wisdom / broken / loose tooth
le dentier / la prothèse, denture
le / la dentiste, dentist
la fausse dent / la dent artificielle, false tooth
la gencive, gum
l'injection *f*, injection

le mal de dents *f*, toothache
le pansement, temporary filling
la plaque dentaire, plaque
le plombage, filling
la racine, root
la rage de dents, violent toothache
le tartre, tartar

arracher/*extraire, to extract (**se *faire arracher une dent**, to have a tooth out)
*avoir mal aux dents *f*, to have toothache
branler, to be loose
ébrécher, to chip
plomber / obturer une dent, to fill a tooth

Chez l'opticien At the optician's

l'étui *m* **à lunettes** *f*, glasses case
le glaucome, glaucoma
les jumelles *f*, binoculars
les lentilles *f* **de contact (dures / souples)**, (hard / soft) contact lenses
le lorgnon / le pince-nez *pl inv*, pince-nez
la loupe, magnifying glass
les lunettes *f* **(de soleil** *m*), (sun)glasses
le monocle, monocle
la monture, frame
le test oculaire, eye-test
le verre / la lentille, lens (**le verre teinté**, tinted lens)
la vue (bonne / faible), (good / weak) sight

contrôler, to check

daltonien *f* **-enne**, colour-blind
myope, short-sighted
presbyte / hypermétrope, long-sighted

SEE ALSO: **Accidents; Disasters; The Human Body; Science; The Senses; Tobacco and Drugs**

23. History L'Histoire

l'âge *m*, age (l'âge de bronze *m* / de fer *m* / de pierre *f* / d'or
  m, bronze / iron / stone / golden age)
l'antiquité *f*, antiquity
l'apogée *m* (de), high point (of)
l'archéologie *f*, archaeology
l'archéologue *m/f*, archaeologist
l'avenir *m* / le futur, future (à l'avenir, in the future)
la chronologie, chronology
la chute, fall
la civilisation, civilization
la conspiration des poudres, Gunpowder Plot
la croisade, crusade
la décennie, decade
le déclin, decline
le développement, development
le document, document
l'époque *f*, epoch / era (à cette époque, at that time;
  l'époque glaciaire, ice-age)
l'ère *f*, era (l'ère chrétienne, the Christian era; de notre ère,
  AD; avant notre ère, BC)
l'événement *m*, event
le fait, fact
la féodalité, feudalism
les fouilles *f*, excavations
l'histoire *f*, history
l'historien *m*; *f* -enne, historian
l'impérialisme *m*, imperialism
le monument, memorial / monument
le moyen âge, Middle Ages (le haut moyen âge, Dark Ages;
  haut, high)
le musée, museum
l'origine *f*, origin (dès l'origine, from the very beginning)
le passé, past (dans le passé, in the past)
la période, period
la préhistoire, prehistory

le présent, present (**à présent**, at the moment)
la Réforme, Reformation
la Renaissance, Renaissance
la Révolution, (French) Revolution
les ruines *f*, ruins
le siècle, century (**au dix-neuvième siècle**, in the
   nineteenth century)
le temps, time (**les temps modernes / passés /
   préhistoriques**, modern / past / prehistoric times; **le bon
   vieux temps**, the good old days; **dans le temps**, in times
   past)

arriver / se passer, to happen
dater de, to date from
durer, to last
il était une fois . . ., once upon a time there was . . .
passer / s'écouler, to pass [of time]
*prendre naissance (dans), to originate (in)(**la
   naissance**, birth)
se *produire / *avoir lieu, to occur (**le lieu**, place)

à ce moment-là, at that moment
en ce temps-là, at that time
actuel *f* **-elle / présent**, present
ancien *f* **-enne**; *used before noun*, former
autrefois, formerly
avant/après J-C (= Jésus Christ), BC /AD
chronologique, chronological
civilisé, civilized
de nos jours *m*, nowadays
en / à ce moment, at the moment
féodal, feudal
futur, future
historique, historic
jadis / naguère, in times past
légendaire, legendary
moderne, modern
moyenâgeux *f* **-euse**, medieval
passé, past

préhistorique, prehistoric
traditionnel f **-elle**, traditional

SEE ALSO: **Art and Architecture; Politics; Time; War, Peace, and the Armed Services**

24. Holidays Les Vacances

Les préparatifs Preparations

l'agence *f* **de voyages** *m* **/ tourisme** *m*, travel agency
les arrhes *f* **/ la caution / l'acompte** *m*, deposit
l'assurance-voyage *f*; *pl* **-s -**, travel insurance
  (**contracter une assurance**, to take out insurance)
les bagages *m*, luggage
le billet, ticket
la carte, map (**la carte d'identité** *f*, identity card)
le chèque de voyage *m*, traveller's cheque
la confirmation, confirmation
le / la juilletiste / l'aoûtien *m*; *f* **-enne**, visitor staying for
  July / August
le passeport, passport (**renouveler**, to renew; **montrer**,
  to show)
le programme, itinerary
la réservation, reservation / booking
le sac de voyage *m* **/ à dos** *m*, travel bag / rucksack
la trousse de toilette *f*, sponge-bag
la valise, suitcase
le visa, visa

annuler, to cancel (**rembourser la caution**, to return the
  deposit)
confirmer (par écrit), to confirm (in writing)
emporter, to take (with one)
*faire ses bagages *m* **/ ses valises** *f*, to pack
louer un logement, to rent accommodation
réserver (d'avance), to book (in advance)

Les destinations Destinations

l'auberge *f*, inn
l'auberge de jeunesse *f*, youth hostel
le camping, campsite

des chambres *f* **chez l'habitant**, bed and breakfast
(accommodation) (**l'habitant** *m*, householder; **héberger
qn.**, to put sb. up; **chambre** *f* **à louer**, room to let)
l'échange *m* **(scolaire)**, (school) exchange
le gîte, self-catering cottage
l'hôtel *m*, hotel
le motel, motel
la pension, guest house
la station (d'hiver / d'été *m* **/ balnéaire / climatique)**,
(ski / summer / seaside / health) resort (**l'hiver** *m*, winter;
balnéaire, bathing)
la station thermale, spa
les vacances *f*, holidays (**un jour de vacances**, a (day's)
holiday; **en vacances**, on holiday)
la villégiature, stay in the country (***être en villégiature**,
be holidaying)
le voyage, trip / journey
le voyage organisé / accompagné, package / conducted
tour (**le groupe**, group / party)
le voyage en mer, voyage (**la mer**, sea)

***partir en vacances**, to go on holiday
voyager, to travel

Ce qu'on y trouve What you find there

l'artisanat *m*, crafts
la brochure, brochure
la cuisine, cooking
les curiosités *f*, sights
le dépliant, leaflet
la douane, customs (**le douanier**, customs officer)
l'étranger *m*; *f* **-gère**, foreigner
l'excursion *f*, walk / excursion / outing
la frontière, border
la gastronomie, gastronomy
le guide, guidebook (**le / la guise**, guide [the person])
l'hospitalité *f*, hospitality

l'office *m* **du / de tourisme / le syndicat d'initiative** *f*,
  tourist office

le pique-nique *pl - -s*, picnic

le séjour (de cinq jours *m***)**, (five-day) stay

le site, site / beauty spot

le souvenir (de), souvenir (of)

la spécialité (de la maison / de la région),
  (house / regional) speciality

la taxe de séjour, (tourist) resort tax (**le séjour**, stay)

le tourisme, tourism

le / la touriste, tourist

la visite (guidée / non-guidée), (guided / independent)
  visit / tour

s'amuser / se divertir, to enjoy oneself

déclarer, to declare

*faire du tourisme, to go sightseeing

se renseigner sur / se documenter sur, to inform oneself
  about

visiter, to visit [place, monument] (**rendre visite à**, to
  visit [person])

pittoresque, picturesque

touristique, tourist (**les renseignements** *m*
  touristiques, tourist information; **le menu touristique**,
  special tourist-menu)

A l'hôtel At the hotel

l'ascenseur *m*, lift

l'aubergiste *m / f*, innkeeper

le bagagiste / le garçon d'hôtel, porter

le balcon, balcony

le bar, bar

la blanchisserie, laundry service

le bureau *pl* **-x**, office

le cabinet de toilette *f*, toilet / (small) bathroom

la catégorie, category

la chambre (pour une personne / à deux lits *m* **/ pour
  deux personnes)**, (single / twin-bedded / double-
  bedded) room

une chambre calme / sur cour, a quiet room/ a room at the back (**la cour**, courtyard)

le chauffage, heating

le chef (de cuisine), chef (**la cuisine**, kitchen/cooking)

la clé / clef, key (**la clé du cinq**, the key of room 5; **la clé est sur la porte**, the key is in the door)

le / la client(e), guest

la climatisation, air-conditioning

le coffre-fort *pl* **-s -s**, safe

la demi-pension, half-board (**la pension complète**, full board)

le directeur *f* **-trice**, manager/manageress

la direction, management

la douche, shower

l'escalier *m*, stairs

l'étage *m*, floor (**au premier (étage)**, on the first floor; **au rez-de-chaussée**, on the ground floor; **au sous-sol**, in the basement)

l'étoile *f*, star [in hotel-rating system]

la femme de chambre, chambermaid

la fiche de voyageur / de renseignements, registration form (**le voyageur**, traveller; **les renseignements** *m*, information; **remplir**, to fill in)

le garage de l'hôtel *m*, hotel garage

le / la gérant(e), manager(ess)

le hall, foyer

l'hôte *m*, host / guest (**la table d'hôte**, set meal; **un hôte payant**, paying guest; **l'hôtesse** *f*, hostess)

l'hôtelier *m*; *f* **-ière**, hotel keeper

le lavabo, washbasin

le lit (d'enfant), bed (cot) (**l'enfant** *m/f*, child)

le lit supplémentaire, extra bed

le logement, accommodation

la note / la facture, bill

le numéro de la chambre, room number

le parking, car-park

le patron *f* **-onne**, proprietor

le / la pensionnaire, resident / permanent guest

la pièce d'identité *f*, means of identification

le portier / le concierge, hall porter

le pourboire, tip

le prix, price (**par jour** *m* / **à partir de trois jours**, per day / for more than two days)

le prix à la semaine, weekly rate

la réception, reception

le/la réceptionnaire / réceptionniste, receptionist

la réclamation, complaint

le reçu, receipt

le repas, meal

le restaurant, restaurant

la salle à manger, dining-room

la salle de bain(s) (particulière), (private) bathroom (**le bain**, bath)

la salle de télévision *f*, television lounge

le salon, lounge

le service, service (**service compris**, service included; **le service d'étage / en chambre** *f*, room service; **l'étage** *m*, floor)

la sortie de secours, emergency exit (**le secours**, help)

le/la standardiste, switchboard operator

le supplément, surcharge

le tarif, tariff

la terrasse, terrace

la vue (sur), view (of)

les **WC** (pronounced [dubl vese] or, often, [vese]), lavatory

*comprendre, to include

déranger, to disturb

*descendre à, to stay at / put up at

donner sur, to look out onto

*faire la chambre, to do the room

*faire monter / descendre les bagages *m*, to have the luggage taken up / brought down

s'*inscrire, to register

passer la nuit, to spend the night

payer d'avance, to pay in advance

se *plaindre de, to complain about

préparer la note, to get the bill ready

recommander, to recommend

réserver / *retenir, to book (in advance)

*rester jusqu'à, to stay until
réveiller, to wake
sonner, to ring
vérifier / rectifier / régler la note, to check / put right /
pay the bill

bruyant, noisy
complet *f* **-plète,** full / no vacancies
compris, included
confortable, comfortable
disponible / libre, available / free
ouvert / fermé, open / closed

Au camping On the campsite

le bac à vaisselle *f*, washing-up sink
le bloc sanitaire / les sanitaires *m*, ablution block /
washing-block
le campeur *f* **-euse,** camper
le camping, camping / campsite
le camping-car *pl* **- -s,** camper / dormobile ℗
le camping sauvage, off-site camping
le canif, pocket-knife
la caravane, caravan
le caravaning / le caravanisme, caravanning
la corde, rope
l'eau *f* **potable,** drinking-water
l'emplacement *m*, (tent) site
l'équipement *m*, facilities
le feu de camp *m*, camp-fire
le gaz, gas (**le dépôt de gaz,** gas retailer; **la bouteille de
gaz,** bottle of gas; **la recharge,** refill)
la lampe de poche *f*, (pocket) torch
la laverie (automatique), launderette
le lit pliant, camp-bed (**pliant,** folding)
le matelas pneumatique, air-bed
le piquet, tent-peg
le portail, front gate
la poubelle, dustbin

le réchaud, stove
la remorque, trailer
le tapis de sol, groundsheet (**le sol**, ground)
le tarif (par jour m **/ par semaine** f**)**, (daily / weekly) charge
la tente, tent
le terrain de camping / caravaning, campsite
le terrain de jeux, playground (**le jeu** pl **-x**, game)

démonter la tente, to take the tent down
***dormir à la belle étoile**, to sleep in the open (**une étoile**, star)
***faire de l'auto-stop** m **/ du stop**, to hitch(-hike)
camper / *faire du camping, to camp
placer la caravane, to park the caravan
planter / monter la tente, to pitch the tent
vider les ordures f, to empty the rubbish

A l'auberge de jeunesse At the youth hostel

la carte de membre m **/ la carte d'AJ**, membership card
la corvée, duty (**le balai**, broom)
le dortoir, dormitory
les formalités f pl **de départ**, check-out (**le départ**, departure)
l'inscription f, registration
le père / la mère aubergiste, warden (**le père**, father; **la mère**, mother)
le règlement, rules
le sac de couchage m, sleeping-bag
la salle commune, day-room
la salle de jeux m; sing **jeu**, games room

SEE ALSO: **Cinema and Photography; Furniture; The Home; Leisure and Hobbies; Nature; Places and Languages; Sports and Games; Transport; The Weather**

25. The Home La Maison

le bail *pl* **baux**, lease
le / la colocataire, joint tenant / fellow resident [of block of flats]
le / la concierge, caretaker (**la loge**, caretaker's room)
le déménagement, removal / move (**le déménageur**, removal man)
l'hypothèque *f*, mortgage
le locataire, tenant
le logement, housing
le loyer, rent
le propriétaire, proprietor

brancher / couper (l'électricité *f*) , to connect / cut off (electricity)
déménager, to move house
donner congé *m*, to give notice
donner sur, to open into [door] / look out on [window]
emménager / déménager, to move in / out
*faire construire, to have built
fermer à clé, to lock (**la clé**, key)
habiter dans, to live in [a house etc.]
hypothéquer, to mortgage
s'installer, to settle in
libérer, to vacate
louer / donner en location *f*, to let (**maison** *f* **à louer**, house to let)
louer / *prendre en location *f*, to rent
*ouvrir / fermer (l'eau *f*) , to turn (the water) on / off
*rentrer (chez soi), to go home
se trouver / *être situé, to be situated

à la maison / chez soi, at home
dedans / à l'intérieur *m*, inside
dehors / à l'extérieur *m*, outside
en bas, downstairs (**les voisins** *m* **d'en bas**, the downstairs neighbours)
en haut, upstairs

voisin / à côté, next-door (**la maison / les gens** *m* **d'à côté**, the house / people next door)

Les habitations Dwellings

l'appartement *m*, flat
le bungalow, bungalow
le chalet, chalet
la chaumière, thatched cottage
le cottage, (country) cottage
la ferme, farm
le gratte-ciel *pl inv*, skyscraper
une HLM (habitation *f* **à loyer modéré)**, council flat (**le loyer**, rent)
l'hôtel *m* **particulier**, (large) town house
l'immeuble *m*, block of flats
la maison (de campagne *f*)**, (country) house
la maison de retraite, old people's home (**la retraite**, retirement)
le meublé, furnished flat
le pavillon, detached house
le pavillon jumelé, semi-detached house (**jumeler**, to twin)
le studio, (one-bedroomed) studio flat

Les parties de la maison Parts of the house

l'ascenseur *m*, lift
le balcon, balcony
la bibliothèque, library
la buanderie, laundry room
le bureau *pl* **-x / le cabinet de travail**, study (**le travail**, work)
la cave, cellar
la chambre (à coucher), bedroom (**coucher**, to go to bed)
la chambre d'amis / d'enfants, guest-room / nursery (**l'ami(e)**, friend; **l'enfant** *m / f*, child)
la cheminée, chimney / fireplace (**le charbon**, coal; **la**

bûche, log; **le bois de chauffage** *m*, logs (literally *heating-wood*); **le feu**, fire; **la fumée**, smoke; **le pot de cheminée**, chimney-pot; **le ramoneur**, chimney-sweep)

le chevron, rafter

le cloison, partition (**le mur de cloison / la paroi**, partition wall)

le coin repas *m* / **le coin salle** *f* **à manger**, dining-area (**le repas**, meal)

le couloir, corridor

la cuisine, kitchen

le débarras, box-room / store-room

l'escalier *m*, stairs / staircase (**dans l'escalier**, on the stairs; **monter / descendre l'escalier**, go up / downstairs)

l'escalier en colimaçon / en spirale *f*, spiral staircase (**le colimaçon**, snail)

l'étage *m*, floor / storey (**au premier (étage)**, on the first floor)

la façade, front

la fenêtre (en baie *f* **/ en saillie)**, (bay) window (**la saillie**, projection)

la fenêtre à guillotine *f* **/ à battants**, sash / casement window (**le battant**, leaf / flap)

le garage, garage

le garde-manger *pl inv*, larder

le grenier, loft

la lucarne, skylight

la mansarde, attic room / garret

la marche, step

le mur, wall

le palier, landing

le parquet / le plancher, (wooden) floor

le patio, patio

le perron, front steps

la pièce, room

le pignon, gable

le plafond, ceiling

la porte (d'entrée *f* **/ de derrière / cochère)**, (front / back / carriage) door

la porte à deux battants / battante / tournante /

coulissante, double / swing / revolving / sliding door (**le battant**, leaf / flap)

la porte-fenêtre *pl* **-s -s**, french window

la poutre (apparente), (exposed) beam

le rez-de-chaussée *pl inv*, ground floor (**au rez-de-chaussée**, on the ground floor)

la salle, (public) room

la salle à manger, dining-room (**manger**, to eat)

la salle de bain(s) *m*, bathroom

le salon, sitting-room

le séjour / la salle de séjour / le living, living-room

le sol, floor

le sous-sol *pl* **- -s**, basement

les toilettes *f* **/ les cabinets** *m* **/ les WC** *m* **/ les waters** *m* (*all usually used as pl*), lavatory

le toit, roof (**l'ardoise** *f*, slate; **la tuile**, tile)

le vasistas, fanlight

la véranda, veranda

le vestibule / l'entrée *f*, entrance hall

Le jardin The garden

l'allée *f*, (garden) path

la brouette, wheelbarrow

la clôture / la barrière, fence

la cour, (court)yard

la fosse septique, septic tank

la grille, (iron) gate / railings

le jardin potager, kitchen / vegetable garden

la pelouse, lawn (**le gazon**, turf; **l'herbe** *f*, grass)

la plate-bande *pl* **-s -s**, flowerbed

la porte (du jardin), (garden) gate

la serre, greenhouse

le seuil, doorstep / threshold

la terrasse, terrace

la tondeuse, lawn-mower

le tuyau d'arrosage *m*, hose (**arroser**, to water)

SEE ALSO: **Plants**

L'aménagement et les accessoires
Equipment and fittings

l'aération *f*, ventilation
l'antenne *f*, aerial
la boîte à fusibles, fuse-box (**le fusible**, fuse)
la boîte aux lettres *f*, letter-box
le cadenas, padlock
la canalisation, mains (**la canalisation sanitaire**, drains)
le carreau *pl* **-x**, (floor) tile / (window) pane
le carrelage, (floor / wall) tiling
le cendrier, ashtray
le chauffe-eau *pl inv*, water-heater
le cintre, coat-hanger
le compteur d'électricité *f* **/ de gaz** *m* **/ d'eau** *f*, electricity / gas / water meter
le coussin, cushion
le crochet, hook
le disjoncteur, mains switch
la fiche, (electric) plug
le garde-fou *pl* **- -s**, balustrade / safety rail [of window]
le gaz butane / propane, butane / propane gas
la girouette, weathercock
le gond / la charnière, hinge
la gouttière, gutter
l'interrupteur *m* **/ le commutateur**, switch (**allumer / *éteindre**, to switch on / off)
le jeu *pl* **-x / le trousseau** *pl* **-x de clés** *f*, set / bunch of keys
la lampe, light / lamp (**l'ampoule** *f*, bulb; **la douille**, (lamp) socket)
le loquet, window catch
le marteau *pl* **-x**, knocker
le papier peint / la tapisserie, wallpaper
la pile, battery
la poignée, door handle / knob
la prise, (electric) plug / socket (**la prise murale / multiple**, wall / multiple point; **la prise de**

raccordement *m*, adaptor; **brancher / débrancher**, to plug in / unplug; **le voltage**, voltage)

le prolongateur / la rallonge, extension lead

le radiateur, radiator

la rampe, handrail / banisters

le rebord (de la fenêtre), window sill

le robinet, tap (**le robinet d'arrêt** *m* **/ de fermeture** *f*, mains stopcock)

la serrure, lock (**le trou de la serrure**, keyhole)

la sonnette, doorbell

le système d'eau chaude, hot-water system

le tuyau *pl* **-x**, pipe (**le tuyau d'écoulement** *m*, drain-pipe / soil-pipe)

le verrou, bolt (**verrouiller la porte**, to bolt the door)

la vitre, window pane

le volet / le contrevent, shutter

Les travaux ménagers Housework

CEUX QUI LES FONT THOSE WHO DO IT

l'aide *f* **ménagère**, home help

la bonne, maid

la femme de ménage, cleaning woman (**le ménage**, household / housework)

le jardinier *f* **-ière**, gardener

la jeune fille au pair, au pair (girl)

la ménagère, housewife

CE QU'ILS FONT WHAT THEY DO

aider / donner un coup de main, to help / give a hand

aspirer, to vacuum

balayer, to sweep

cirer, to polish

débarrasser (la table), to clear the table

épousseter, to dust (**la poussière**, dust)

essorer, to spin-dry

essuyer, to dry [dishes]

*faire le lit, to make the bed
***faire le ménage / la cuisine / la vaisselle / la lessive /
le repassage,** to do the housework / cooking / washing-
up / washing / ironing
laver, to wash
*mettre la table, to set / lay the table
nettoyer, to clean
passer l'aspirateur *m,* to vacuum
raccommoder, to mend
ranger, to put away / tidy
rapiécer, to patch
récurer, to scour
repasser, to iron
repriser, to darn
rincer, to rinse
sécher / *faire sécher, to dry [clothes]

CE DONT ILS SE SERVENT WHAT THEY USE

l'aspirateur *m,* vacuum cleaner
le balai (mécanique), broom / carpet sweeper
le balai à franges / en caoutchouc, mop / squeegee (**la
frange,** fringe; **le caoutchouc,** rubber)
la balayette, (hearth)brush
la brosse (pour la vaisselle), (washing-up) brush
le chiffon, duster
la corde à linge *m,* clothes-line
la cuvette (pour la vaisselle), washing-up bowl
le désinfectant, disinfectant
le détergent, detergent
l'eau *f* **de Javel,** bleach
l'égouttoir *m,* (crockery) drainer
le fer (à repasser), iron (**repasser,** to iron)
le lave-vaisselle *pl inv,* dishwasher
la lavette, dish-mop
le liquide pour la vaisselle, washing-up liquid
la machine à laver, washing-machine
les ordures *f,* rubbish (**ramasser les ordures,** collect
the rubbish)

la pelle (à poussière), dustpan (**la poussière**, dust)
la pince (à linge *m*), clothes-peg
la planche (à repasser), (ironing-)board
la poubelle, waste-bin
la poudre à lessive / la lessive, washing-powder
le récureur, scourer
le seau *pl* **-x**, bucket
le sèche-linge *pl inv*, tumble-drier
le séchoir, clothes-horse
la serpillière, floor-cloth
le sopalin®, kitchen paper
le torchon, duster / tea-towel

SEE ALSO: **Accidents; Cooking and Eating; Furniture; Plants; Relationships**

26. The Human Body
Le Corps Humain

la tête The head

la bouche, mouth
le cerveau *pl* **-x**, brain (**la cervelle**, brain [as matter])
les cheveux *m*, hair
le cil, eyelash
le crâne, skull
la dent (**de lait** *m* / **de sagesse** *f*), (milk / wisdom) tooth
la figure / le visage, face
la fossette, dimple
le front, forehead
la gencive, gum
le globe oculaire, eyeball
la joue, cheek
la langue, tongue
la lèvre, lip
la mâchoire (**supérieure / inférieure**), (upper / lower) jaw
le menton, chin
la mine, look
la narine, nostril
le nez, nose
l'œil *m*; *pl* **yeux**, eye
l'oreille *f*, ear
le palais, palate
la paupière, eyelid
la pommette, cheek-bone
la prunelle / la pupille, pupil
la ride, wrinkle
la salive, saliva
le sourcil, eyebrow
le teint, complexion
la tempe, temple
le trait, feature
la voix, voice

Le corps　The body

l'aisselle *f*, armpit
les amygdales *f*, tonsils
l'annulaire *m*, ring-finger
l'appendice *m*, appendix
l'artère *f*, artery
l'articulation *f*, joint
l'avant-bras *m*; *pl inv*, forearm
le bassin, pelvis
la bile, bile
le bras, arm
la chair, flesh
la cheville, ankle
la circulation, circulation
la clavicule, collar-bone
le cœur, heart
la colonne vertébrale, spine
la côte, rib
le côté, side
le cou, neck
le coude, elbow
le cou-de-pied, *pl* -s - -, instep
la cuisse, thigh
le derrière, behind / bottom
la digestion, digestion
le disque, disc
le doigt, finger
le doigt de pied, toe
le dos, back
l'épaule *f*, shoulder
l'estomac *m*, stomach [the organ] (**le ventre**, stomach [exterior protuberance])
les fesses *f*, buttocks
le foie, liver
le genou *pl* -**x**, knee
la glande, gland
la gorge, throat
l'haleine *f* / **le souffle**, breath

la hanche, hip
l'index *m*, index finger
les intestins *m*, bowels
la jambe, leg
le larynx, larynx
la main, hand
le majeur / le médius, middle finger
le membre, limb
le métabolisme, metabolism
le mollet, calf
le muscle, muscle
le nerf, nerve
la nuque, nape [of neck]
l'omoplate *f*, shoulder-blade
l'ongle *m*, nail
l'organe *m*, organ
l'orteil *m*, toe (**le gros orteil**, big toe)
l'os *m*, bone
le pancréas, pancreas
la paume, palm
la peau *pl* **-x**, skin
le pénis, penis
le petit doigt / l'auriculaire *m*, little finger
le pied, foot (**sur la pointe des pieds**, on tiptoe)
la plante (du pied), sole
le poignet, wrist
le poing, fist
la poitrine, chest / bust
le pouce, thumb
le pouls, pulse
le poumon, lung
les règles *f*, menstruation
le rein, kidney
la respiration, breathing
la rotule, kneecap
le sang, blood
le sein, breast
le squelette, skeleton
la sueur, sweat

le système nerveux, nervous system
la taille, waist / height
le talon, heel
le tendon, sinew / tendon
le testicule, testicle
le tibia, shin
la trachée, windpipe
le tronc, trunk
le tympan, ear-drum
l'urine *f*, urine
le vagin, vagina
la veine, vein
la vésicule, gall bladder
la vessie, bladder

Les actions du corps Actions of the body

s'accouder à, to lean (elbows) on
s'accroupir, to squat
s'adosser à, to lean (back) against
s'agenouiller, to kneel
s'allonger, to stretch out
s'appuyer contre, to lean against
s'*asseoir, to sit down
avaler, to swallow
bâiller, to yawn
baisser, to lower
se baisser, to stoop
*battre, to beat [heart]
boiter, to limp
bondir, to leap
bouger, to move
se casser, to break
cligner des yeux, to blink (**les yeux** *m*, eyes)
se coucher, to lie down
se courber, to bend
*courir, to run
se dépêcher / se hâter, to hurry

digérer, to digest

donner un coup de pied / de poing, to kick / punch (**le coup**, blow; **le pied**, foot; **le poing**, fist)

donner une gifle, to slap (**la gifle**, slap)

écouter, to listen to

entendre, to hear

s'étirer, to stretch

étouffer, to choke

***faire oui / non de la tête**, to nod / shake one's head

***faire un clin d'œil** *m*, to wink (**un clin d'œil**, a wink of the eye)

***faire une grimace**, to make a face

se fouler, to sprain

frapper, to hit

froncer les sourcils, to frown (**le sourcil**, eyebrow)

goûter, to taste

se gratter, to scratch

haleter, to pant

hausser les épaules, to shrug (**l'épaule** *f*, shoulder)

hocher la tête, to shake one's head / nod

jeter, to throw

jeter un coup d'œil, to glance (**un coup d'œil**, a glance)

lancer, to throw

lever, to raise

se lever, to get up

lever / baisser les yeux, to look up / down (**les yeux** *m*, eyes)

mâcher, to chew

marcher, to walk

montrer du doigt, to point (**le doigt**, finger)

se moucher, to blow one's nose

***partir du bon pied**, to put one's best foot forward

pencher de côté / sur le côté, to lean sideways

se pencher sur, to lean over

se précipiter, to rush

***prendre**, to take

reculer, to step back

regarder, to look at (**regarder fixement / furieusement**, to stare / glare at)

se reposer, to rest

respirer, to breathe
*rire, to laugh
sauter, to jump
sautiller, to hop
secouer la tête, to shake one's head
*sentir, to smell
serrer la main (à qn.), to shake hands (with sb.)
serrer les poings *m*, to clench one's fists
*sourire, to smile
sursauter, to (give a) start
tituber, to stagger
*tomber à la renverse, to fall on one's back (**à la renverse**, backwards)
toucher, to touch
tourner le dos à qn., to turn one's back on sb.
trébucher, to trip
*voir, to see

Les positions Positions

accoudé, leaning [on one's elbows]
accroupi, squatting
adossé (à), leaning [back against]
agenouillé, kneeling
à genoux, on one's knees (**le genou**, knee)
allongé, lying down
à plat ventre, face down (**le ventre**, stomach)
appuyé (sur), leaning (on)
à quatre pattes, on all fours (**la patte**, paw)
assis, sitting
les bras croisés, with arms folded
bras dessus bras dessous, arm in arm (**dessus**, over; **dessous**, under)
côte *f* **à côte**, side by side
couché, lying
coude à coude, shoulder to shoulder (**le coude**, elbow)
courbé en deux, bent double
debout, standing

étendu, [lying] stretched out
la main dans la main, hand in hand
penché (sur), leaning (over)
suspendu (à), hanging (from)

SEE ALSO: **Accidents; Adornment; Clothing; Describing People; Hair; Health and Sickness; Identity; The Senses; Tobacco and Drugs**

27. Identity L'Identité

Le nom Name

comment vous appelez-vous? / quel est votre nom?, what is your name?

quel est votre prénom?, what's your first name?

je m'appelle . . ., my name is . . .

l'identité *f*, identity

l'initiale *f*, initial

le nom (de famille *f* **/ de jeune fille** *f* **/ de mariage** *m***)**, (sur- / maiden / married) name

le nom de guerre / le pseudonyme, pen-name (**la guerre**, war)

le nom d'emprunt / de théâtre, assumed / stage name (**l'emprunt** *m*, loan)

le paraphe, initials [as signature] (**parapher**, to initial)

le prénom / le petit nom, first name

la signature, signature

Madame Untel / Mme Untel, Mrs X (also used for *Ms X*)

Mademoiselle Untel / Mlle Untel, Miss X

Monsieur Untel / M. Untel / Mr Untel, Mr X

monsieur le docteur X / monsieur le comte de X, Doctor X / the Earl of X

Mesdames *abb* **Mmes**, ladies

mesdames et messieurs / messieurs-dames, ladies and gentlemen

Mesdemoiselles *abb* **Mlles**, young ladies

Messieurs *abb* **Mrs**, gentlemen

s'appeler / se nommer, to be called

baptiser, to christen

nommer, to name

signer, to sign (**le / la soussigné(e)**, the undersigned)

surnommer, to nickname

L'adresse Address

où habitez-vous?, where do you live?

j'habite cinq, rue Lamartine, I live at five, rue Lamartine

l'adresse *f*, address
l'annuaire *m* **/ le bottin** [Ⓟ], telephone directory
l'avenue *f*, avenue
le boulevard, boulevard
le code postal *pl* **-aux**, postcode
les coordonnées *f*, address and phone number
le domicile, place of residence
l'étage *m*, storey
le lieu *pl* **-x**, place [town]
le numéro (de téléphone *m***)**, (phone) number
la place, square
la rue, street

habiter, to live at
loger (à), to be living (in / at)
louer, to rent (**le locataire**, tenant)
partager, to share
posséder, to own

à la campagne, in the country
au bord de la mer, at the seaside
au bout du monde, at the ends of the earth
en banlieue *f*, in the suburbs
en ville *f*, in town

L'âge Age

quel âge avez-vous?, how old are you?
j'ai cinquante ans passés, I'm over fifty
j'ai huit ans et demi, I'm eight and a half

l'adolescence *f*, adolescence
l'adolescent *m; f* **-te**, adolescent
l'adulte *m / f*, adult

l'âge *m*, age (**d'un certain âge**, elderly; **entre deux âges**, middle-aged)

l'aîné *m*; *f* **-ée**, the older (**il est de deux ans mon aîné**, he's two years older than me)

l'an *m*, year

l'anniversaire *m*, birthday

le bébé, baby

le / la cadet(te), the younger

le / la centenaire, hundred-year-old

le / la contemporain(e), contemporary

l'enfant *m* / *f* **(au-dessous de quatorze ans)**, child (under fourteen)

le / la gamin(e), kid

une grande personne, a grown-up

la jeune femme, young woman

la jeune fille, girl

le jeune homme, young man

la jeune femme, young lady

les jeunes *m*, young people

la jeunesse, youth

la limite d'âge *m*, age limit

la longévité, longevity

le mois, month

la naissance, birth (**la date de naissance**, date of birth; **anglais de naissance**, English by birth)

la personne âgée, old person

le troisième âge, old age

le vieillard / le vieil homme / le vieux, old man (**les vieillards**, old people)

la vieillesse, age

*atteindre sa majorité, to come of age

*être majeur *f* **-e**, to be of age

grandir, to grow up / grow tall

*mourir, to die

*naître, to be born

vieillir, to grow old

*vivre, to live

adulte, adult
âgé, old
enfantin, childish
jeune, young
juvénile, juvenile
mineur, under-age / a minor
mûr, mature
sénile, senile
suranné, outdated
vieillot *f* **-otte**, oldish
vieux *m sing before vowel* **vieil**; *f* **vieille**, old

Le sexe Sex

la dame, lady
la féminité, femininity
le féminisme, feminism
la femme, woman
la (jeune) fille, girl
le garçon, boy
l'homme *m*, man
la masculinité, masculinity
le monsieur *pl* **messieurs**, gentleman

femelle, female
féminin, feminine
mâle, male
masculin, masculine

SEE ALSO: **Birth, Marriage, and Death; Describing People;
The Human Body; Jobs; Places and Langua␣es;
Relationships**

28. Jobs Les Emplois

Ce qu'on fait dans la vie
What you do for a living

Only the words shown have feminine forms; if femaleness needs to be specified with the others use **femme: une femme architecte; une femme docteur.**

l'acteur *m*; *f* **-trice,** actor / actress
l'agent *m*, agent (**l'agent secret / d'assurances** *f* **/ de change** *m*, secret agent / insurance agent / stockbroker)
l'agent *m* **de police** *f* **/ le gendarme,** policeman / -woman
l'agriculteur *f* **-trice,** farmer
l'ambulancier *f* **-ière,** ambulance man / woman
l'architecte *m* / *f*, architect
l'armurier *m*, gunsmith
l'artiste *m* / *f*, artist
l'assistant social (*f* **l'assistante sociale**), social worker (**l'assistance** *f* **sociale,** social security)
l'astronaute *m* / *f* / **le / la cosmonaute,** astronaut / cosmonaut
l'astronome *m* / *f*, astronomer
l'avocat *m*; *f* **-te,** lawyer
l'avoué *m*, solicitor
le balayeur (municipal *pl* **-aux),** street sweeper
le berger *f* **-gère,** shepherd(ess)
le / la bibliothécaire, librarian
le bijoutier *f* **-ière,** jeweller
le blanchisseur *f* **-euse,** laundry man / laundress
la bonne, maid
le boucher *f* **-chère,** boucher
le boulanger *f* **-gère,** baker
le brasseur, brewer
le camionneur / le routier, lorry driver
le chanteur *f* **-euse,** singer

le charbonnier, coal-merchant
le charcutier *f* **-ière**, pork butcher / delicatessen keeper
le charpentier, carpenter
le chauffeur (d'autobus *m* **/ de taxi** *m***)**, (bus- / taxi-)driver
   m or f
le chef de train *m*, guard
le cheminot, railwayman
le chiffonnier, rag-and-bone merchant
le chirurgien, surgeon
le clochard *f* **-e**, tramp
le coiffeur *f* **-euse**, hairdresser
le colporteur *f* **-euse**, door-to-door salesman / hawker
le comédien *f* **-enne**, comedian / actor
le / la commerçant(e), shopkeeper
le commis, clerk
le / la comptable, accountant
le / la concierge, caretaker
le conducteur *f* **-trice**, driver
le conseiller *f* **-llère**, counsellor (**le conseiller**
   d'orientation *f*, careers adviser)
le constructeur, (structural) engineer (**le constructeur**
   automobile *f* **/ de navires** *m*, car manufacturer /
   shipbuilder)
le contremaître *f* **-tresse**, foreman / -woman
le contrôleur *f* **-euse**, ticket inspector
le cordonnier *f* **-ière**, shoemaker
le coutelier *f* **-ière**, cutler
le couturier *f* **-ière**, couturier / dressmaker
le cuisinier *f* **-ière**, cook (**le chef cuisinier**, chef)
le curé, priest
la dactylo, typist *f or m*
le décorateur *f* **-trice**, interior decorator
le déménageur *f* **-euse**, furniture remover
le / la dentiste, dentist
le député, MP
le dessinateur *f* **-trice**, draughtsman / -woman / cartoonist
le docteur, doctor
le / la domestique, servant

le douanier *f* -**ière**, customs officer
l'ébéniste *m*, cabinet maker
l'éboueur *m*, dustman / street cleaner
l'écrivain *m*, writer
l'éditeur *f* -**trice**, publisher
l'électricien *f* -**enne**, electrician
l'employé *m*; *f* -**ée** (**de bureau** *m*; *pl* -**x**), employee
  (**l'employé de banque** *f* **/ des postes** *f* **/ de magasin** *m* **/
  du gaz**, bank clerk / post-office clerk / shop assistant / gas-
  man)
l'enseignant *m*; *f* -**te**, teacher
l'épicier *m*; *f* -**ière**, grocer
l'étudiant *m*; *f* -**te**, student
le facteur *f* -**trice**, postman / -woman
la femme de chambre *f* **/ de ménage** *m*, chambermaid /
  cleaner
le fermier *f* -**ière**, farmer
le / la fleuriste, florist
le / la fonctionnaire, civil servant
le forgeron, blacksmith
le fruitier *f* -**ière**, fruiterer / greengrocer
le / la garagiste, garage owner / mechanic
le garçon (de café *m*) (*f* **la serveuse**), waiter
le garde forestier, forester
le gazier, gas-fitter
le / la grossiste, wholesaler
le guide, guide
l'homme *m* **/ la femme d'affaires** *f*, businessman / -woman
l'homme *m* **politique**, politician
l'horloger *m*; *f* -**gère**, watchmaker / clockmaker
l'hôtesse *f* **de l'air** *m* (*m* **le steward**), air hostess / cabin
  steward
l'imprimeur *m*, printer
l'infirmier *m*; *f* -**ière**, nurse
l'informaticien *m*; *f* -**enne** **/ le programmeur** *f* -**euse**,
  computer programmer (**l'informatique** *f*, computing)
l'ingénieur *m*, engineer
l'instituteur *m*; *f* -**trice**, primary-school teacher
l'interprète *m* **/** *f*, interpreter

le jardinier *f* **-ière**, gardener (**la jardinière d'enfants** *m*, kindergarten teacher)

le / la journaliste, journalist

le juge, judge

le laveur de vitres *f*, window-cleaner

le / la libraire, bookseller

le livreur *f* **-euse**, delivery man / woman

le maçon, bricklayer

le maître *f* **-tresse** (**d'école** *f*), (primary-school) teacher (**le maître de conférences** *f*, lecturer; **le maître-nageur** *pl* **-s -s**, swimming instructor)

le mannequin, model *m or f*

le manœuvre, labourer

le maraîcher *f* **-chère**, market gardener

le / la marchand(e) (de), shopkeeper / merchant / dealer (in) (**le marchand des quatre saisons**, barrow boy / costermonger; **la saison**, season)

le marin / le matelot, sailor

le mécanicien *f* **-enne**, mechanic

le médecin, doctor

le / la mendiant(e), beggar

le menuisier, joiner

le mercier *f* **-ière**, haberdasher

le métallurgiste, metalworker

le meunier *f* **-ière**, miller

le militaire, serviceman (**l'ancien militaire**, ex-serviceman; **les militaires**, the military)

le mineur, miner

le ministre, (cabinet) minister *m or f* (**le premier ministre**, prime minister)

la modiste, milliner

le moine, monk

le moniteur *f* **-trice** (**d'auto-école** *f*), (driving-)instructor

le musicien *f* **-enne**, musician

le négociant en gros / en vins *m pl* **/ en blés** *m pl*, wholesaler / wine-merchant / corn-merchant

le notaire, notary

la nurse, nanny

l'**officier** *m* (**de l'armée** *f* **de terre** *f* **/ de l'armée de l'air** *m* **/ de marine** *f*), (army / air-force / naval) officer

l'**opérateur** (*f* **-trice**) **de prise de vues**, cameraman (l'**opérateur** (*f* **-trice**) **du sons** *m*, sound mixer)

l'**opticien** *m*; *f* **-enne**, optician

l'**orfèvre** *m*, goldsmith / silversmith

l'**ouvreuse** *f*, usherette

le **papetier** *f* **-ière**, stationer

le **pasteur**, (Protestant) minister

le **pâtissier** *f* **-ière**, pastrycook / confectioner

le **pêcheur**, fisherman

le **peintre**, painter (le **peintre en bâtiment(s)** *m* **/ le peintre décorateur**, house-painter)

le **pharmacien** *f* **-enne**, chemist

le **/ la photographe**, photographer

le **physicien** *f* **-enne**, physicist

le **pilote**, pilot

le **plombier**, plumber

le **poissonnier** *f* **-ière**, fishmonger

le **pompier**, fireman

le **potier**, potter

le **présentateur** *f* **-trice**, announcer

le **prêtre**, priest

le **professeur**, (secondary-school) teacher / lecturer / professor *m or f*; *but* la **prof** *colloquial for* female teacher

le **/ la psychiatre**, psychiatrist

le **/ la psychologue**, psychologist

le **quincailler / le droguiste**, ironmonger

le **ramoneur**, chimney-sweep

le **/ la réceptionniste**, receptionist

la **religieuse / la nonne / la sœur**, nun

le **reporter**, reporter

le **/ la représentant(e)**, representative

la **sage-femme** *pl* **-s -s** (*m* l'**homme sage-femme**), midwife

le **savant**, scholar *m or f*

le **/ la scientifique**, scientist

le **sculpteur**, sculptor

le **/ la secrétaire**, secretary

le serrurier, locksmith
le serviteur, [male] servant
le soldat, soldier
le speaker *f* **-erine**, TV announcer
le / la standardiste, (switchboard) operator
le / la sténodactylo, shorthand-typist
le tailleur, tailor
le / la tisserand(e), weaver
le technicien *f* **-enne**, technician
le traducteur *f* **-trice**, translator
le traiteur, caterer
le tricoteur *f* **-euse**, knitter
la vedette, star *m or f*
le vendeur *f* **-euse**, shop assistant
le / la vétérinaire, vet
le vigneron *f* **-onne**, wine-grower
le voyageur de commerce *m*, commercial traveller

Ce qu'on est What you are

l'apprenti *m; f* **-ie**, apprentice
le cadre, executive
le chef d'atelier *m*, overseer (**l'atelier** *m*, workshop)
le chômeur *f* **-euse**, unemployed person
le / la collègue, colleague
le demandeur (*f* **-euse**) **d'emploi** *m*, job-seeker
le directeur *f* **-trice**, director / manager / headteacher (**le
(président) directeur général** *pl* **-s -s -aux / le PDG**,
managing director)
l'employé *m; f* **-ée**, employee (**de bureau** *m*, office
worker)
l'employeur *m*, employer
le fabricant, manufacturer
les gens *m* **de métier** *m*, professionals (**les gens**, people)
le / la gérant(e), manager(ess)
le / la gréviste, striker
l'industriel *m*, industrialist
le jaune, blackleg / scab

l'ouvrier *f* -ière, (blue-collar) worker (**la classe ouvrière**, working class)
le patron *f* -onne, boss
le / la retraité(e), retiree / pensioner
le / la salarié(e), wage-earner
le / la spécialiste (en), specialist (in)
le / la stagiaire, trainee
le / la syndicaliste, trade-unionist
le / la syndiqué(e), union member
le technicien *f* -enne, technician
le travailleur *f* -euse, worker

Où on travaille Where you work

l'administration *f*, management (**dans l'Administration**, in the civil service)
les affaires *f*, business (**dans les affaires**, in business; **le voyage d'affaires**, business trip)
l'atelier *m*, workshop
le bureau *pl* -x, office
le chantier, construction site
le commerce (de gros *m* / de détail *m*), (wholesale / retail) trade
le dépôt / un entrepôt, warehouse
l'entreprise *f* / la société / la compagnie, company (**la société anonyme [SA]**, public company; **la société à responsabilité limitée [SARL]**, public limited liability company [plc])
la firme / la maison de commerce *f*, firm
l'industrie (**lourde / légère**), (light / heavy) industry
le laboratoire, laboratory (**la recherche**, research)
le magasin, shop
le secteur (de vente *f*), (sales) area
le siège social *pl* -aux, head office
la succursale, branch
l'usine *f*, factory

Ce qu'on fait What you do

administrer, to administer
chercher / trouver / accepter / refuser un emploi, to
  look for / find / accept / refuse a job
chômer / *être sans emploi *m* **/ *être en chômage** *m* **/
  *être au chômage**, to be unemployed
congédier / licencier / *renvoyer, to dismiss
démissionner, to resign
diriger, to run
embaucher / engager, to take on
*faire la grève / *être en grève, to be on strike
*faire la grève perlée / du zèle, to go slow / work to rule
  (**perler**, to execute to perfection; **le zèle**, zeal)
*faire une demande d'emploi *m*, to apply for a job
gagner / toucher, to earn (**gagner sa vie**, to earn one's
  living)
gérer, to manage
*mettre à la porte, to sack [= put to the door]
*mettre au chômage, to make redundant
se *mettre en grève *f*, to go on strike
peiner, to toil / slog
*prendre sa retraite, to retire
*suivre une formation, to follow a training course
travailler, to work

La vie industrielle Industrial life

l'allocation *f* **chômage**, unemployment benefit
l'apprentissage *m*, apprenticeship
l'augmentation *f* **de salaire** *m*, pay rise
la carrière, career
le conflit (social), (industrial) dispute
les congés *m* **/ les vacances** *f*, holidays (**les congés
  payés**, paid holidays)
le contrat de travail *m*, contract of employment
le curriculum vitae *pl inv*, curriculum vitae, CV
le débouché, opening
la demande d'emploi *m*, job application
la direction, management

l'emploi *m* **à mi-temps / à plein temps / permanent /
temporaire**, (part-time / full-time / permanent /
temporary) job

l'entretien *m* **/ l'entrevue** *f*, interview

la formation, training (**la formation permanente**,
continuing education / training)

l'horaire *m* **à la carte**, flexitime [= selective timetable]

les impôts *m*, taxes

le licenciement, dismissal

le lock-out *pl inv*, lock-out

**le main-d'œuvre (non spécialisée / spécialisée /
qualifiée)**, (unskilled / semi-skilled / skilled) labour

la manifestation, demonstration

le métier, job / trade (**. . . de métier**, . . . by trade)

une offre d'emploi *m*, vacancy (**les offres d'emploi**,
situations vacant)

le patronat, employers

le personnel, staff / personnel

la place du tout repos, soft job (**le repos**, rest)

la profession, profession

la retraite, retirement (**la caisse de retraite**, pension
fund; **la pension de retraite**, retirement pension)

le salaire, wages

la sécurité sociale, social security

la situation / le poste, post

le stage (de formation *f*), (training-)course

le syndicat, trade union

le traitement, salary

le travail, work (**le travail aux pièces** *f*, piece-work)

SEE ALSO: **Describing People; Education; Identity;
Tools**

29. Justice and Law
La Justice et la loi

La poursuite du criminel
Pursuit of the criminal

l'agent *m* **(de police** *f*) **/ le gardien de la paix**,
  policeman (**la paix**, peace)
les agents *m* **de la circulation**, traffic police
l'agent secret, secret agent
l'arrestation *f*, arrest
l'aveu *m*, confession
le bouclier, shield
le butin, loot
le casque, helmet
la cellule, cell
le chien policier, police dog
le commissaire, superintendent
le constat, report
le CRS (= **Compagnies républicaines de sécurité**),
  riot police (**le CRS**, riot policeman)
la déposition / la déclaration, statement
le détective (privé), (private) detective
le / la détenu(e), prisoner
les empreintes *f* **digitales**, fingerprints
l'enquête *f*, enquiry
l'enquêteur *m*, investigator
l'évadé *m; f* **-ée**, escaped prisoner
l'évasion *f*, escape
la femme policier, policewoman / woman police-officer
le flic *colloq*, cop
la fourgonnette de police *f* **/ le panier à salade** *f colloq*,
  police van (**le panier**, basket)
le fugitif *f* **-ive**, fugitive
le garde, guard [group] (**le garde**, guard [soldier])
le gardien de nuit, night-watchman
le gaz lacrymogène, tear-gas

le gendarme, policeman [outside main towns]

la gendarmerie / le poste de police / le commissariat, police station

l'indicateur *m*, informer

l'inspecteur *m* **(de police)**, (police) inspector

l'interrogatoire *m*, examination

le mandat (de perquisition *f* **/ d'arrêt** *m***)**, (search / arrest) warrant

la matraque, truncheon

les menottes *f*, handcuffs

le motard, motor-cycle policeman

la police, police

la police judiciaire [PJ], criminal investigation department [CID]

le policier (en civil), (plain-clothes) policeman

la prise (de), capture (of)

la procédure, procedure / proceedings

le procès-verbal *pl* **- -aux**, police report

la rafle, raid

les recherches *f*, investigation(s)

la récompense, reward

le sauvetage, rescue

le sauveteur, rescuer

le signalement, description

la surveillance, surveillance

le suspect, suspect

la tentative, attempt

la victime, victim *f or m*

la voiture de police *f*, police car

arrêter, to arrest

avouer, to confess

confisquer, to confiscate

déranger, to disturb

déposer une plainte, to make a complaint

désarmer, to disarm

dresser un procès-verbal *pl* **- -aux**, to make a report

enquêter sur qch., to investigate sth.

*être en état *m* **d'arrestation** *f*, to be under arrest

*être sur la piste de, to be on the track of

s'évader, to escape
*****faire qn. prisonnier** *m*, to take sb. prisoner
*****faire une perquisition chez qn.**, to search sb.'s premises
inculper de, to charge with
intercepter, to intercept
interpeller, to challenge
interroger, to question
libérer / *mettre en liberté *f*, to free
*****maintenir / rétablir l'ordre** *m*, to keep / restore order
nier, to deny
porter plainte *f* **contre qn.**, to lodge a complaint against
  sb.
*****prendre en flagrant délit** *m*, to catch red-handed
*****prendre la fuite**, to take flight
rapporter, to report
récompenser, to reward
surveiller, to watch

Le procès et la punition
Trial and punishment

l'accusation *f*, charge
l'accusé *m*; *f* **-ée**, the accused
l'acquittement *m*, acquittal
l'affaire *f*, case
l'alibi *m*, alibi
l'amende *f*, fine
l'appel *m*, appeal
l'avocat *m*; *f* **-te**, lawyer
la barre des prévenus / des témoins *m*, dock / witness-
  box (**le / la prévenu(e)**, person charged)
le bourreau *pl* **-x**, executioner
la caution, bail
la chaise électrique, electric chair
le code civil / pénal, civil / penal law
la condamnation (à vie *f* **/ à mort** *f* **/ avec sursis** *m***)**, (life /
  death / suspended) sentence
la contravention, minor offence

la cour, court
la culpabilité, guilt
la défense, defence
la délinquance (juvénile), (juvenile) delinquency
le / la délinquant(e), delinquent
le délit, offence
les dépens *m*, costs
la détention (préventive), (remand in) custody
les dommages-intérêts *m*, damages
le droit, law [e.g. as subject of study] (**une loi**, a law)
l'échafaud *m*, scaffold / gallows
l'emprisonnement *m* (**à vie** *f*), (life) imprisonment
l'erreur *f* **judiciaire**, judicial error
l'exécution *f*, execution
le forçat, convict
le geôlier, jailer
la grâce, pardon
le greffier, clerk of the court
la guillotine, guillotine
l'huissier *m*, (court) usher
l'incarcération *f*, imprisonment
l'infraction *f*, offence
le juge, judge
le juge d'instruction *f*, investigation magistrate
le jugement, judgment / sentence
le jury / les jurés *m*, jury
la loi, law
le magistrat, magistrate
le méfait, misdeed
le notaire, notary / solicitor
l'ordonnance *f*, decree
le palais de justice *f*, law courts
la peine capitale, capital punishment
la peine de mort *f*, death penalty
la poursuite, prosecution
la préméditation, premeditation
la preuve, proof / piece of evidence
la prison, prison

le prisonnier *f* **-ière**, prisoner
le procès, trial
la réclusion criminelle (à perpétuité *f***)**, imprisonment (for life)
la remise de peine *f*, reduced sentence
la salle d'audience *f*, courtroom
le serment, oath
le sursis, suspended sentence / reprieve
le témoin (oculaire), (eye)witness
le témoignage, evidence
les travaux forcés, hard labour (**le travail** *pl* **-aux**, work / labour)
le tribunal (*pl* **-aux**) **civil**, civil court
le verdict, verdict

accuser (de), to accuse (of)
acquitter, to acquit
condamner à une amende, to fine
condamner à mort *f* **/ à dix ans** *m* **de prison** *f*, to sentence to death / to 10 years in prison
défendre, to defend
emprisonner, to imprison
*être coupable de / innocent de, to be guilty / innocent of
exécuter, to execute
exécuter sa peine, to serve one's sentence
grâcier, to pardon / reprieve
juger une affaire / un accusé, to try a case / sentence a prisoner
jurer, to swear
*mettre en cause, to implicate (**la cause**, suit / case)
*mettre en prison *f*, to put in prison
payer la caution de qn., to stand bail for sb.
plaider, to plead
prouver, to prove
rendre un jugement, to pass judgment
suborner (un témoin), to suborn (a witness)

SEE ALSO: **Arguing For and Against; Crimes and Criminals**

30. Leisure and Hobbies
Les Loisirs et les passe-temps

l'activité *f*, activity
le club, club (**la réunion**, meeting)
l'enthousiasme *m*, enthusiasm
le hobby *pl* **-s**, hobby
l'intérêt *m*, interest
le loisir, leisure (**les loisirs** *m*, leisure time)
le passe-temps *pl inv*, pastime
le violon d'Ingres, dominating interest [the painter Ingres was a gifted violinist]

s'amuser à (faire qch.), to enjoy (doing sth.)
s'ennuyer à (faire qch.), to get bored (doing sth.)
s'intéresser à, to be interested in
*être passionné(e) de, to be keen on
*faire du / de la . . ., to do . . .
*faire partie *f* **de**, to be in / belong to
participer à, to take part in
passer son temps à (faire qch.), to spend one's time (doing sth.)
se réunir, to meet [club, group]

amusant, amusing
captivant / passionnant, fascinating
ennuyeux *f* **-euse**, boring
intéressant, interesting

Les loisirs Leisure-time activities

le bal *pl* **-s**, dance (**danser**, to dance; ***aller danser**, to go dancing)
le ballet, ballet (**la danse**, dancing; **le danseur** *f* **-euse**, dancer)
le bar, bar
le billard, billiard hall

la boîte de nuit *f* **/ le cabaret**, night-club (**le videur**, bouncer)

le boulodrome / le bowling, bowling alley

la boum / la fête / la surprise-partie *pl* -s -s, party (**l'invitation** *f*, invitation; **l'invité** *m*; *f* -ée, guest)

le café, café (**le babyfoot**, table football; **le flipper**, pinball machine; **l'appareil** *m* **à sous**, slot-machine; **le sou**, penny)

le casino, casino

le cinéma, cinema (**le film**, film)

le cirque, circus (**le clown**, clown)

le club de jazz *m*, jazz club

le concert de rock *m* **/ de musique** *f* **classique**, rock / classical concert (**le groupe**, group; **le chanteur** *f* -euse, singer; **le fan**, fan; **l'orchestre** *m*, orchestra; **le / la soliste**, soloist)

le dancing, dance-hall (**la piste de danse** *f*, dance-floor)

la discothèque, disco (**le disc-jockey** *pl* - -s, DJ; **le juke-box** *pl inv*, jukebox)

le disque, record (**écouter**, to listen to; **passer**, to play)

la fête foraine, fun-fair (**forain**, travelling; **la fête champêtre**, village fair)

le feu *pl* -x **d'artifice** *m*, firework display

la galerie d'art *m*, art gallery (**la collection**, collection)

l'hippodrome *m*, race-course (**le cheval** *pl* -aux, horse; **la course**, race)

le jardin botanique / le jardin des plantes *f*, botanical gardens

la maison des jeunes *m*, youth club

le match *pl* -s **de football** *m* **/ de rugby** *m* **/ de cricket** *m*, football / rugby / cricket match

le minigolf, minigolf(-course)

le musée, museum (**une exposition**, exhibition)

le music-hall *pl* - -s, variety theatre

l'opéra *m*, opera

le parc / le jardin public, park (**le parc d'attractions** *f*, amusement park)

la patinoire, ice rink (**patiner**, to skate)

le pique-nique *pl* - -s, picnic

la piscine, swimming-pool

la radio, radio
le restaurant, restaurant
le spectacle, show
le sport, sport (*faire du sport, to play games; les sports d'hiver *m*, winter sports)
le stade, sports stadium
la télévision, television (regarder, to look at; la chaîne, channel; le magnétoscope, video recorder)
le théâtre, theatre (la pièce, play)
le zoo, zoo

accompagner, to go with
*aller à, to go to
*avoir rendez-vous *m* avec qn., to be meeting sb.
déposer, to drop off
donner rendez-vous *m* à qn., to make a date with sb.
inviter, to invite
se rencontrer, to meet
*rentrer, to go home
se *revoir, to meet again
*sortir (seul / ensemble / avec . . .), to go out (alone / together / with . . .)
se *voir, to see each other (*aller voir des ami(e)s, to visit friends)

Les hobbys Hobbies

l'art *m*, art
le ballet, ballet
le bricolage, DIY (le bricoleur *f* -euse, handyman / DIY enthusiast)
la broderie, embroidery
les cartes *f*, cards (*faire une partie de, to have a game of)
le cerf-volant *pl* -s -s, kite (*faire voler, to fly)
le chant, singing (la chanson, song)
la chorale, choir
le club de . . . , . . . club (le membre, member; la réunion, meeting; la cotisation, subscription)
la collection de, collecting / collection of

le concours, competition
la construction (de maquettes *f* **)**, building (models)
la couture, dressmaking
la cuisine, cooking
le cyclisme, cycling (**le vélo**, bicycle)
le dessin, drawing
les échecs *m*, chess
l'équitation *f*, (horse-)riding
l'excursion *f* **(à pied)**, outing / hike (**le pied**, foot)
le film (vidéo), (video) film
l'informatique *f*, computing (**l'ordinateur** *m*, computer;
  le micro, micro; **les jeux** *m* **électroniques**, computer
  games)
le jardinage, gardening
le jardin ouvrier / le lopin (de terre *f* **)**, allotment (**ouvrier**,
  workman's)
le jeu *pl* **-x**, game / gambling (**miser sur**, to bet on)
le jeu *pl* **-x de société** *f*, party game
la lecture, reading
le loto, bingo
les mots croisés *always pl*, crossword
la musique, music
l'ornithologie *f*, bird-watching
la pêche, fishing (***aller à la pêche**, to go fishing)
la peinture, painting
la philatélie, stamp-collecting (**l'album** *m*, album; **le
  timbre**, stamp)
la photo(graphie), photography
la poterie, pottery
la promenade, walk / walking
le puzzle, jigsaw
la randonnée (à cheval), ramble / ride (**le cheval** *pl* **-aux**,
  horse)
le scoutisme, scouting (**le scout / l'éclaireur** *m*, scout;
  l'éclaireuse *f*, guide)
la tapisserie, tapestry
le tricot, knitting
le tour en voiture, drive (**la voiture**, car)
la vidéo, video

le yachting / la voile, sailing

bricoler, to do DIY
broder, embroider
chanter, to sing
collectionner, to collect
*construire, to make
*coudre, to sew
cuisiner, to cook
dessiner, to draw
*écrire, to write
*faire des photos *f*, to take photographs
*faire du vélo / de la voile, etc., to cycle / sail, etc.
jardiner, to garden
jouer de [+ musical instrument] / **à** [+ game], to play
*lire, to read (**le roman (policier)**, (detective) novel; **la poésie**, poetry)
*monter à cheval, to ride [horse]
pêcher, to fish (***aller à la pêche**, to go fishing)
se promener, to walk
tricoter, to knit

SEE ALSO: Art and Architecture; Cinema and Photography; Cooking and Eating; Holidays; The Media; Music; Nature; Reading and Writing; Sports and Games; Theatre; Tools; Transport

31. Liking, Disliking, Comparing
Aimer, ne pas aimer, comparer

Aimer Liking

l'**affection** *f* **(pour)**, affection (for)
l'**amitié** *f*, friendship
l'**amour** *m* **(de / pour)**, love (of / for)
l'**attachement** *m* **(à)**, attachment (to)
la **bienveillance (envers / pour)**, benevolence / kindness (to)
le **besoin (de)**, need (of)
la **camaraderie**, comradeship
le **coup de foudre** *f*, love at first sight [literally, *thunderbolt*]
le **désir**, desire
l'**envie** *f* **(de faire qch.)**, wish, desire (to do sth.)
la **familiarité**, familiarity
le **goût (de)**, taste (for) (**à mon goût**, to my liking)
l'**inclination** *f* **(à faire qch.)**, inclination (to do sth.)
l'**intention** *f*, intention
la **passion**, passion
le **penchant (pour qch.)**, liking (for sth.)
le **plaisir**, pleasure (**cela me fait grand plaisir (de faire qch.)**, it gives me great pleasure (to do sth.); **avec plaisir**, with pleasure)
le **souhait**, wish / desire
la **sympathie (pour qn.)**, liking (for sb.)
la **tendresse (pour)**, fondness (for)

aimer, to like / love (**aimer bien**, to like; **aimer d'amour**, to love)
admirer, to admire
adorer, to adore
affectionner, to be fond of
apprécier, to appreciate
*avoir besoin de, to need
*avoir envie de, to want / feel like

*avoir l'intention *f* **de,** to intend to
chérir, to cherish
se *complaire à faire qch., to delight in doing sth.
désirer, to want
*être fou (*f* **folle) d'amour (pour),** be madly in love (with)
idolâtrer, to idolize
*plaire (à qn.), to please (sb.) (**cela me plaît,** I like it; **il
me plaît,** I like him)
raffoler de, to be mad on
souhaiter, to wish
*tomber amoureux *f* **-euse de,** to fall in love with
*vouloir, to want / wish

admirable, admirable
adorable, delightful
agréable, pleasant
amical *pl* **-aux,** friendly
bien disposé (envers), well-disposed (towards)
bienveillant, benevolent
charmant, charming
désirable, desirable
épris / amoureux *f* **-euse (de),** in love (with)
formidable, terrific
magnifique, magnificent
merveilleux *f* **-euse,** marvellous
plaisant, pleasant / agreeable
ravissant, delightful

Ne pas aimer Disliking

l'animosité *f,* animosity
l'antipathie *f,* antipathy
l'aversion *f* **(pour),** aversion (to)
le dégoût (pour), disgust (of)
le dépit, spite
le désagrément, annoyance
la haine, hate
l'hostilité *f,* hostility
l'indifférence *f* **(envers),** indifference (towards)

l'inimitié f, enmity
le mécontentement (de), dissatisfaction (with)
le mépris, scorn
la rancune, resentment (**garder rancune**, to bear a grudge)
la réclamation, complaint
la répugnance (pour / à), repugnance (for)
la répulsion, repulsion
le ressentiment (de), resentment (of)

abhorrer, to detest / abhor
abominer, to loathe
***avoir / éprouver du dégoût pour qch.**, not to be able to stand sth.
***avoir honte** f **de**, be ashamed of
***avoir horreur** f **de**, to have a horror of
se désaffectionner de, to grow cold towards
détester, to hate / detest
exécrer, to detest / find repellent
***faire qch. à contrecœur**, to do sth. reluctantly
***haïr**, to hate (**comme la peste**, like the plague)
mépriser, to despise
ne pas aimer, to dislike
***prendre qn. / qch. en aversion** f / **en dégoût** m, to take a dislike to sb. / sth.
réclamer (contre), to complain / object (to)
rejeter, to reject
réprouver qn. / qch., to disapprove of sb. / sth.

abominable, abominable
détestable, detestable
ennuyeux f **-euse**, boring
exécrable, execrable
fâcheux f **-euse**, annoying
haineux f **-euse**, full of hatred / spiteful
indifférent à, indifferent (to)
indigné de / par, indignant at
mal disposé (envers), ill-disposed (towards)
mécontent (de), dissatisfied (with)
odieux f **-euse**, hateful
peu désirable, undesirable

rancunier *f* **-ière**, resentful
vindicatif *f* **-ive**, vindictive

Comparer Making comparisons

le choix, choice
la comparaison, comparison
le contraire, opposite
le contraste, contrast
la différence, difference
le jugement, judgement
la préférence, preference
la similitude, similarity

aimer mieux, to prefer
peser (des idées *f* **etc.),** to weigh (ideas etc.)
choisir (entre), to choose (between)
comparer (avec), to compare (with)
décider (entre), to decide (between)
différer (de), to differ (from)
hésiter (entre), to hesitate (between)
incliner à faire qch., to be inclined to do sth.
pencher (pour / vers), to lean towards
préférer (qch. à qch.), to prefer (sth. to sth.)

comparable (à), comparable (to)
comparatif *f* **-ive (à),** comparative / compared (with / to)
différent (de), different (from)
égal *pl* **-aux (à),** equal (to)
favori *f* **-ite / préféré,** favourite
identique (à), identical (to)
pareil *f* **-eille (à),** like / the same (as)
préférable (à), preferable (to)
semblable (à), like / similar (to)

aussi . . . que, as . . . as
autant de [+ NOUN] **que,** as much / many . . . as
moins de [+ NOUN] **que,** less / fewer . . . than
moins . . . que, less . . . than

pas (aus)si . . . que, not so . . . as
plus de [+ NOUN] **que**, more . . . than
plus . . . que, more . . . than

autant que (moi etc.), as much / many as (me etc.)
beaucoup (de) / bien (des), a lot (of)
beaucoup moins / bien moins, a lot less
beaucoup plus / bien plus, a lot / many more
comme, like / as
de préférence *f* **/ plutôt**, preferably / rather
en comparaison *f* **de**, in comparison to / compared with
mieux que, better than
pire que, worse than
tant, so much

SEE ALSO: **Arguing For and Against; Describing
 People; Feelings**

32. **Materials** Les Matériaux

la composition, composition
l'étoffe *f*, material / fabric
le gaz (*pl* -) **(naturel)**, (natural) gas
le liquide, liquid
la matière / la substance, material / substance / matter
  (**la matière première**, raw material)
le matériau *pl* -x, construction material
le métal *pl* -aux, metal
le minéral *pl* -aux, mineral
le produit, product
le solide, solid

argileux *f* -euse, clayey
artificiel *f* -elle, artificial
compact / dense, compact / dense
de bois m / d'or *m* etc., wooden / golden etc. (also **en bois / en or** etc.)
fait (à la) main, hand-made
grand teint *inv*, colour-fast
marbré, marbled / mottled
naturel *f* -elle, natural
pétrifié, petrified
pierreux *f* -euse / **rocailleux** *f* -euse, stony
plastique, plastic
poreux *f* -euse, porous
sableux *f* -euse / **sablonneux** *f* -euse, sandy
synthétique, synthetic
taillé, carved / hewn
velouté, velvety
véritable, real

Les noms de matériaux Names of materials

l'acier *m*, steel
l'acrylique *m*, acrylic
l'air *m*, air

l'**aluminium** *m*, aluminium
l'**argent** *m*, silver
l'**argile** *f*, clay
le **bambou**, bamboo
le **béton**, concrete
le **bitume**, bitumen / asphalt
le **bois**, wood
la **brique**, brick
le **bronze**, bronze
le **calcaire / la pierre à chaux**, limestone (la **chaux**, lime)
le **caoutchouc (mousse)**, (foam) rubber (les **bottes** *f* de **caoutchouc**, gumboots / wellingtons)
le **carton**, cardboard
le **charbon**, coal (le **mineur**, miner; la **mine / la fosse**, mine; le **puits**, shaft; le **terril**, spoil-heap)
le **ciment**, cement
la **cire**, wax
le **coke**, coke
la **colle**, glue
le **(bois) contre-plaqué**, plywood (**contre-plaqué en trois**, three-ply; **en contre-plaqué**, laminated)
la **corde**, rope
le **coton**, cotton
le **crêpe**, crêpe
le **cristal**, crystal
le **cuir**, leather
le **cuivre (rouge)**, copper
le **cuivre jaune / le laiton**, brass
la **dentelle**, lace
le **diamant**, diamond
le **drap**, (woollen) cloth
l'**eau** *f*; *pl* **-x**, water
l'**étain** *m*, tin / pewter (le **papier d'étain**, silver paper)
la **faïence**, earthenware / crockery
le **fer (forgé)**, (wrought) iron
le **fer-blanc**, tin (plate)
le **feutre**, felt
la **ficelle**, string
le **fil**, thread (le **fil de fer** *m*, wire)

la flanelle, flannel
la fourrure, fur
le goudron, tar
le granit, granite
le gravier, gravel
le grès, sandstone / earthenware
la houille, coal (**la houille blanche,** hydroelectric power;
  blanc *f* **-nche,** white)
l'huile *f,* oil
le kaolin, china-clay / kaolin
la laine, wool
la lave, lava
le lignite, brown coal / lignite
le lin, linen / flax
le marbre, marble
le mastic, putty
le mica, mica
le minerai, ore
le nylon, nylon
l'or *m,* gold
l'osier *m,* wicker(work)
la paille, straw
le papier, paper
la peau (de porc *m* **/ de veau** *m),* (pig / calf)skin
la peluche, plush
le pétrole, oil / paraffin (**le gisement pétrolifère,** oil-field)
la pierre, stone (**la pierre précieuse,** precious stone)
le plastique, plastic
le plâtre, plaster
le plomb, lead
le polyester, polyester
la porcelaine, porcelain / china
la roche, rock
le rotin, cane
le satin, satin
le silex, flint
la soie, silk
le tergal[Ⓟ]**/ le térylène**[Ⓟ]**,** terylene[Ⓟ]

la terre, earth (**la terre cuite**, earthenware; **cuit**, cooked)
le tissu (naturel / synthétique), (natural / man-made) fabric
la toile, canvas / linen (**la toile cirée**, oilcloth)
la tourbe, peat
le velours, velvet
le verre, glass
le vinyle, vinyl

SEE ALSO: **Adornment (for jewels and metals); Clothing (for types of cloth); Plants (for woods); Science (for gases and chemicals)**

33. The Media Les Média

La télévision, la radio, la vidéo
Television, radio, video

l'**annonceur** *m*, advertiser
l'**antenne** *f*, aerial / *colloq* radio set (**le temps d'antenne**, air-time; **l'antenne parabolique**, dish aerial)
l'**audience** *f*, audience
l'**auditeur** *m*; *f* **-trice**, listener
le **bulletin d'information** / **les informations** *f*, news (broadcast)
la **caméra** / **le caméscope**, video camera / camcorder
le **canal** *pl* **-aux**, channel
la **chaîne**, channel / network
le **clip vidéo**, video clip
le / la **correspondant(e)**, correspondent
le **décodeur**, decoder (**l'abonnement** *m*, subscription ; **l'abonné** *m*; *f* **-ée**, subscriber)
le **documentaire**, documentary
l'**écran** *m*, screen
l'**émission** *f* / **le programme**, programme / broadcast
l'**enregistrement** *m*, recording
le **feuilleton**, soap
le **film (vidéo)**, (video) film
le **flash (publicitaire)**, commercial
la **FM**, FM (**sur la FM**, on FM)
le **générique**, credits
l'**image** *f*, picture
l'**interview** *f*, interview
le **(télé)journal** *pl* **-aux**, news (broadcast)
le **magnétoscope**, video recorder (**la cassette**, cassette)
les **média** *m*, media
le **microphone**, microphone
les **ondes** *f* **courtes** / **moyennes** / **longues**, short / medium / long wave
les **parasites** *m*, interference

la perturbation, breakdown
la pièce radiophonique / télévisée, radio / television play
le présentateur *f* **-trice,** presenter / newsreader
le producteur *f* **-trice,** producer
la pub(licité) radio / télé, radio / TV advertising / advertisements / commercial(s)
la radio / le poste, radio (set) (**une radio,** a radio station)
la radio périphérique / libre, independent radio station
la réception, reception
la rediffusion, repeat
le son, sound
le speaker *f* **-erine,** announcer
la station, (TV / radio) station
le studio, studio
le téléspectateur *f* **-trice,** viewer
la télévision / la télé, television [the service] (**à la télé,** on TV)
la télévision / le téléviseur / le poste, television [the set]
la télévision en couleurs *f* **/ en noir** *m* **et blanc** *m* **/ par câble** *m* **/ scolaire / satellite** *m*, colour / black and white / cable / schools / satellite television
le transistor, transistor

allumer / *mettre, to switch on
brancher sur, to tune to (**branché,** switched on)
changer de chaîne *f*, to change stations / channels
diffuser (en direct), to broadcast (live)
écouter, to listen to
enregistrer, to record
essuyer, to wipe
*éteindre / arrêter, to switch off
passer (à la télé / à la radio), to be on TV / radio
passer une cassette, to play a video / a cassette
programmer, to programme
regarder, to watch
téléviser, to televise

La presse The press

l'agence *f* (de presse *f*), press agency
les (petites) annonces *f*, small ads / classified
l'article *m* (de tête / de fond), (leading / in-depth) article
(la tête, head; le fond, in-depth knowledge)
le collaborateur *f* -trice, contributor
la conférence de presse *f*, press conference
la coquille, misprint
le courrier, letters (le courrier du cœur, agony column)
le critique, critic (la critique, criticism)
l'éditeur *m*; *f* -trice, publisher
l'en-tête *m*; *pl* - -s, headline (le gros titre, main headline)
l'hebdomadaire *m*, weekly (magazine / newspaper)
l'illustré *m*, (photo) magazine
le journal *pl* -aux (du matin / du soir / du dimanche
m), (morning / evening / Sunday) newspaper
le / la journaliste, journalist
le magazine / la revue, magazine
les (dernières) nouvelles *f*, the (latest) news (une
nouvelle, a piece of news)
le périodique, periodical
le / la photographe de presse *f*, newspaper photographer
la presse (écrite), press (écrit, written; la presse à
sensation *f*, gutter press)
la publicité, advertisements
le rédacteur *f* -trice (en chef), editor
le reportage / le compte rendu *pl* -s -s, report (le
compte, account)
le reporter, reporter
la rubrique, column / section
le service de presse *f*, publicity department
le supplément (en couleurs *f*), (colour) supplement
le tirage, circulation
la une, the front page

*avoir bonne / mauvaise presse, to have a good / bad press
éditer / publier, to publish
imprimer, to print

SEE ALSO: **Cinema and Photography; Music; Politics;
Theatre**

34. Money L'Argent

l'achat *m*, purchase
l'action *f*, share [in company]
le bénéfice, profit
le budget, budget
le capital *sometimes found in pl* **-aux**, capital
le coût (de la vie), cost (of living) (le niveau *pl* **-x de vie**, standard of living)
le crédit, credit (**acheter à crédit**, to buy on hire-purchase; ***faire crédit**, to give credit)
la dépense, expense
la dépréciation, depreciation
la dette, debt
la facture, invoice
le faux-monnayeur *pl* **- -s**, counterfeiter
la fluctuation, fluctuation
les frais *m*, expenses
l'inflation *f*, inflation
l'investissement *m*, investment
la loterie, lottery (le tirage, draw; le gros lot, first prize)
le montant, amount/sum
le paiement, payment
le portefeuille, wallet
le porte-monnaie *pl inv*, purse
le pourcentage, percentage
le prix (coûtant/élevé/bas), (cost/high/low) price (les prix montent/baissent, prices rise/fall)
la quittance/le reçu, receipt
la somme, sum
la taxe, charge/tax (la taxe à la valeur ajoutée [TVA], value added tax [VAT])
la valeur, value (les valeurs, shares/stocks/assets)
la vente, sale

accepter, to take/accept
acheter, to buy
changer (en), to change (into)

coûter, to cost
dépenser, to spend
*faire, to come to/add up to (**ça fait dix francs** *m*, that comes to ten francs)
*faire payer qch. à qn., to charge sb. sth.
gagner, to earn
*mettre en circulation *f*, to put into circulation
payer, to pay (**payer qn.**, to pay sb.; **payer qch.**, to pay for sth.; **payer qch. à qn.**, to pay sb. for sth.)
se payer qch., to treat oneself to sth.
payer comptant/par chèque *m*/**par carte** *f* **de crédit** *m*, to pay cash/by cheque/by credit card
payer la note/une tournée, to foot the bill/stand a round
*valoir, to be worth
vendre, to sell

à court *inv* **d'argent** *m*, short of cash
bon marché *inv*, cheap (**meilleur marché**, cheaper)
cher *f* **chère**, dear
fauché, broke
faux (*f* **fausse**)/**contrefait**, forged/counterfeit
pauvre, poor
pile ou face, heads or tails
riche, rich
valable, valid (**de valeur** *f*, valuable)

Les devises Currency

l'argent *m* (**de poche** *f*), (pocket-)money (**l'argent liquide**, cash)
le billet (**de banque** *f*/**de cent francs** *m*), (bank/100-franc) note
le centime, centime [coin]
la coupure, note (**les grosses/petites coupures**, large/small notes)
les devises *f* (**étrangères**), (foreign) currency
le dollar, dollar
les espèces *f*, cash (**en espèces**, in cash)
le franc français/belge/suisse, French/Belgian/Swiss franc

la **livre sterling**, pound sterling
la **monnaie (de)**, change (for) (la **monnaie française**,
  French currency; l'**hôtel** *m* de la **Monnaie**, the Mint)
la **pièce**, coin

Les institutions financières
Financial institutions

la **banque**, bank (le **guichet**, position / counter)
la **bourse**, stock exchange [also *purse*]
le **bureau** *pl* -x de change *m*, bureau de change (le **change**,
  exchange; le **taux de change** / le **cours**, exchange rate)
la **caisse d'épargne** *f*, savings bank (le **livret d'épargne**,
  savings book)
la **compagnie d'assurances**, insurance company
  (l'**assurance** *f*, insurance; la **police**, policy [also means
  police]; la **prime**, premium)

Votre compte en banque Your bank account

la **caisse**, till / cashier's desk (le **caissier** *f* -ière, cashier)
la **commission**, commission
le **compte (en banque** *f*), (bank) account (*faire ses
  comptes**, to do one's accounts; *être à couvert** / à
  découvert, to be in the black / red; **découvert**, uncovered /
  overdrawn)
le **compte courant** / d'épargne *f* / à terme *m* / de chèques *m*
  postaux, current / savings / deposit / Giro account (le
  relevé, statement)
le **découvert (de)**, overdraft (of)
les **économies** *f*, savings
l'**emprunt** *m*, loan [taken out]
les **frais bancaires**, bank charges
l'**hypothèque** *f* / un **emprunt-logement**, mortgage
l'**intérêt** *m*, interest
le **prêt**, loan
le **retrait**, withdrawal

le solde, balance
le versement, deposit
le virement / le transfert, transfer

créditer, to credit
déposer, to deposit
économiser / *faire des économies f / **épargner**, to save
emprunter (à), to borrow (from)
encaisser, to cash
prêter, to lend
rembourser, to pay back
retirer (de l'argent m**)**, to draw (money) out
toucher, to cash / get [money]
transférer, to transfer
verser (de l'argent à . . .), to pay / put (money in . . .)

Les cartes et les chèques Cards and cheques

la carte bancaire, bank card
la carte de crédit m, credit card
le chèque (de mille francs m**)**, cheque (for 1,000 francs)
le chèque de voyage m / **barré** / **ouvert** / **en blanc** m / **sans
  provision** f, traveller's / crossed / open / blank / dud cheque
le chéquier / le carnet de chèques m, cheque-book
le distributeur (de billets), cash dispenser (**le billet**, bank-
  note)
l'eurochèque m, Eurocheque
le mandat postal pl -aux, postal order
la pièce d'identité f, identity card

SEE ALSO: **Crimes and Criminals; Numbers and
  Quantities; Shops and Shopping**

35. Music La Musique

le **bâton**, baton
bis!, encore!
la **cassette**, cassette
la **corde**, string
la **discothèque**, disco
le **disque** (**CD** / **compact**), (CD) record
l'**électrophone** *m* / le **tourne-disque(s)** *pl* - -s, record-player
l'**instrument** *m*, instrument
le **juke-box** *pl inv*, juke-box
le **magnétophone**, cassette recorder
le **magnétoscope**, video recorder (la **vidéocassette**,
   videocassette)
le **45 tours** (**simple**) *pl inv*, single
la **salle de concert**, concert hall
le **super 45 tours** *pl inv*, EP [record]
la **touche**, key [of instrument]
le **33 tours** *pl inv*, LP [record]

Les musiciens Musicians

l'**accompagnateur** *f* -**trice**, accompanist
l'**alto** *m*, alto / counter-tenor
le **baryton**, baritone
la **basse** *always f*, bass [singer, voice, or part]
le **chanteur** *f* -**euse** / la **cantatrice**, singer
le **chef d'orchestre** *m*, conductor
le **chœur**, chorus
le **compositeur**, composer
le **contralto** *always m*, contralto
le **joueur** *f* -**euse** (**de** . . .), (. . .) player
le **musicien** *f* -**ienne**, musician
le / la **pianiste**, pianist
lé **premier violon**, leader (of orchestra)
le / la **soliste**, soloist

le/la soprano, soprano voice/soprano [singer]
le ténor, tenor

Les ensembles Ensembles

la (société) chorale, choir
le duo, duet
la fanfare, brass band
le groupe, group/band
l'orchestre *m* **(de chambre)**, (chamber) orchestra
le quatuor, quartet
le trio, trio

Ce qu'on joue What they play

l'accord *m*, chord
l'air *m*, tune
l'aria *f*, aria
la chanson, song
le chant, singing
le concert (symphonique/de rock *m*), (symphony/rock) concert
la dissonance, discord
la gamme, scale
l'harmonie *f*, harmony
le hit-parade *pl* **--s/le palmarès**, hit parade; top twenty
le jazz, jazz
le morceau *pl* **-x**, piece
la musique classique/pop/légère/folklorique/de chambre *f*, classical/pop/light/folk/chamber music
la (fausse) note, (wrong) note
l'opéra *m*, opera
l'opérette *f*, operetta
l'ouverture *f*, overture
la partition, score
le récital *pl* **-s (de . . .)**, (. . .) recital
le rock, rock

la sonate, sonata
la symphonie, symphony

Ce qu'on fait What they do

chanter, to sing
diriger / *conduire, to conduct
*faire partie ƒ de, to play / sing in
interpréter, to interpret
jouer de, to play [an instrument]
jouer juste / faux, to play in / out of tune
passer un disque / une cassette, to put on a record / cassette
travailler un instrument, to practise an instrument

Les instruments The instruments

l'accordéon *m*, accordion
le basson, bassoon
la batterie, drums / drum-kit
les bois *m*, the woodwind
le clairon, bugle
la clarinette, clarinet
le clavecin, harpsichord
le clavier, keyboard(s)
la contrebasse, (double-)bass
le cor anglais, cor anglais
le cor d'harmonie *f*, French horn
les cordes *f*, the strings [group of instruments]
la cornemuse, bagpipes
les cuivres *m*, the brass [group of instruments]
les cymbales *f*, cymbals
la flûte, flute
la flûte à bec, recorder (**le bec**, beak / nozzle)
la grosse caisse, bass drum
la guitare, guitar
l'harmonica *m*, mouth-organ

l'harmonium *m*, harmonium
la harpe, harp
le hautbois, oboe
les instruments *m* **à percussion** *f*, the percussion
les instruments *m* **à vent** *m*, wind instruments / the winds
l'orgue *m*, organ (**les orgues** *f pl*, church organ)
le piano (droit / à queue), (upright / grand) piano (**la queue**, tail)
le saxophone, saxophone
le tambour, drum
le tambourin, tambourine
les timbales *f*, the timpani
le triangle, triangle
le trombone, trombone
la trompette, trumpet
le violon, violin
le violoncelle, cello
le xylophone, xylophone

La gamme The scale

ut [**do** when singing solfa], C
ré, D
mi, E
fa, F
sol, G
la, A
si, B
bémol, flat
dièse, sharp
majeur, major
mineur, minor

SEE ALSO: **Leisure and Hobbies; The Media; The Senses; Theatre**

36. **Nature** La Nature

L'espace Space

l'astéroïde *m*, asteroid
le ciel *pl usually* **cieux**, sky
la comète, comet (**comme le vin de la comète**, once in a blue moon)
la constellation, constellation
l'éclipse *f*, eclipse
l'espace *m*, space
l'éternité *f*, eternity
l'étoile *f*, star
la galaxie, galaxy
l'horizon *m*, horizon
la (nouvelle / pleine) lune, (new / full) moon (**le clair de lune**, moonlight)
le monde, world
la navette, (space) shuttle
la nébuleuse, nebula
l'observatoire *m*, observatory
la planète, planet
le satellite, satellite
le soleil, sun / sunlight (**au soleil**, in the sun; **le lever / le coucher du soleil**, sunrise / sunset; **l'aube** *f* **/ l'aurore** *f*, dawn; **le crépuscule**, dusk)
le télescope, telescope
l'univers *m*, universe
le vaisseau *pl* **-x spatial** *pl* **-aux**, spaceship
le voyageur (*f* **-euse**) **de l'espace** *m*, spaceman / -woman
briller, to shine
*croître / *décroître, to wax / wane
*étinceler, to sparkle
se lever / se coucher, to rise / set
*parcourir l'espace *m*, to travel through space
scintiller, to twinkle

tourner autour de, to revolve around
voyager dans l'espace *m*, to travel in space

Le paysage The countryside

l'abîme *m*, abyss
l'affluent *m*, tributary
le barrage, dam
le bois, wood
la bruyère, heath [also means *heather*]
la campagne, country (**à la campagne**, in the country;
  en pleine campagne, in open country)
le canal *pl* **-aux**, canal (**une écluse**, lock)
la caverne, cave
la chaîne de montagnes *f*, mountain chain
le champ, field
le chemin, path / road / way (**le chemin rural** *pl* **-aux**,
  country lane)
la chute d'eau *f*, waterfall
la clairière, clearing
le col, pass
la colline, hill
le coteau *pl* **-x**, slope / hillside
le cours d'eau *f*, waterway / stream
le creux, hollow
le delta, delta
le désert, desert
la dune, dune
l'étang *m*, pool
la ferme, farm
le fleuve, (major) river
la forêt (vierge / pluviale), (virgin / rain) forest
le fossé, ditch
le glacier, glacier
la gorge, gorge
le gouffre, chasm
le gué, ford
la jungle, jungle

le **lac**, lake
la **lande**, sandy moor / heath
le **maquis**, scrub
le **marais**, marsh
la **mare**, pond
le **marécage**, swamp
le **massif**, mountain range
le **mont**, mount
la **montagne**, mountain (**à la montagne**, in the mountains)
l'**oasis** *f occasionally m*, oasis
le **parc national** *pl* **-aux**, national park
la **passerelle**, foot-bridge
la **pente**, slope
le **pic**, peak
la **pierre**, stone
la **plaine**, plain
le **plateau** *pl* **-x**, plateau
le **pont (suspendu / tournant)**, (suspension / swing) bridge
la **prairie**, meadow / prairie
le **pré**, meadow (**les prés salés**, salt meadows / saltings)
le **précipice**, precipice
le **raccourci**, short-cut
le **ravin**, ravine
la **rivière**, river (**la rive**, bank; **le lit**, bed; **en amont**,
    upstream; **en aval**, downstream)
la **route**, road (**la grand-route** *pl* **- -s**, highway)
la **ruelle**, lane
le **ruisseau** *pl* **-x**, stream
la **savane**, savannah
le **sentier (de grande randonnée)**, (long-distance) path
    (**la randonnée**, excursion)
le **sol / le terroir**, soil
le **sommet**, summit
la **source**, spring
la **steppe**, steppe
le **terrain**, ground
le **tertre**, knoll
le **torrent**, torrent
la **vallée / le val** *pl usually* **-s**, valley

le verger, orchard
le vignoble, vineyard / vine plantation
le volcan (éteint / inactif / en activité *f*), (extinct / dormant / active) volcano (**le cratère**, crater)

*aller à travers champs, to go across country (**le champ**, field)
barrer / endiguer, to dam
border, to border
couler, to flow
déborder, to overflow
se dresser, to stand
s'élever, to rise
entourer (de), to surround (with)
s'étendre, to stretch
inonder, to flood
se jeter dans, to flow into [a river etc.]
passer à gué *m*, to ford / wade
se trouver / *être situé, to be situated

accidenté, hilly
à pic, vertical / precipitous
déchiqueté / dentelé, jagged
escarpé / raide, steep
inégal *pl* **-aux**, uneven
luxuriant, lush
montagneux *f* **-euse**, mountainous
navigable, navigable
nu, bare
pierreux / rocailleux *both f* **-euse**, stony
plat, flat
poussiéreux *f* **-euse**, dusty
rugueux / raboteux *both f* **-euse**, rough
sablonneux *f* **-euse**, sandy
uni, smooth

La mer et la côte The sea and the coast

l'archipel *m*, archipelago
la baie, bay
le banc de sable *m*, sandbank

le bas-fond *pl* **- -s**, shoal
le bord de mer, seaside
le cap, cape
le coquillage, shell
le courant, current
le détroit, strait
l'écume *f*, foam
les embruns *m*, spray
l'estuaire *m*, estuary
la falaise, cliff
le front de mer, promenade
le galet / le caillou *pl* **-x**, pebble
le golfe, gulf
la grève, strand / beach
la houle, swell
l'île *f*, island
l'îlot *m*, islet
l'isthme *m*, isthmus
la jetée, jetty / pier
la marée (haute / basse), (high / low) tide (**la marée monte / descend**, the tide's coming in / going out)
la mer, sea (**une mer calme / mauvaise / agitée**, smooth / rough / choppy sea)
le niveau *pl* **-x de la mer**, sea-level
l'océan *m*, ocean
le phare, lighthouse
la plage, beach
le port, port
la presqu'île *pl* **-s**, peninsula
le promontoire, promontory
le quai, quay
le récif, reef
le ressac, surf
le rivage, shore
le rocher, rock
le sable, sand
la station balnéaire, seaside resort (**balnéaire**, bathing)
la vague, wave

Le monde des hommes The world of men

le canton, [France] canton / district
la commune, [France] commune [= parish]
le comté, [England] county
le continent, continent
le département, [France] department [= county]
l'équateur *m*, equator
l'état *m*, state
à l'étranger *m*, abroad
la frontière, frontier
le globe, globe
l'hémisphère *m* **nord / sud**, northern / southern hemisphere
la nation, nation
la patrie, native land
le pays, country
le pôle (nord / sud / magnétique), (north / south / magnetic) pole
la province, province(s) (***vivre en province**, to live in the provinces)
la région, region
la terre, earth
les tropiques *f*, tropics (**sous les tropiques**, in the tropics)

SEE ALSO: **Animals; Disasters; Places and Languages; Plants; Science; The Weather**

37. Numbers and Quantities
Les Nombres et les quantités

le calcul, calculation / arithmetic / calculus
la calculatrice, calculator [the machine]
le chiffre, figure / numeral (**les chiffres romains / arabes**, roman / arabic numerals)
la différence, difference
la fraction, fraction
l'infini *m*, infinity
la moyenne, average
le nombre, number (**un nombre entier / pair / impair**, a whole / even / odd number)
le numéro, number [= several figures put together, e.g. **le numéro de téléphone** *m*, telephone number]
une partie, a part
le tout, the whole
l'unité *f*, unit

ajouter (à), to add (to)
augmenter, to increase / augment
calculer, to calculate
compter, to count
doubler, to double
diminuer, to lessen / diminish
distribuer, to distribute
diviser (par / en), to divide (by / into)
égaler, to equal
évaluer, to estimate
mesurer, to measure
multiplier (par), to multiply (by)
partager / répartir, to share (out)
peser (lourd), to weigh (a lot)
remplir, to fill
*soustraire (de), to subtract (from)
*suffire, to be enough
tripler, to triple
vider, to empty

à peine, scarcely
à peu près / autour de / environ, about
approximativement, approximately
au moins, at least
au plus, at most
davantage, more
encore, again / more
plus ou moins, more or less
seulement, only
tout à fait / complètement, completely
tout au plus, at the very most
tout juste, just

(in)défini, (in)definite
(in)égal *pl* **-aux**, (un)equal
(in)exact / (im)précis, (in)exact
innombrable, countless
nombreux *f* **-euse**, numerous
rare, rare / infrequent
seul, only / single
suffisant, sufficient
superflu, superfluous / excessive

au carré, squared
divisé par, divided by
fois, times
moins, minus
plus, plus
pour cent, per cent

Les nombres cardinaux Cardinal numbers

0	zéro	8	huit
1	un(e)	9	neuf
2	deux	10	dix
3	trois	11	onze
4	quatre	12	douze
5	cinq	13	treize
6	six	14	quatorze
7	sept	15	quinze

16 seize	41 quarante et un(e)
17 dix-sept	50 cinquante
18 dix-huit	51 cinquante et un(e)
19 dix-neuf	60 soixante
20 vingt	61 soixante et un(e)
21 vingt et un(e)	70 soixante-dix
22 vingt-deux	71 soixante et onze
23 vingt-trois	72 soixante-douze
24 vingt-quatre	80 quatre-vingts
25 vingt-cinq	81 quatre-vingt-un(e)
26 vingt-six	90 quatre-vingt-dix
27 vingt-sept	91 quatre-vingt-onze
28 vingt-huit	92 quatre-vingt-douze
29 vingt-neuf	100 cent
30 trente	101 cent un(e)
31 trente et un(e)	200 deux cents
32 trente-deux	201 deux cent un(e)
40 quarante	

1000	mille
1001	mille un(e)
1002	mille deux
2000	deux mille
1 000 000	un million
1 000 200	un million deux cents
2 000 000	deux millions
1 000 000 000	un milliard
2 000 000 000	deux milliards

There is no **-s** on the plural of **vingt** and **cent** when these are followed by another number. **Million** and **milliard** are nouns: **un million de soldats**, *a million soldiers*. All other numbers are adjectives and invariable, except that those ending in **un** change it to **une** before a feminine noun. Before **huit** and **onze**, **le** does not become **l'**: **le onze juin**, *the eleventh of June*.

In Belgium, Switzerland, and Canada **septante**, **octante** or **huitante**, and **nonante** are used for 70, 80, and 90.

une fois, once
deux fois, twice

trois fois, three times / thrice
quatre fois, four times
x fois, umpteen times

simple / unique, single
double, double
triple, triple
quadruple, quadruple
quintuple, quintuple
décuple, tenfold
centuple, a hundredfold
multiple, multiple

Les nombres ordinaux Ordinal numbers

premier *f* **-ière**, first
deuxième / second *f* **-e**, second
troisième, third
quatrième, fourth
cinquième, fifth
sixième, sixth
septième, seventh
huitième, eighth
neuvième, ninth
dixième, tenth

onzième, eleventh
douzième, twelfth
treizième, thirteenth
quatorzième, fourteenth
quinzième, fifteenth
seizième, sixteenth
dix-septième, seventeenth
dix-huitième, eighteenth
dix-neuvième, nineteenth
vingtième, twentieth

vingt et unième, twenty-first
vingt-deuxième, twenty-second
trentième, thirtieth
quarantième, fortieth
cinquantième, fiftieth
soixantième, sixtieth
soixante-dixième, seventieth
soixante et onzième, seventy-first
quatre-vingtième, eightieth
quatre-vingt-unième, eighty-first
quatre-vingt-dixième, ninetieth
quatre-vingt-onzième, ninety-first
centième, hundredth
cent unième, hundred and first

deux centième, two hundredth
deux cent unième, two hundred and first
millième, thousandth
mille unième, thousand and first
deux millième, two thousandth
millionième, millionth
milliardième, billionth

dernier *f* **-ière**, last

premièrement, firstly
deuxièmement, secondly
troisièmement, thirdly

Henri premier, Henri I
Henri deux, Henri II
Henri trois, Henri III

Les nombres approximatifs
Approximate numbers

une huitaine, about eight / a week
une dizaine, about ten (**les dizaines**, the tens [when doing sums])
une douzaine, a dozen (**une demi-douzaine d'œufs** *m*, half a dozen eggs)
une quinzaine, about fifteen / a fortnight
une vingtaine, about twenty / a score
une trentaine, about thirty
une quarantaine, about forty
une cinquantaine, about fifty
une soixantaine, about sixty
une centaine, about a hundred
un millier, about a thousand

Les fractions Fractions

un(e) demi(e), a half (**une heure et demie**, an hour and a half; **un kilo et demi**, a kilo and a half; **une demi-heure** [**demi** *inv* before noun], half an hour / a half-hour)

la moitié (de), (the) half (of)
un tiers (de), a third (of) (**deux tiers**, two-thirds)
un quart (de), a quarter (of) (**trois quarts**, three-quarters)
un cinquième, a fifth
un sixième, a sixth
trois huitièmes, three-eighths
trois et quatre cinquièmes, three and four-fifths (3⅘)
neuf sur dix, nine out of ten
un virgule cinq (1,5), one point five (1·5) (**la virgule**, comma)
trente-cinq mille deux cent trois (35 203), thirty-five thousand two hundred and three (35,203)

Les expressions de quantité
Expressions of quantity

assez (de), enough
autant (de), as much / many (of)
beaucoup (de), a lot (of) / much / many
bien des, a lot of
bon nombre (de / des), a fair number (of / of the)
encore (du / de la / des), more
la plupart (des), most (of the)
moins (de), less / fewer (of)
ne . . . pas de / ne . . . aucun ƒ -e / ne . . . nul ƒ nulle, no
ne . . . plus (de), no more (of)
peu (de), little / few
plus (de), more (of)
plusieurs, several
quelque(s), some
quelque chose (de . . .), something (. . .)
rien (de . . .), nothing (. . .)
trop (de), too much / many (of)

une assiette (de), a plate (of)
une bande (de), a flock / gang (of)
une boîte (de), a can (of)
un bol (de), a bowl (of)
une bouchée (de), a mouthful [food] (of)

un bout de, a bit of
une bouteille (de), a bottle (of)
une cuillerée (de), a spoonful (of)
une foule (de), a crowd (of)
une gorgée (de), a mouthful [drink] (of)
un grand nombre (de / des), a large number (of / of the)
un morceau *pl* **-x (de)**, a piece (of)
une paire (de), a pair (of)
un paquet (de), a packet (of)
un peu (de), a little (of)
une pile (de), a stack (of)
une poignée (de), a handful (of)
une portion (de), a helping (of)
un pot (de), a jar / pot (of)
une quantité (de), a quantity (of)
un rouleau *pl* **-x (de)**, a roll (of)
un sac (de), a bag (of)
une tablette (de), a bar (of)
un tas (de), a lot (of)
une tasse (de), a cup (of)
une tranche (de), a slice (of)
un troupeau *pl* **-x (de)**, a herd / flock (of)
un tube (de), a tube (of)
un verre (de), a glass / jar (of)

Les poids et les mesures
Weights and measures

l'ampère *m*, ampere
la calorie, calorie
le centimètre (carré / cube), (square / cubic) centimetre
le gramme, gram
l'hectare *m*, hectare
le kilo(gramme), kilo(gram)
le kilomètre, kilometre
le litre, litre
la livre, pound [= half a kilo]
le mètre, metre [also means *tape-measure*]

l'once *f*, ounce
le pouce, inch
la tonne, (metric) ton
le volt, volt
le watt, watt

la dimension, dimension
la distance, distance
l'épaisseur *f*, thickness
la grandeur, size
la hauteur, height
la largeur, breadth / width
la longueur, length
la mesure, measure(ment)
le poids, weight
la profondeur, depth
la quantité, quantity
la surface, area
la taille, size [in clothing; also means *height* and *waist*]
le volume, volume

mesurer, to measure

bas *f* **basse**, low
court, short
creux *f* **creuse**, hollow
étroit, narrow
grand, large / tall
gros *f* **grosse**, large / bulky
haut, high
large, broad / wide
léger *f* **légère**, light
long *f* **longue**, long
lourd, heavy
petit, small
plat, flat
profond, deep (**peu profond**, shallow)

Les dimensions Dimensions

quelle est la longueur / la largeur / la hauteur de cette pièce?, how long / wide / high is this room?

elle a / fait trois mètres de long(ueur) / large(ur) / haut(eur), it's 3 metres long / wide / high

quelle taille faites-vous?, what size are you?

je fais / porte du 36, I take size 36

combien mesurez-vous?, what is your height?

quel est votre tour de poitrine *f* / de taille *f* / de hanches *f*?, what is your bust / waist / hip size? (**le tour**, circumference)

quelle pointure chaussez-vous / faites-vous?, what is your shoe size?

je fais / chausse du 42, I take size 42

trois mètres sur quatre, three metres by four

long de trois mètres / d'une longueur de trois mètres, three metres long

SEE ALSO: **Money; Post and Telephone; Time**

38. Places and Languages
Les Lieux et les langues

Les océans et les mers Oceans and seas

l'**Atlantique** *m*, Atlantic
la **Baltique**, Baltic
le **golfe de Gascogne**, Bay of Biscay (la **Gascogne**,
  Gascony)
le **lac Léman**, Lake Geneva
la **Manche**, English Channel
la **Méditerranée**, Mediterranean
la **mer des Antilles**, Caribbean (les **Antilles** *f*, West Indies)
la **mer d'Irlande** *f*, Irish Sea
la **mer du Nord**, North Sea
l'**océan** *m* **Indien**, Indian Ocean
le **Pacifique**, Pacific

Les continents et leurs habitants
Continents and their inhabitants

l'**Afrique** *f*, Africa   **africain** / **un(e) Africain(e)**, African
l'**Amérique** *f* (**du Nord** / **du Sud**), (North / South)
  America   **américain** / **un(e) Américain(e)**, American
l'**Antarctique** *m*, Antarctica   **antarctique**, antarctic
l'**Asie** *f*, Asia   **asiatique** / **un(e) Asiatique**, Asiatic
l'**Australie** *f*, Australia   **australien** *f* -**enne** / **un(e)
  Australien(ne)**, Australian
l'**Europe** *f*, Europe   **européen** *f* -**enne** / **un(e)
  Européen(ne)**, European

Les fleuves et les montagnes
Rivers and mountains

les **Alpes** *f*, Alps   **alpin**, Alpine
les **Cévennes** *f*, Cevennes   **cévenol**, Cévenne *adj*

le **Danube**, Danube   **danubien** *f* **-enne**, Danubian
la **Garonne**, Garonne   **garonnais**, Garonne *adj*
le **Jura**, Jura mountains   **jurassien** *f* **-enne**, Jura *adj*
la **Loire**, Loire
le **Massif Central**, Central Massif
les **Pyrénées** *f*, Pyrenees   **pyrénéen** *f* **-enne**, Pyrenean
le **Rhin**, Rhine   **rhénan** *f* **-anne**, Rhineland *adj*
le **Rhône**, Rhone   **rhodanien** *f* **-enne**, Rhone *adj*
la **Seine**, Seine
la **Tamise**, Thames
les **Vosges** *f*, Vosges   **vosgien** *f* **-enne**, Vosge *adj*

Les villes, les îles, les régions
Towns, islands, regions

Alger, Algiers
l'**Alsace** *f*, Alsace   **alsacien** *f* **-enne**, Alsatian
Anvers, Antwerp
l'**Arabie** *f*, Arabia   **arabe**, Arab
l'**Asie** *f* **mineure**, Asia Minor
Athènes, Athens
Bâle, Basle
Barcelone, Barcelona
la **Bourgogne**, Burgundy   **bourguignon** *f* **-onne**,
  Burgundian
Brême, Bremen
la **Bretagne**, Brittany   **breton** *f* **-onne**, Breton
Bruxelles, Brussels
Cantorbéry, Canterbury
le **Caire**, Cairo
Coblence, Koblenz
Cologne, Cologne (Köln)
la **Communauté Européenne**, the European
  Community. **communautaire**, Community *adj*
Copenhague, Copenhagen
Cordoue, Cordoba
la **Cornouailles**, Cornwall
la **Corse**, Corsica **corse**, Corsican

la Côte d'Azur, the Riviera
la Crimée, the Crimea
Douvres, Dover
Dresde, Dresden
Édimbourg, Edinburgh
la Flandre, Flanders **flamand**, Flemish
Flessingue, Flushing
Gand, Ghent
la Gascogne, Gascony **gascon** *f* **-onne**, Gascon
la Gaule, Gaul **gaulois**, Gallic
Gênes, Genoa
Genève, Geneva
la Haye, The Hague
les îles *f* **Anglo-Normandes**, the Channel Islands
les îles *f* **Britanniques**, the British Isles
Lisbonne, Lisbon
Livourne, Leghorn
Londres, London **londonien** *f* **-enne**, London *adj*
Lyon, Lyons
le Maghreb, the Maghreb [Morocco, Algeria, and
  Tunisia] **maghrebin**, North-African
Majorque, Majorca
Marseille, Marseilles
Mayence, Mainz
la Mecque, Mecca
le Midi, South of France **méridional** *pl* **-aux**, southern
  French
Moscou, Moscow
Munich, Munich (München)
la Normandie, Normandy **normand**, Norman
Padoue, Padua
Paris, Paris **parisien** *f* **-enne**, Parisian
la Picardie, Picardy **picard**, Picard
l'Orient *m*, the East (**le Proche-Orient**, the Near East; **le
  Moyen-Orient**, the Middle East; **l'Extrême-Orient**,
  the Far East) **oriental** *pl* **-aux**, oriental
le Québec, Quebec **québecois**, Quebec *adj*
Reims, Rheims
le Sahara, the Sahara

la Sardaigne, Sardinia **sarde**, Sardinian
la Savoie, Savoy
la Saxe, Saxony **saxe**, Saxon
la Scandinavie, Scandinavia **scandinave**, Scandinavian
la Sicile, Sicily **sicilien** *f* **-enne**, Sicilian
Tanger, Tangiers
le Tiers Monde, the Third World
Varsovie, Warsaw
Venise, Venice
Vienne, Vienna [also Vienne, in France]
la Wallonie, Wallonia [French-speaking Belgium]
   wallon *f* **-onne**, Walloon

Les pays et leurs habitants
Countries and their inhabitants

l'Afrique *f* **du Sud**, South Africa **sud-africain / un(e)
   Sud-africain(e)**, South African
l'Algérie *f*, Algeria **algérien** *f* **-enne / un(e)
   Algérien(ne)**, Algerian
l'Allemagne *f*, Germany **allemand / un(e)
   Allemand(e)**, German
l'Angleterre *f*, England **anglais**, English; **un(e)
   Anglais(e)**, Englishman / -woman
les Antilles *f*, West Indies **antillais / un(e)
   Antillais(e)**, West Indian
l'Argentine *f*, Argentina **argentin / un(e) Argentin(e)**,
   Argentinian
l'Autriche *f*, Austria **autrichien** *f* **-enne / un(e)
   Autrichien(ne)**, Austrian
le Bangladesh, Bangladesh **bangladeshi / un(e)
   Bangladeshi**, Bangladeshi
la Belgique, Belgium **belge / un(e) Belge**, Belgian
le Brésil, Brazil **brésilien** *f* **-enne / un(e)
   Brésilien(ne)**, Brazilian
la Bulgarie, Bulgaria **bulgare / un(e) Bulgare**, Bulgarian
le Canada, Canada **canadien** *f* **-enne / un(e)
   Canadien(ne)**, Canadian

le Chili, Chile   **chilien** *f* **-enne** / **un(e) Chilien(ne)**, Chilean

la Chine, China   **chinois**, Chinese; **un(e) Chinois(e)** Chinese man / woman

la Corée, Korea   **coréen** *f* **-enne** / **un(e) Coréen(ne)**, Korean

le Danemark, Denmark   **danois**, Danish; **un(e) Danois(e)**, Dane

l'Écosse *f*, Scotland   **écossais**, Scottish; **un(e) Écossais(e)**, Scotsman / -woman

l'Égypte *f*, Egypt   **égyptien** *f* **-enne** / **un(e) Égyptien(ne)**, Egyptian

l'Espagne *f*, Spain   **espagnol**, Spanish; **un(e) Espagnol(e)**, Spaniard

les États-Unis (d'Amérique *f*) / **les USA** *m*, the United States (of America)

la Finlande, Finland   **finlandais**, Finnish; **un(e) Finlandais(e)**, Finn

la France, France   **français**, French; **un(e) Français(e)**, Frenchman / -woman

la Grande-Bretagne, Great Britain   **britannique**, British; **un(e) Britannique**, Brit / Briton

la Grèce, Greece   **grec** *f* **grecque** / **un(e) Grec(que)**, Greek

la Hollande, Holland; **les Pays-Bas** *m*, the Netherlands **hollandais**, Dutch; **un(e) Hollandais(e)**, Dutchman / -woman

la Hongrie, Hungary   **hongrois** / **un(e) Hongrois(e)**, Hungarian

l'Inde *f sometimes* **les Indes**, India   **indien** *f* **-enne** / **un(e) Indien(ne)**, Indian

l'Irlande *f* (**du Nord**), (Northern) Ireland;   **irlandais**, Irish; **un(e) Irlandais(e)**, Irishman / -woman

l'Islande *f*, Iceland   **islandais**, Icelandic; **un(e) Islandais(e)**, Icelander

Israël *m*, Israel   **israélien** *f* **-enne** / **un(e) Israélien(ne)**, Israeli; **juif** *f* **-ive**, Jewish; **le Juif** / **la Juive**, Jew

l'Italie *f*, Italy   **italien** *f* **-enne** / **un(e) Italien(ne)**, Italian

le Japon, Japan   **japonais / un(e) Japonais(e)**, Japanese

la Libye, Libya   **libyen** *f* **-enne / un(e) Libyen(ne)**, Libyan

le Luxembourg, Luxemburg   **luxembourgeois,**
   Luxemburg *adj*; **un(e) Luxembourgeois(e)**,
   Luxemburger

le Maroc, Morocco   **marocain / un(e) Marocain(e)**,
   Moroccan; **le / la Maure**, Moor; **mauresque**, Moorish

le Mexique, Mexico   **mexicain / un(e) Mexicain(e)**,
   Mexican

Monaco, Monaco   **monégasque**, Monaco *adj*; **un(e)**
   Monégasque, Monacan / Monegasque

la Norvège, Norway   **norvégien** *f* **-enne / un(e)**
   Norvégien(ne), Norwegian

la Nouvelle-Zélande, New Zealand   **néo-zélandais**, New
   Zealand *adj*; **un(e) Néo-Zélandais(e)**, New Zealander

le Pakistan, Pakistan   **pakistanais / un(e)**
   Pakistanais(e), Pakistani

la Palestine, Palestine   **palestinien** *f* **-enne / un(e)**
   Palestinien(ne), Palestinian

le Pays de Galles, Wales   **gallois**, Welsh; **un(e)**
   Gallois(e), Welshman / -woman

le Pérou, Peru   **péruvien** *f* **-enne / un(e)**
   Péruvien(ne), Peruvian

la Pologne, Poland   **polonais**, Polish; **un(e)**
   Polonais(e), Pole

le Portugal, Portugal   **portugais / un(e) Portugais(e)**,
   Portuguese

la Roumanie, Romania   **roumain / un(e)**
   Roumain(e), Romanian

le Royaume-Uni, United Kingdom

la Russie, Russia   **russe / un(e) Russe**, Russian

la Suède, Sweden   **suédois**, Swedish; **un(e)**
   Suédois(e), Swede

la Suisse, Switzerland   **suisse / un(e) Suisse**, Swiss

la Tchécoslovaquie, Czechoslovakia   **tchécoslovaque**,
   Czechoslovak; **un(e) Tchèque**, Czech; **un(e) Slovaque**,
   Slovak

la Turquie, Turkey   **turc** *f* **turque**, Turkish; **un Turc /**
   une Turque, Turk

l'Union *f* des républiques *f* socialistes soviétiques /
  URSS, Union of Soviet Socialist Republics / USSR;
  l'Union soviétique, Soviet Union
le Vietnam, Vietnam   vietnamien *f* -enne / un(e)
  Vietnamien(ne), Vietnamese
la Yougoslavie, Yugoslavia   yougoslave / un(e)
  Yougoslave, Yugoslav

Les Langues Languages

le français, French
  [and similarly all other languages that correspond to
  adjectives in the 'Countries' list above]

l'accent *m*, accent
le dialecte, dialect
le gaélique, Gaelic
la grammaire, grammar
le grec ancien / moderne, classical / modern Greek
la langue (étrangère / vivante / morte), (foreign /
  modern / dead) language (vivant, living; la langue
  maternelle, mother tongue)
le latin, Latin
la linguistique, linguistics (le / la linguiste, linguist)
les pays *m* francophones / anglophones, French-
  speaking / English-speaking countries
la phonétique, phonetics
la prononciation, pronunciation
le vocabulaire, vocabulary

*apprendre (le français), to learn (French)
*comprendre (le français), to understand (French)
s'exprimer (en français), to express oneself (in French)
parler (français), to speak (French) (parler
  couramment, to speak fluently)
prononcer, to pronounce
*traduire, to translate
*vouloir dire / signifier, to mean

SEE ALSO: **Identity; Nature; Towns**

39. Plants Les Plantes

l'arbre *m* **(forestier / fruitier / d'agrément** *m* **/ de Noël**
   m **/** *f***)**, (forest / fruit / ornamental / Christmas) tree
l'arbuste *m*, shrub
la baie, berry
le bois, wood [both senses]
le bouquet, bunch
le bourgeon / le bouton, bud
la branche, branch
le brin, sprig / blade [of grass]
la brindille, twig
les broussailles *f*, brushwood / scrub
le buisson, bush
la cime, tree-top
la clairière, clearing
le conifère, conifer
la couronne, wreath
le déboisement, deforestation (**le reboisement**,
   reafforestation)
l'écorce *f*, bark
l'épine *f*, thorn
le feuillage, foliage
la feuille, leaf
la fleur (sauvage), (wild) flower / blossom (**en fleurs /**
   fleuri, in blossom / in flower)
la floraison, blossoming
la forêt (vierge), (virgin) forest
le fourré, thicket
le fruit, fruit
le gazon, turf
la graine / la semence, seed
la guirlande, garland
la haie, hedge
le noyau *pl* **-x**, (fruit)-stone
la plate-bande *pl* **-s -s / le parterre**, flower-bed
la pelouse, lawn

le pépin, pip
la pépinière, nursery
le pétale, petal
la plantation, plantation
la plante, plant
le pollen, pollen
la pousse / le germe, shoot
la racine, root
le rameau *pl* **-x,** bough
la récolte, harvest
la sève, sap
la souche, tree-stump
le sous-bois, undergrowth
le taillis, copse
la tige, stem
le tronc, trunk
la vendange, grape-harvest
le verger, orchard

*abattre, to fell
arracher, to uproot
arroser, to water
creuser (un trou), to dig (a hole) (**bêcher le jardin,** to
  dig the garden)
*cueillir, to pick
cultiver, to cultivate
défricher, to clear
désherber, to weed
élaguer / émonder, to prune
s'épanouir, to blossom / open
se faner, to fade
se flétrir, to wither
fleurir, to flower / blossom
germer, to shoot
greffer, to graft
labourer, to plough
mûrir, to ripen (**mûr,** ripe)
planter, to plant
pourrir, to rot

pousser / *croître, to grow (***faire pousser des plantes**,
to grow plants)
ratisser, to rake
récolter, to harvest
repiquer, to thin out
semer, to sow
tailler, to trim
transplanter / déplanter, to transplant

Les arbres forestiers et d'agrément, les arbustes
Forest and ornamental trees, shrubs

l'acajou *m*, mahogany tree [also the wood]
l'aubépine *f*, hawthorn (**l'aubépine noire**, blackthorn)
l'au(l)ne *m*, alder
le bambou, bamboo
le bouleau *pl* **-x**, (silver) birch
le buis, box
le camélia, camellia
le cèdre, cedar
le charme, hornbeam
le chêne, oak (**le gland**, acorn)
le chèvrefeuille, honeysuckle
le cyprès, cypress
le cytise, laburnum
l'érable *m*, maple
le frêne, ash
le hêtre (pourpre / rouge), (copper) beech (**rouge**, red;
pourpre, crimson)
l'hortensia *m*, hydrangea
le houx, holly
l'if *m*, yew
le jasmin, jasmine
le laurier, laurel
la lavande, lavender
le lierre, ivy
le lilas, lilac

le **magnolia**, magnolia
le **marronnier (d'Inde)**, (horse-)chestnut (**l'Inde** *f*, India)
le **myrte**, myrtle
l'**orme** *m*, elm
le **peuplier**, poplar
le **pin**, pine (**la pomme de pin**, pine-cone; **une aiguille de pin**, pine needle)
le **platane**, plane tree
le **rhododendron**, rhododendron
le **sapin**, fir
le **saule (pleureur)**, (weeping) willow
le **sureau** *pl* -x, elder
le **tilleul**, lime
le **tremble**, aspen
le **troène**, privet

Les arbres fruitiers Fruit trees

l'**abricotier** *m*, apricot tree
l'**amandier** *m*, almond tree
le **bananier**, banana tree
le **cerisier**, cherry tree
le **châtaignier**, (sweet) chestnut
le **citronnier**, lemon tree
le **cocotier**, coconut palm
le **dattier**, date palm
le **figuier**, fig tree
le **fraisier**, strawberry plant
le **framboisier**, raspberry cane
le **grenadier**, pomegranate (tree)
le **groseillier**, currant bush (**le cassis**, blackcurrant bush)
le **groseillier à maquereau**, gooseberry bush (**le maquereau**, mackerel)
le **noisetier**, hazel tree
le **noyer**, walnut tree
l'**olivier** *m*, olive tree
l'**oranger** *m*, orange tree
le **palmier**, palm tree

le pêcher, peach tree
le poirier, pear tree
le pommier, apple tree
le prunier, plum tree
la ronce, blackberry bush
la vigne, vine

Les fleurs Flowers

l'anémone *f*, anemone
l'aster *m*, aster
le bleuet, cornflower
le bouton d'or / la renoncule, buttercup (**le bouton**, button; **l'or** *m*, gold)
le chrysanthème, chrysanthemum
le coucou, cowslip [also means *cuckoo*]
le crocus, crocus
le dahlia, dahlia
la digitale, foxglove
le géranium, geranium
la giroflée, stock / wallflower
l'iris *m*, iris
la jacinthe, hyacinth (**la jacinthe des bois**, bluebell; **le bois**, wood)
le jasmin, jasmine
la jonquille, daffodil
le lis, lily
la marguerite / la pâquerette, daisy
le muguet, lily of the valley
le myosotis, forget-me-not
le narcisse, narcissus
le nénuphar, water-lily
l'œillet *m*, carnation
l'orchidée *f*, orchid
le pavot, poppy (**le coquelicot**, red / corn poppy)
la pensée, pansy

le [*sometimes* la] **perce-neige** *pl inv*, snowdrop (**percer**, to pierce)
la **pervenche**, periwinkle
le **pétunia**, petunia
le **pissenlit**, dandelion
la **pivoine**, peony
le **pois de senteur**, sweetpea (la **senteur** *literary*, scent)
la **rose**, rose (le **rosier**, rose-bush; l'**églantier** *m*, wild rose; l'**épine** *f*, thorn)
le **tournesol**, sunflower
la **tulipe**, tulip
la **violette**, violet

Les plantes sauvages Wild plants

l'**ajonc** *m*, gorse
l'**algue** *f* / le **goémon**, seaweed
la **bruyère**, heather
le **chardon**, thistle
le **chiendent**, couchgrass
la **fougère**, fern
le **genêt**, broom
le **gui**, mistletoe
l'**herbe** *f*, grass (la **mauvaise herbe**, weed; les **fines herbes**, herbs)
la **mousse**, moss
l'**ortie** *f*, nettle
le **roseau** *pl* -**x**, reed
le **trèfle**, clover

SEE ALSO: **Cooking and Eating (for herbs); Food (for fruits, vegetables, nuts); Nature**

40. Politics La Politique

l'**administration** *f*, administration
l'**aristocratie** *f*, aristocracy
l'**arrêté** *m*, decree
la **barricade**, barricade
le **bien public**, the public good / public welfare
la **bourgeoisie**, middle classes
le **budget**, budget
la **campagne**, campaign
le **centre**, the centre
la **circonscription**, constituency
la **classe ouvrière**, working class
la **conférence**, conference
la **constitution**, constitution
la **coopération**, co-operation
le **coup (d'état** *m***)**, coup
le **couronnement**, coronation (**la couronne**, crown)
la **crise**, crisis
le **débat**, debate
le **devoir**, duty
la **discussion**, discussion / debate
le **drapeau** *pl* **-x**, flag
le **droit**, right
l'**économie** *f*, economy
l'**égalité** *f*, equality
l'**élection** *f*, election (l'**électeur** *m*; *f* **-trice**, elector)
l'**électorat** *m*, electorate
l'**émeute** *f*, riot
la **foule**, crowd / mob
la **fraternité**, fraternity
l'**impôt** *m*, tax (**les impôts**, taxation)
l'**inflation** *f*, inflation
la **liberté**, liberty
la **loi**, law
la **majorité**, majority (**une faible majorité**, a narrow majority)

la manifestation, demonstration
la minorité, minority
la mission, function
la nationalité, nationality
la noblesse, nobility
l'opinion *f* **publique**, public opinion
l'opposition *f*, opposition
le parti, party (**un parti de (la) droite / gauche**, a party of
the right / left)
la patrie / homeland
le pays, country
le peuple, the people
la politique, policy / politics
le pouvoir, power
le progrès [often plural], progress
le projet de loi *f*, bill
le rassemblement, rally
le référendum, referendum
le régime, regime
la responsabilité, responsibility
la révolution, revolution
le scrutin, poll
le siège, seat [in parliament]
la solidarité, solidarity
le sondage, opinion poll
le statut, status
le (premier / second) tour, (first / second) ballot
le tricolore, the (French) Tricolour
l'union *f*, union
l'unité *f*, unity
l'urne *f*, ballot box
le vote, vote

abolir / supprimer, to abolish
adopter, to pass
(dé)centraliser, to (de)centralize
démissionner, to resign
*dissoudre, to dissolve
*élire, to elect
*entrer en vigueur, to come into effect

gouverner, to govern
manifester, to demonstrate
nationaliser, to nationalize
nommer, to appoint
organiser, to organize
*prendre le pouvoir, to take power
privatiser, to privatize
régner, to rule
repousser, to reject
réprimer, to repress
se révolter, to revolt
siéger, to sit [= be in session]
*soutenir, to support
taxer, to tax
voter, to vote / pass [a law]

autonome, self-governing
de gauche *f* / **de droite** *f*, left- / right-wing (**d'extrême-droite** / **d'extrême-gauche**, extreme right- / left-wing)
du centre, centrist
politique, political
unanime, unanimous

Les institutions The institutions

l'Assemblée *f* Nationale, [French] National Assembly
la Chambre des Députés *m*, Chamber of Deputies [French lower house]
la Communauté européenne (CE), European Community (EC)
le Conseil des ministres *m*, Council of Ministers [of the EC]
le conseil municipal *pl* **-s -aux**, town council
l'état *m*, State (**l'état** *m* **providence** *f*, Welfare State)
le gouvernement, government
le Marché commun, Common Market
la monarchie, monarchy
la nation, nation
l'Organisation *f* des Nations Unies (ONU), United Nations Organization (UNO) (**les Nations Unies**, United Nations)

le parlement, parliament
la république, republic
le Sénat, Senate [French upper house]

Les hommes et les femmes
The men and women

l'ambassadeur *m*, ambassador (**l'ambassade** *f* **de France**, French Embassy)
le / la candidat(e), candidate
le chef d'état *m*, head of state
le citoyen *f* **-enne**, citizen
le / la compatriote, fellow-countryman / -woman
le / la démocrate, democrat
le député, Deputy [= MP]
le dictateur, dictator
l'empereur *m* (*f* **l'impératrice**), emperor (**l'empire** *m*, empire)
le / la fonctionnaire, civil servant
l'homme *m* **d'état** *m*, statesman
l'homme politique, politician [**le politicien** *f* **-enne**, *politician*, is usually pejorative, especially when masculine]
le maire *always m*, mayor [**la mairesse**, usually used humorously, means *wife of the mayor*]
le ministre *always m*, minister (**le premier ministre**, prime minister; **le ministre des affaires** *f* **étrangères / des finances** *f*, foreign minister / Chancellor of the Exchequer)
le / la président(e), president
le prince / la princesse prince / princess (**le Prince de Galles**, the Prince of Wales; **Son Altesse** *f* **Royale [SAR]**, His / Her Royal Highness [HRH])
la reine (mère), queen (mother) (**Sa Majesté [SM]**, His / Her Majesty [HM])
le roi, king (**le royaume**, kingdom; **le trône**, throne)
le / la souverain(e), sovereign

Les idéologies Ideologies

l'anarchisme *m*, anarchism
l'antisémitisme *m*, anti-Semitism
le capitalisme, capitalism
le chauvinisme, chauvinism
le communisme, communism
le conservatisme, conservatism
la démocratie (sociale), (social) democracy
la dictature, dictatorship
le fascisme, fascism
l'idéologie *f*, ideology
l'impérialisme *m*, imperialism
l'internationalisme *m*, internationalism
le libéralisme, liberalism
le marxisme, marxism
le monarchisme, monarchism
le nationalisme *m*, nationalism
le patriotisme, patriotism
le racisme, racism
le républicanisme, republicanism
le socialisme, socialism
le syndicalisme *m*, trade-unionism (**le syndicat**, trade union)
la tyrannie, tyranny (**le tyran**, tyrant)

anarchiste, anarchist
chauvin, chauvinist
communiste, communist
conservateur *f* **-trice**, conservative
démocratique, democratic
fasciste, fascist
impérial *pl* **-aux**, imperial
international *pl* **-aux**, international
libéral *pl* **-aux**, liberal
marxiste, marxist
national *pl* **-aux**, national
patriotique, patriotic
radical *pl* **-aux**, radical
républicain, republican

royal *pl* -aux, royal
socialiste, socialist

SEE ALSO: **Arguing For and Against; History; Justice and
Law; The Media; War, Peace, and the Armed Services**

41. Post and Telephone
La Poste et le téléphone

La poste The post

l'accusé *m* **de réception** *f*, acknowledgement of receipt [= recorded delivery]

l'adresse *f*, address

l'aérogramme *m*, air letter

la bande, wrapper

la boîte aux lettres, post-box / letter-box (**la fente**, slot; **boîte postale 66**, PO Box 66)

le bureau *pl* **-x de poste / la poste / les PTT** *f*, post office

le cachet d'oblitération *f*, postmark

la carte (postale / d'anniversaire *m* / **de Noël** *m or f*), (post / birthday / Christmas) card

la carte-lettre *pl* **-s -s**, letter-card

la circulaire, circular

le code postal *pl* **-aux**, post-code

la correspondance, correspondence

le courrier, mail

la déclaration de douane *f*, customs declaration

le / la destinataire, addressee / recipient

la distribution, delivery

l'employé *m*; *f* **-ée**, counter clerk

l'enveloppe *f*, envelope

l'expéditeur *m*; *f* **-trice**, sender [abbreviation **exp** = *from*]

le facteur / la factrice, postman (**lever**, to collect; **distribuer**, to deliver; **la sacoche**, mail-bag)

le faire-part *pl inv*, announcement

le formulaire / la fiche, form (**la formule**, telegram form; **remplir**, to fill in)

le guichet, counter / position

les imprimés *m*, printed matter

la lettre, letter

la levée, collection

le mandat(-poste) *pl* **-s -**, postal order

les messageries *f*, parcel post

le paquet / le colis, parcel (**le papier d'emballage**, brown / wrapping paper; **l'emballage** *m*, wrapping)

le pèse-lettres *pl inv* / **le pèse-paquets** *pl inv*, post-office scales

les P et T (Postes et télécommunications) / les PTT [*f*; technically obsolete form, still in everyday use] (**Postes, télégraphes et téléphones**), post office

le pli, cover / envelope (**sous ce pli / ci-inclus**, enclosed; **sous pli séparé**, under separate cover)

le pneumatique, express letter [delivered in Paris by pneumatic tubes]

le port / l'affranchissement *m*, postage

la poste, post / mail (**la poste aérienne**, airmail; **la poste restante**, poste restante)

le tarif normal / réduit, first-class / second-class postage

le télégramme / la dépêche (réponse payée), (reply-paid) telegram

le télex, telex

le timbre / le timbre-poste *pl* -s - (**à deux francs**), (two-franc) stamp (**la série**, set)

le tri, sorting / sorting office

addresser, to address

affranchir, to stamp [= put a stamp on] (**à combien faut-il affranchir une lettre?**, what does a letter cost?)

cacheter, to seal

coller, to stick

*envoyer, to send

expédier, to send off

*faire suivre, to forward / send on

peser, to weigh

poster, to post (***mettre une lettre à la poste**, to post a letter)

aux bons soins de . . ., care of . . .

ci-joint, attached

exprès *inv*, express (**en exprès**, express delivery)

(non-)timbré, (un)stamped

oblitéré, postmarked

par avion, by airmail (**un avion**, aeroplane)
par retour *m* du courrier *m*, by return of post
par voie de terre, by surface mail (**la voie**, way; **la terre**, land)
postal *pl* **-aux**, postal
prière de faire suivre, please forward (***suivre**, to follow)
recommandé, registered (**en recommandé**, by registered letter)
urgent, urgent
voir au verso, see overleaf

Le téléphone   The telephone

l'abonné *m*; *f* -ée, subscriber
l'annuaire *m*, phone book (**le minitel**, electronic directory)
l'appel *m* / le coup de téléphone *m* / le coup de fil *m*, (phone) call (**le fil**, wire)
l'appel avec préavis, personal call (**le préavis**, advance notice)
la cabine téléphonique, phone box
le cadran, dial
le central (téléphonique), (telephone) exchange (**l'international *m***, international exchange / operator)
le combiné / le récepteur, receiver (**le crochet**, hook / cradle)
la communication locale / interurbaine / à l'étranger, local / long-distance / international call (**à l'étranger *m***, abroad)
la communication SCC (sur compte courant), credit-card call (**le compte courant**, current account)
l'écouteur *m*, supplementary earpiece [on French phone]
l'indicatif *m*, dialling code
la ligne (encombrée), (crossed / busy) line
le numéro (de téléphone *m* / d'urgence *f*), (telephone / emergency) number (**le faux numéro**, wrong number)
le poste, extension
le renseignements *m*, directory enquiries
le signal d'appel / la tonalité d'appel / la sonnerie, ringing tone (**un appel**, call)

le / la standardiste, switchboard operator
le taxiphone, payphone
la télécarte, phonecard
le téléphone (à touches *f* **/ à cadran** *m* **/ sans fil** *m***)**,
 (push-button / dial / cordless) telephone
le / la téléphoniste, operator
la tonalité, dialling tone
la touche *f*, push-button / key

appeler, to call
composer un numéro, to dial a number
décrocher, to lift the receiver
donner un coup de fil à qn., to ring sb.
*être au bout du fil, to be on the line / phone (**au bout,** at
 the end)
*faire une communication en PCV, to reverse the
 charges [**PCV = à PerCeVoir à l'arrivée**, to be charged
 on arrival]
*introduire, to insert
*prendre un message, to take a message
raccrocher, to hang up
rappeler, to ring back
répondre, to answer
sonner, to ring [of phone]
téléphoner à qn. / donner un coup de téléphone *m* **à
 qn.**, to phone / ring sb.
se tromper de numéro *m*, to misdial

Ce qu'on dit What you say

allô, hello
de la part de qui?, who's calling?
excusez-moi, je me suis trompé(e) de numéro, sorry,
 wrong number
ici X, this is X
il n'y a personne, no answer
je vais vous brancher sur un autre numéro, I'm going
 to put you through to another number
je vous passe X, I'm connecting you with X

je vous redonne la communication, I'm reconnecting you

le numéro est occupé / est en dérangement *m* **/ ne répond pas,** the number is engaged / is out of order / doesn't answer

lui-même! / elle-même! / j'écoute!, speaking!

mon numéro est le . . ., my number is . . .

ne quittez pas! / ne raccrochez pas!, hang on! / one moment, please!

on m'a débranché / coupé, I've been disconnected / cut off

pas libre, line engaged

qui est à l'appareil *m*?, who's speaking?

un instant, s'il vous plaît, just a minute, please

votre correspondant *m* **ne répond pas,** no reply

vous êtes en communication *f*, you're through

Pour épeler au téléphone Spelling code

épeler, to spell

A comme (as in) **Anatole**	N comme **Nicolas**
B comme **Berthe**	O comme **Oscar**
C comme **César**	P comme **Pierre**
D comme **Désiré**	Q comme **Québec**
E comme **Eugène**	R comme **Robert**
É comme **Émile**	S comme **Suzanne**
F comme **François**	T comme **Thérèse**
G comme **Gaston**	U comme **Ursule**
H comme **Henri**	V comme **Victor**
I comme **Irma**	W comme **William**
J comme **Joseph**	X comme **Xavier**
K comme **Kléber**	Y comme **Yvonne**
L comme **Louis**	Z comme **Zoé**
M comme **Marcel**	

SEE ALSO: **Greetings and Replies; Reading and Writing**

42. Reading and Writing
Lire et écrire

Ceux qui le font Those who do it

l'auteur *m*, author
le / la biographe, biographer
le bouquiniste, second-hand bookseller (**le bouquineur**, lover of old books / avid reader)
le / la correspondant(e), pen-friend
l'éditeur *m; f* **-trice**, publisher
le / la journaliste, journalist
le lecteur *f* **-trice**, reader
le / la libraire, bookseller (**la librairie**, bookshop)
le poète, poet
le romancier *f* **-ière**, novelist

Ce qu'ils font What they do

bouquiner, to browse / collect old books / read for pleasure
citer, to quote
correspondre, to correspond
créer, to create
*distraire / divertir, to entertain
*écrire, to write
emprunter (à), to borrow (from)
*faire des vers *m*, to write poetry
griffonner, to scribble
imprimer, to print
inventer, to invent
*lire, to read
noter, to jot down
publier, to publish / bring out
rimer, to rhyme
signer, to sign
souligner, to underline
taper (à la machine), to type

Ce dont ils se servent What they use

l'agrafeuse *f*, stapler (**les agrafes** *f*, staples)
la bibliothèque, library
le bic®, ballpoint
le bloc, writing-pad
le bloc-notes *pl* **-s -**, notebook
le bouquin, (old) book
le brouillon, rough draft
le cahier, exercise book
le carnet, notebook
la carte, card / map
la cartouche d'encre *f* / **la recharge**, (pen) cartridge
le chapitre, chapter
la citation, quotation
le crayon (de couleur *f*), (coloured) pencil
la description, description
l'écriture *f* (**lisible** / **illisible**), (legible / illegible)
 handwriting
l'encre *f*, ink
l'enveloppe *f*, envelope
l'extrait *m*, extract
le feutre, felt-tip pen
la gomme, rubber / eraser
l'illustration *f*, illustration
l'intrigue *f*, plot
la librairie, bookshop
la ligne, line
la locution, phrase / expression
la machine à écrire, typewriter (**le ruban**, ribbon)
la machine à traitement *m* **de texte(s)** *m*, word processor
la majuscule, capital letter
la marge, margin
la minuscule, small letter
le mot, word
la note, note
la papeterie, stationer's
le papier machine *f* / **à écrire** / **à lettre** *f*, typing / writing /
 note paper
le paragraphe, paragraph

la photocopie, photocopy
la photocopieuse, photocopier
la phrase, sentence
les pièces jointes *f*; *abb.* **pj**, enclosures
la poésie, poetry
le porte-mine *pl* **- -s**, propelling pencil
la prose, prose
la rime, rhyme
le rythme, rhythm
le scotch $^{®}$, sellotape$^{®}$
la signature, signature
la strophe, verse [of poem]
le style, style
le stylo (à bille), (ball-point) pen (**la bille**, ball-bearing)
le taille-crayon *pl* **- -s**, pencil-sharpener
la télécopie, fax
la télécopieuse, fax machine
le titre, title
le trombone, paper-clip
le vers, line [of poem]

Leurs créations   Their products

l'autobiographie *f*, autobiography
la ballade, ballad
la bande dessinée, strip cartoon (**dessiner**, to draw)
la biographie, biography
la carte postale, postcard
le catalogue, catalogue
le chef-d'œuvre *pl* **-s -**, masterpiece
le conte / la nouvelle, short story
le conte de fée *f*, fairy-tale
le dictionnaire, dictionary
l'édition *f*, edition
la fable, fable
le guide, guidebook
la lecture, reading
la légende, legend / caption

la lettre (de la part de . . .), letter (from . . .)
la littérature (classique / romantique), (classical / romantic) literature
le livre (d'occasion / relié / de poche / pour enfants *m* / *f*)**, (second-hand / hardback / paperback / children's) book (**l'occasion** *f*, bargain; **la poche**, pocket)
le manuel, handbook
l'ode *f*, ode
l'ouvrage *m* **de référence** *f*, reference book
le poème, poem
le polar, detective story / whodunit
le récit, narrative
le recueil (de poèmes *m* / **de contes** *m*)**, (poetry / short-story) collection
la revue / le magazine, magazine
le roman (policier), (crime) novel
le sonnet, sonnet
le texte, text
le volume, volume

Les formules de politesse   Conventional beginnings and endings to letters

Cher (*f* **Chère) X**, Dear X
Cher (*f* **Chère) X, cher Y / Chers amis (***f* **Chères amies) / Chers tous deux (***f* **Chères toutes deux)**, Dear X and Y
(Mon) chéri *f* **(Ma) chérie**, Darling
Madame / Monsieur / Messieurs, Dear Madam / Dear Sir / Dear Sirs
Salut!, Dear X [to close friends]
TSVP (tournez s'il vous plaît), PTO (please turn over)
A bientôt, Cheers
affectueusement / Je t'embrasse / Bons baisers / Grosses bises, Love (**le baiser / la bise**, kiss; **embrasser**, to kiss)
Amitiés / Bien amicalement à vous, Kind regards / Best wishes

Croyez à mes sentiments respectueux[†], Yours sincerely
Veuillez agréer, cher Monsieur / chère Madame,
l'expression f **de mes sentiments les plus distingués**[†],
Yours faithfully (**agréer**, to approve of)

SEE.ALSO: **Arguing For and Against; Education; The
Media; Post and Telephone**

[†] The formal letter-endings are not fixed, as in English, and
considerable variations on the forms given are found, in equally
flowery style.

43. Relationships
Les Liens de parenté

l'adulte *m / f*, adult (**les grandes personnes** *f*, the grown-ups)

l'amant *m*; *f* **-te**, lover

l'ami *m*; *f* **-ie**, friend

l'ancêtre *always m* **/ l'aïeul** *m*; *pl* **-eux**; *f* **-eule**, ancestor

le bébé *always m*, baby

le / la camarade, pal / schoolfriend

le / la célibataire, bachelor / spinster

le / la collègue, colleague / fellow-worker

une connaissance, an acquaintance

le copain / la copine *colloq*, friend / mate

le couple, couple

le / la descendant(e), descendant

l'enfant *m / f*, child (**un(e) enfant unique**, an only child)

la famille, family (**le membre**, member; **le chef de famille**, head of the family; **la famille Bloggs**, the Bloggs family)

l'orphelin *m*; *f* **-ine**, orphan

le / la petit(e) ami(e), boyfriend / girlfriend

le veuf / la veuve, widower / widow

adoptif *f* **-ive**, adopted

adulte, adult

aîné, elder

cadet *f* **-ette**, younger

fraternel *f* **-elle**, fraternal

jumeau *pl* **-x**; *f* **-elle**, twin

maternel *f* **-elle**, maternal (**du côté maternel**, on the mother's side)

mineur, under age / a minor (**majeur**, of age)

paternel *f* **-elle**, paternal

unique, only

La famille The family

le / la cousin(e) (germain(e) / au second degré), (first / second) cousin

la femme / l'épouse *f*, wife

le / la fiancé(e), fiancé(e)

la fille, daughter

le / la filleul(e), godson / goddaughter

le fils, son

le frère, brother (**le demi-frère** *pl* - -s, half-brother)

le gendre, son-in-law [**la bru**, *daughter-in-law*, is old-fashioned or regional: **la belle-fille**, see below, is used]

la grand-mère *pl* - -s, grandmother (**grand-maman** *f*; *pl* - -s, grandma)

le grand-père *pl* -s -s, grandfather (**grand-papa** *m*; *pl* -s -s, grandad)

les grands-parents *m*; *no sing*, grandparents

le jumeau *pl* -x *f* -elle, twin

le mari / l'époux *m*, husband

la marraine, godmother

la mère, mother (**maman** *f*, mum)

le neveu *pl* -x, nephew (**le petit-neveu** *pl* -s -x, great-nephew)

la nièce, niece (**la petite-nièce** *pl* - -s, great-niece)

l'oncle *m*, uncle (**le grand-oncle** *pl* - -s, great-uncle)

le / la parent(e), relative (**un parent proche / éloigné**, a near / distant relative; **les parents** parents)

le parrain, godfather

le père, father (**papa** *m*, dad)

la petite-fille *pl* -s -s, grand-daughter

le petit-fils *pl* -s -s, grandson

les petits-enfants *m*; *no sing*, grandchildren

la sœur, sister (**la demi-sœur** *pl* - -s, half-sister)

la tante, aunt (**la grand-tante** *pl* - -s, great-aunt)

le / la triplé(e), triplet

le / la trisaïeul(e), great-great-grandfather / grandmother

Arrière- *pl inv* can be added to the **grand-** / **petit-** relationships above, to mean *great-*; **beau-** *pl* **-x** can be added to male relationships and **belle-** *pl* **-s** to female relationships above, to mean *step-* or *-in-law* Examples follow:

l'arrière-grand-mère *pl* **- - -s**, great-grandmother
l'arrière-grand-père *pl* **- -s -s**, great-grandfather
le beau-fils *pl* **-x -**, son-in-law / stepson
le beau-père *pl* **-x -s**, father-in-law / stepfather
la belle-fille *pl* **-s -s**, daughter-in-law / stepdaughter
la belle-mère *pl* **-s -s**, mother-in-law / stepmother

SEE ALSO: **Birth, Marriage, and Death**

44. **Religion** La Religion

Jésus-Christ, Jesus Christ (**le Christ,** Christ)
Mahomet, Mahomet
Moïse, Moses
le Tout-Puissant, the Almighty

l'ange *m*, angel
l'apôtre *m*, apostle
le blasphème, blasphemy
le ciel *pl* **cieux,** heaven
la conversion, conversion
la création, creation (**le créateur,** creator)
la croyance, belief
le démon, demon
le diable, devil
le dieu *pl* **-x,** god (**la déesse,** goddess)
le disciple, disciple
la doctrine, doctrine
l'enfer *m*, hell
la foi, faith
l'hérétique *m* / *f*, heretic (**l'hérésie** *f*, heresy)
l'hymne *m*, hymn (**l'hymne national** *pl* **-s -aux,** national
  anthem)
l'idole *f*, idol (**l'idolatrie** *f*, idolatry)
la magie, magic (**le magicien** *f* **-enne,** magician)
le / la martyr(e), martyr (**le martyre,** martyrdom)
la messe, mass
le miracle, miracle (***faire un miracle,** to work a miracle)
le païen *f* **-enne,** pagan
le paradis (terrestre), (earthly) paradise
le péché, sin (**le pécheur** *f* **pécheresse,** sinner)
le pèlerin, pilgrim (**le pèlerinage,** pilgrimage)
le prophète *f* **prophétesse,** prophet (**la prophétie,**
  prophecy)
la providence, providence
le purgatoire, purgatory
le revenant / le fantôme, ghost

le / la **saint(e)**, saint
le **salut**, salvation
le **secte**, sect
le **sermon**, sermon
la **sorcellerie**, witchcraft (**la sorcière**, witch; **le sorcier**, wizard)
le **sort**, fate
la **superstition**, superstition
la **tentation**, temptation

***absoudre (de)**, to absolve (from)
bénir, to bless
chanter, to sing
***commettre**, to commit
confesser, to confess (**se confesser**, to confess one's sins)
convertir, to convert
***croire (à / en)**, to believe (in)
crucifier, to crucify
damner, to damn
expier, to atone for
pécher, to sin
prêcher, to preach
prier, to pray
se repentir, to repent

Ce qu'on est What you are

agnostique, agnostic (**l'agnosticisme** *m*, agnosticism)
anglican, Anglican / Church of England (**l'anglicanisme** *m*, Anglicanism)
athée, atheist (**l'athéisme** *m*, atheism)
baptiste, Baptist
béni, blessèd
bouddhiste, Buddhist (**le bouddhisme**, Buddhism)
catholique, Catholic (**le catholicisme**, Catholicism)
chrétien *f* **-enne**, Christian (**le christianisme**, Christianity; **la Bible**, the Bible; **le Nouveau / l'Ancien Testament**, the New / Old Testament; **la Croix**, the Cross; **le Crucifiement / la Crucifixion**, Crucifixion)

converti, converted (**le / la converti(e)**, convert)
croyant, believing (**le / la croyant(e)**, believer)
juif *f* **juive**, Jewish (**le judaïsme**, Judaism)
méthodiste, Methodist (**le méthodisme**, Methodism)
musulman, Muslim (**l'islamisme**, Islam; **le Coran**, the Koran)
pieux *f* **-euse**, pious
protestant, Protestant (**le protestantisme**, Protestantism)
puritain, puritan (**le puritanisme**, puritanism)
quaker *f* **-eresse**, Quaker (**le quakerisme**, Quakerism)
saint, holy (**la sainteté**, holiness)
sceptique, sceptical (**un(e) sceptique**, a sceptic; **le scepticisme**, scepticism)
superstitieux *f* **-euse**, superstitious (**la superstition**, superstition)
unitarien *f* **-enne**, Unitarian (**l'unitarisme** *m*, Unitarianism)

Les lieux de culte et le clergé
Religious buildings and clergy

l'abbaye *f*, abbey
l'abbé *m*, abbot
l'archevêque *m*, archbishop
le cardinal *pl* **-aux**, cardinal
la cathédrale, cathedral
le curé, (parish) priest (**le vicaire**, curate)
l'église *f*, (catholic) church
l'évêque *m*, bishop
le moine, monk / friar
la mosquée, mosque
le muezzin, muezzin
le Pape, Pope
le pasteur, minister
le prêtre, priest
le rabbin, rabbi (**le Grand Rabbin**, Chief Rabbi)
la religieuse, nun
la synagogue, synagogue

le temple, (protestant) church

SEE ALSO: **Art and Architecture; Birth, Marriage, and Death; History**

45. Science Les Sciences

l'acide *m* **(nitrique / sulfurique)**, (nitric / sulphuric) acid
l'acoustique *f*, acoustics
l'algèbre *f*, algebra
l'ammoniaque *f*, ammonia
l'arithmétique *f*, arithmetic
l'atome *m*, atom
l'azote *m*, nitrogen
le calcul **(différentiel)**, (differential) calculus
le carbone, carbon
la chaleur, heat
le chlore, chlorine
l'électricité *f*, electricity **(le courant**, current)
l'élément *m*, element
l'équation *f*, equation
l'expérience *f*, experiment
la force, force
la formule, formula
le frottement, friction
la géométrie, geometry
la gravité, gravity **(le centre de gravité**, centre of gravity)
l'hydrogène *m*, hydrogen
l'invention *f*, invention **(l'inventeur** *m*; *f* **-trice**, inventor;
  le brevet, patent)
l'iode *m*, iodine
le laboratoire, laboratory
la lumière, light
le magnétisme, magnetism **(l'aimant** *m*, magnet)
le microscope **(électronique)**, (electron) microscope
la molécule, molecule
l'onde *f* **(lumineuse / sonore)**, (light- / sound-)wave
l'optique *f*, optics
l'oxygène *m*, oxygen
le point de congélation *f* / d'ébullition *f*, freezing- /
  boiling-point

la pression, pressure
le produit chimique, chemical
le rayon, ray (**les rayons X**, X-rays)
le rayonnement, radiation
la réaction, reaction
les recherches *f* **scientifiques**, scientific research
la science (pure / appliquée / physique / sociale), (pure /
  applied / physical / social) science
le / la scientifique, scientist
le son, sound
le soufre, sulphur
le télescope, telescope (**la lentille**, lens)
la trigonométrie, trigonometry

Les noms des sciences Names of sciences

l'anthropologie *f*, anthropology
l'archéologie *f*, archaeology
l'astronomie *f*, astronomy
la biologie (moléculaire), (molecular) biology
la botanique, botany
la chimie (organique / minérale), (organic / inorganic)
  chemistry
l'électronique *f*, electronics
la géologie, geology
l'informatique *f*, computer science (**l'ordinateur** *m*,
  computer)
les mathématiques, mathematics
la mécanique, mechanics
la métallurgie, metallurgy
la minéralogie, mineralogy
la physique (nucléaire / quantique), (nuclear /
  quantum) physics
la psychologie, psychology
la sociologie, sociology
la technique / la technologie, technology
la zoologie, zoology

Les savants Scientists

l'anthropologiste *m / f* **/ anthropologue** *m / f*,
  anthropologist
l'archéologue *m / f*, archaeologist
l'astronome *m*, astronomer
le / la biologiste, biologist
le / la botaniste, botanist
le / la chimiste, chemist
le / la géologue, geologist
l'informaticien *m*; *f* **-enne**, computer scientist
le mathématicien *f* **-enne**, mathematician
le / la métallurgiste, metallurgist
le / la minéralogiste, mineralogist
le physicien *f* **-enne**, physicist
le / la psychologue, psychologist
le / la sociologue, sociologist
le / la technologiste / technologue, technologist (**le
  technicien** *f* **-enne**, technician)
le / la zoologiste, zoologist

SEE ALSO: **Animals; Art and Architecture; Education;
  Health and Sickness; The Human Body; Materials;
  Nature; Numbers and Quantities; Plants; The
  Senses**

46. The Senses Les Sens

La vue Sight

l'aspect *m* / **l'air** *m*, look [= appearance]
la clarté, brightness
la couleur, colour
les jumelles *f; occasionally sing.* binoculars
la longue-vue *pl* -s -s, (field) telescope
la loupe, magnifying glass
la lueur, gleam / flash
la lumière, light
les lunettes *f* (**de soleil** *m* / **solaires**), spectacles
  (sunglasses)
le monocle, monocle
l'obscurité *f*, darkness
l'œil *m*; *pl* **yeux**, eye (**le coup d'œil (rapide)**, glance /
  glimpse; **le clin d'œil**, wink)
le regard, look [= glance] (**un regard de côté**, a sidelong
  look; **le côté**, side)
la visibilité, visibility
la vision, vision
la vue, sight / view (**s'abîmer la vue**, to spoil one's
  eyesight; **à première vue**, at first sight; **à perte de vue**,
  as far as the eye can see; ***connaître qn. de vue**, know
  sb. by sight)

*apercevoir, to catch sight of / set eyes on (**s'*apercevoir
  de**, to notice)
*avoir l'air *m* **de**, to look like
chercher, to look for (**chercher qch. dans**, to look sth.
  up in)
cligner (des yeux), to wink
clignoter, to blink
contempler, to contemplate
discerner, to discern
distinguer, to make out
éclairer, to light up
*entrevoir, to catch a glimpse of
*étinceler, to sparkle

examiner, to examine
jeter un coup d'œil sur, to glance at
jeter une lueur / des lueurs, to flash
lever / baisser les yeux, to look up / down [to raise / lower the eyes]
loucher, to squint
observer, to watch / observe
*percevoir, to perceive
perdre de vue f, to lose sight of
regarder, to look at (**regarder fixement**, to stare at; **regarder du coin de l'œil**, to give a sidelong glance at; **regarder en arrière**, to look back)
remarquer, to notice
*voir, to see (***revoir**, to see again; **rien à *voir**, nothing to be seen)

aveugle (d'un œil), blind (in one eye) (**le braille**, Braille)
aveuglé (par), blinded (by)
borgne, one-eyed
brillant, bright
clair, light
ébloui, dazzled
incolore, colourless
myope, short-sighted
obscur / sombre, dark
presbyte / hypermétrope, long-sighted
(in)visible, (in)visible

SEE ALSO: **Health and Sickness (At the optician's)**

L'ouïe Hearing

le bourdonnement, buzzing
le bruissement, rustling [leaves] / humming [machinery]
le bruit, noise
le chant, singing (**la chanson**, song)
le chuchotement, whisper
le crépitement, crackling
le cri, cry

l'**écho** *m*, echo
le **fracas**, crash
le **grincement**, creaking
l'**oreille** *f*, ear
l'**ouï-dire** *m inv*, hearsay (**par ouï-dire**, from hearsay)
l'**ouïe** *f*, hearing
le **son**, sound
la **sonnerie**, ringing
la **surdité**, deafness (**la prothèse auditive**, hearing-aid)
le **vacarme**, din
la **voix**, voice (**à / hors de portée** *f* **de voix**, within / out of
  earshot)

bourdonner, to buzz
***bruire**, to rustle
chanter, to sing
chuchoter, to whisper
écouter, to listen to (**n'écouter que d'une oreille**, to
  listen with half an ear)
entendre, to hear (**entendre dire que . . .**, to hear that . . .;
  entendre parler de, to hear about)
fredonner, to hum
grincer, to creak
insonoriser, to soundproof
retenir, to resound
siffler, to whistle
sonner, to sound / ring
se *taire, to be quiet
tendre l'oreille *f*, to prick up one's ears
tonner, to thunder
vrombir, to buzz / throb

aigu *f* **-guë**, sharp
assourdissant, deafening (**sourd**, deaf)
bruyant, noisy
dur d'oreille *f*, hard of hearing
faible, faint
fort, loud
insonore, soundproof

perçant, piercing
perceptible, audible
silencieux *f* **-euse**, silent
sourd, deaf / dull [sound] (**sourd-muet** *f* **sourde-muette**
pl **-s -s**, deaf and dumb)
strident, shrill

Le toucher Touch

la caresse, caress
le chaud, heat
le coup, blow (**un coup de pied / de poing**, kick / punch (**le
pied**, foot; **le poing**, fist))
le froid, cold
la sensation (de), sensation / feeling (of)
le toucher, touch

caresser, to stroke
chatouiller, to tickle
chercher qch. à tâtons, to feel for sth.
cogner, to knock
éprouver, to experience
frapper, to hit
frotter, to rub
gratter, to scratch
promener ses doigts sur, to finger (**le doigt**, finger)
*sentir qch., to feel sth. [a sensation] [also means *smell*]
(***ressentir qch.**, to feel sth. [mentally]; **tâter qch.**, to feel
sth. [by touching])
toucher, to touch

chaud, hot
doux *f* **douce / mou** *m sing before vowel* **mol**; *f* **molle**, soft
dur, hard
froid, cold
lisse, smooth
rugueux *f* **-euse / rude**, rough

L'odorat Smell

l'arôme *m*, aroma
l'odeur *f*, scent (**une odeur**, a smell)
l'odorat *m*, smell [the sense]
le parfum, perfume [also *flavour*]
la puanteur, stench / reek

empester, to reek (of)
exhaler, to give off [a smell]
flairer, to smell out
parfumer, to perfume
puer, to stink (of)
renifler, to sniff
*sentir (bon / mauvais), to smell (nice / bad) (also means *feel*) (**ça sent le gaz ici**, it smells of gas here; **ça ne sent rien**, it has no smell)

âcre, pungent
embaumé, fragrant
enfumé, smoky
infect, (smelling or tasting) bad / off
inodore, scentless
parfumé, perfumed
puant, stinking

Le goût Taste

le goût, taste [the sense] (**un goût**, a taste; **le bon goût**, good taste)
la saveur, savour / flavour (**un parfum**, a flavour [also *perfume*])
*avoir un goût de, to taste of
*boire, to drink
déguster, to sample / savour
goûter, to taste
lécher, to lick
manger, to eat
savourer, to savour

acide, acid
aigre, sharp / tart / sour
aigrelet *f* -**ette**, sourish
alléchant, mouth-watering
amer *f* **amère**, bitter
doux *f* **douce** / **sucré**, sweet
épicé, spicy
fade, tasteless
fort, strong
insipide, tasteless
piquant, piquant
rance / ranci, rancid
salé, salt(y) / savoury
savoureux *f* -**euse**, tasty
sur, sour

SEE ALSO: **Adornment (for perfume); Cooking and Eating; Drinks; Health and Sickness; The Human Body; Music; Tobacco and Drugs**

47. Shops and Shopping
Les Magasins et les courses

l'achat *m*, purchase

l'article *m*, article

le bon, (money-off) coupon (**le bon d'achat** *m*, gift voucher)

la boutique, (small) shop

la braderie, (rummage) sale

le cabas, shopping-bag / -basket

le caddy / caddie, (supermarket) trolley

la caisse, till / cash-desk / check-out

le centre commercial *pl* **-s -aux**, shopping-centre

le / la client(e), customer

la commande, order

le / la commerçant(e), trader

le commerce, trade

le comptoir, counter

la consommateur *f* **-trice**, consumer

la date limite *f* **de vente** *f*, sell-by date (**consommer de préférence** *f* **avant . . .**, best before . . .; **consommer**, to consume)

le directeur / le gérant, manager

l'échantillon *m*, sample

l'emballage-cadeau *m*; *pl* **-s -x**, gift-wrapping

la garantie, guarantee

l'hypermarché *m*, hypermarket

la livraison, delivery (***faire / *prendre livraison de**, deliver / take delivery of)

la location, rental

le magasin, shop

le / la marchande, shopkeeper

les marchandises *f*; *sometimes sing*, goods

le marché (couvert / en plein air / aux fleurs *f* **/ aux puces** *f***)**, (covered / open-air / flower / flea) market (**le jour de marché**, market-day)

le panier, basket

le prix (réduit / spécial / de gros / de détail), (reduced / special / wholesale / retail) price

la queue, queue (***faire la queue,** to queue up)

le rabais, reduction / rebate

le rayon de . . ., the . . . department

la réduction, reduction

les soldes, sales (**le solde,** surplus stock / remnant)

la succursale, branch

le supermarché, supermarket

la taille / la pointure, size

la vente, sale(s) (**le service après-vente,** after-sales service; **en vente,** on sale)

la vente aux enchères, auction (**l'enchère** f, bid(ding); **le commissaire-priseur** pl **-s -s,** auctioneer)

la vitrine / la devanture, shop window

acheter, to buy

*aller à [+ shop: **à la boulangerie**] / **chez** [+ shopkeeper: **chez le boulanger**], to go to [the baker's]

choisir, to choose

commander, to order

coûter, to cost (**ils coûtent 12 francs (la) pièce,** they cost 12 francs apiece)

dépenser, to spend

échanger (contre), to exchange (for)

*faire des courses f / **des achats** m / **ses commissions** f / **son marché** / **du shopping,** to go shopping

*faire du lèche-vitrine, to go window-shopping (**lécher,** to lick)

se *faire rembourser qch., to get a refund for sth.

*faire réparer, to have repaired

garantir, to guarantee

livrer, to deliver

marchander, to haggle

payer, to pay (for) (**payer en espèces** f / **par chèque** m / **par carte** f **de crédit** m, to pay cash / by cheque / by credit card)

solder, to sell at cut price

vendre, to sell (**à vendre,** for sale)

cher *f* **chère**, dear
en promotion *f*, on special offer
en solde *m*, cut-price / reduced
épuisé, out of stock
fermé, closed
gratuit, free
ouvert, open
peu cher *f* **chère / bon marché** [*inv*, = a good buy], cheap
  (**moins cher / meilleur marché**, cheaper)

Les magasins et ceux qui vous servent
The shops and those who serve you

l'agence *f* **de voyages** *m*, travel agency   **l'agent** *m* **de voyages**, travel agent
l'agence *f* **immobilière**, estate agency   **l'agent** *m* **immobilier**, estate agent
l'alimentation *f* **générale / l'épicerie** *f*, grocer's   **l'épicier** *f* **-ière**, grocer
la banque, bank (**la caisse d'épargne**, savings bank)
la bibliothèque, library   **le / la bibliothécaire**, librarian
le bijoutier, jeweller's   **le bijoutier** *f* **-ière**, jeweller
la blanchisserie, laundry   **le blanchisseur** *f* **-euse**, laundryman / laundress
la boucherie, butcher's   **le boucher** *f* **-chère**, butcher
la boulangerie, baker's   **le boulanger** *f* **-gère**, baker
le bureau *pl* **-x de poste / la poste / les P et T** *f*, post office   **l'employé** *f* **-ée**, clerk
le bureau *pl* **-x / le débit de tabac**, tobacconist's   **le / la marchand(e) de tabac**, tobacconist
la charcuterie, delicatessen   **le charcutier** *f* **-ière**, delicatessen keeper
la confiserie, sweet shop / confectioner's   **le confiseur** *f* **-euse / le chocolatier** *f* **-ière**, confectioner
la cordonnerie, shoe-repairer's   **le cordonnier** *f* **-ière**, cobbler / shoe-repairer
la crémerie / la laiterie, dairy   **le crémier** *f* **-ière / le laitier** *f* **-ière**, dairyman / -woman

la fruiterie, fruiterer's / greengrocer's **le fruitier** *f* -ière, fruiterer; **le / la marchand(e) de légumes** *m* **/ de primeurs** *f*, greengrocer

le grand magasin, department store **le vendeur** *f* -euse, salesman / -woman

l'horlogerie *f*, watchmaker's **l'horloger** *f* -gère, watchmaker / -repairer

l'institut *m* **de beauté** *f*, beauty salon **l'esthéticien** *f* -nne, beautician

le kiosque à journaux, news-stand (**le journal** *pl* -aux, newspaper)

la laverie automatique, launderette

la librairie (d'occasion *f*), (second-hand) bookshop **le / la libraire**, bookseller

le libre-service *pl* -s -s, self-service shop

le magasin d'antiquités *f*, antique shop **l'antiquaire** *m*, antique dealer

le magasin de chaussures *f*, shoe shop

le magasin de diététique *f*, health-food shop

le magasin de disques *m*, record shop **le disquaire**, record dealer

le magasin d'électroménager *m*, electrical shop

le magasin de fleurs *f*, flower shop **le / la fleuriste**, florist

le magasin de jouets *m*, toy-shop

le magasin de meubles *m*, furniture shop

le magasin de modes *f*, milliner's / hat-shop **le / la modiste**, milliner

le magasin de musique *f*, music shop

le magasin d'appareils-photo *m*, camera shop **le / la photographe**, photographer

le magasin de porcelaine *f*, china shop

le magasin de prêt-à-porter, clothes shop (**le prêt-à-porter** *no pl*, ready-made clothes)

le magasin de sport *m*, sports shop

le magasin de vins *m* (**et spiritueux** *m*), off-licence / wine store **le / la marchand(e) de vins**, wine merchant

le magasin du tailleur, tailor's **le tailleur** *f* -euse, tailor

la maison de confection *m*, clothes shop

la maison de la presse, newsagent's   **le / la marchand(e) de journaux** *m*; *sing* **-al**, newsagent

la maroquinerie, leather shop   **le maroquinier** *f* **-ière**, dealer in leather goods

la mercerie, draper's / haberdasher's   **le mercier** *f* **-ière**, draper / haberdasher

la papeterie, stationer's   **le papetier** *f* **-ière**, stationer

la parfumerie, perfume shop   **le parfumeur** *f* **-euse**, perfumer

la pâtisserie, cakeshop   **le pâtissier** *f* **-ière**, pastrycook

la pharmacie, chemist's   **le pharmacien** *f* **-ienne**, chemist / pharmacist

la poissonnerie, fish shop   **le poissonnier** *f* **-ière**, fishmonger

le pressing / la teinturerie, dry-cleaner's (**le nettoyage à sec**, dry-cleaning; **sec**, dry)

la quincaillerie / la droguerie, hardware shop / ironmongery   **le quincailler / le droguiste**, ironmonger

le salon de coiffure, hairdresser's   **le coiffeur** *f* **-euse**, stylist

le tabac-journaux *pl* **-s -**, newsagent and tobacconist's

Ce que dit le marchand
What the shopkeeper says

avez-vous de la monnaie?, do you have change?

ça fait . . ., that comes to

c'est pour emporter?, will you take it with you?

c'est pour offrir?, would you like it gift-wrapped?

et avec ça?, anything else?

monsieur / madame désire? / vous désirez?, can I help you?

Ce qui vous dites   What you say

ça fait combien?, what does that come to?

ça ne me plaît pas / ça me plaît beaucoup, I don't like it / I like it a lot

ceci coûte combien?, what does this cost?

ce n'est pas ce qu'il me faut, it's not what I'm looking for

c'est dans la vitrine, it's in the window

c'est tout, that's all

combien vous dois-je?, what do I owe you?

en avez-vous d'autres?, have you any more of these?

je ne fais que regarder, I'm only looking

je veux quelque chose de plus . . ., I want something more . . .

je veux rendre ceci: voici le reçu, I want to return this: here's the receipt

je voudrais / je désire . . ., I should like . . .

pourriez-vous m'aider?, can you help me?

pourriez-vous me montrer quelque chose de moins cher / de plus grand . . .?, could you show me something cheaper / bigger . . .?

puis-je avoir un reçu / un autre sac s'il vous plaît?, could I have a receipt / another bag please?

quel est le prix de . . .?, what is the price of . . .?

vous prenez / acceptez les cartes *f* de crédit *m* ?, do you take credit cards?

SEE ALSO: **Adornment; Cinema and Photography; Clothing; Drinks; Food; Hair; Health and Sickness; Leisure and Hobbies; The Media; Money; Music; Numbers and Quantities; Post and Telephone; Sport and Games; Tobacco and Drugs; Towns**

48. Sports and Games
Les Sports et les jeux

l'adversaire *m*, opponent

l'amateur *m*; *no f*, amateur (**un amateur de . . .**, a . . . lover)

l'arbitre *m*, referee

le but, goal (**le gardien de but**, goalkeeper; **le filet**, net; **le poteau** *pl* **-x**, goal-post; **la barre**, crossbar)

le champion, *f* **-onne**, champion

le championnat, championship

la cible, target

le combat, fight

la compétition / le concours, competition

le / la concurrent(e), competitor

le coup de pied, kick (**le coup d'envoi** *m*, kick-off; **le coup franc**, free kick; **le pied**, foot)

la coupe, cup

le / la débutant(e), beginner

la défaite, defeat

le détenteur *f* **-trice**, holder [of cup, record, etc.]

l'éliminatoire *f*, heat

l'entraînement *m*, training

l'entraîneur *m*, coach

l'épreuve *f* (**sur terrain** *m* **/ sur piste** *f*), (field / track) event (**une arrivée ex aequo**, a dead heat)

l'équipe *f*, team

l'étape *f*, stage / lap

un(e) fan(atique) de . . . / un(e) passionné(e) de . . ., a . . . fan

la finale, final

le / la gagnant(e), winner

le jeu *pl* **-x**, game (**les jeux olympiques**, Olympic games; **le jouet**, toy / plaything)

le joueur *f* **-euse de . . .**, . . . player

le marathon, marathon

le match, match (**le match nul**, draw)

la médaille, medal

la mêlée, scrum
la mi-temps *pl inv*, half-time (**la première / seconde mi-temps,** first / second half)
le moniteur *f* **-trice,** instructor
la partie, game
la passe (en avant / en arrière), (forward / backward) pass
le peloton, pack
le penalty, penalty
le / la perdant(e), loser
la performance, performance
le professionnel *f* **-elle,** professional
la prolongation, (period of) extra time (**jouer les prolongations,** to play extra time)
le rallye, rally
le record, record
la reprise, round [boxing etc.]
le résultat, result
la réunion (hippique), (race) meeting
le saut, jump
le score, score
le service, serve
le set, set
le spectateur *f* **-trice,** spectator
le sport, sport (**les sports d'hiver** *m*, winter sports)
le sportif *f* **-ive,** sportsman / -woman
le sprint, sprint
le supporter, supporter
la touche, touch
le tournoi, tournament
la victoire, victory

acclamer, to cheer
*aller au trot / au petit galop, to trot / canter / gallop
assister à, to be at (event)
*battre / *vaincre, to beat
entraîner qn., to train sb.
*être en tête, to be in the lead (***prendre la tête,** to take the lead)
s'exercer à, to practise
*faire de / *aller à, to go (***faire de l'alpinisme** *m*, to go

mountaineering; **aller à la chasse**, to go hunting)
faire du sport, to play games
faire match *m* nul, to draw
franchir la ligne d'arrivée *f*, to cross the finishing-line
gagner, to win
huer, to boo
jouer à, to play
marquer un but / X points *m*, to score a goal / X points
(**marquer les points**, to keep score)
mener, to be ahead
parier, to bet (**miser sur**, to bet on; **la cote**, odds)
participer à, to take part in
perdre, to lose
prendre part à, to take part in
rebondir, to bounce
servir, to serve (**retourner**, to return)
siffler, to blow the whistle

Les Sports Sports

l'aérobic *m*, aerobics
l'alpinisme *m*, mountaineering
l'athlétisme *m*, athletics (**le saut en hauteur *f* / en longueur**
***f* / à la perche**, high / long / pole jump; **le javelot**, javelin)
l'aviron *m*, rowing
le badminton / le volant, badminton
le ball-trap, clay-pigeon shooting
le basket(ball), basketball
la boule / la pétanque, [French] bowls
le bowling, bowling
la boxe, boxing
le canoë, canoeing
le canotage, dinghy sailing / rowing
le char à voile, sand-yachting (**la voile**, sail)
la chasse, (game-)shooting (**la chasse à courre**, hunting;
la chasse au renard, fox-hunting)
la course, race (**la course à pied**, running; **les courses
automobile / d'autos *f***, car racing; **les courses de
lévriers**, dog racing; **les courses de trot *m***, trotting;

la **course de taureaux**, bullfight; **le pied**, foot;
  le lévrier, greyhound; **le taureau** *pl* **-x**, bull)
le **cricket**, cricket
le **croquet**, croquet
le **cross à pied / à cheval**, cross-country / point-to-point
  (**à pied** *m*, on foot; **à cheval** *m*; *pl* **-aux**, on horseback)
la **culture physique**, physical training
le **cyclisme**, cycling (**le cyclotourisme**, cycle touring)
le **delta(plane)**, hang-gliding (**l'ULM** *m* [= ultra-léger
  motorisé])
l'**équitation** *f* **l'hippisme** *m*, horse-riding (**la course de
  chevaux** *m*; *sing* **-al**, horse-race)
l'**escalade** *f*, climbing (**la varappe**, rock-climbing)
l'**escrime** *f*, fencing
le **foot(ball)**, football
le **footing**, walking [racing]
le **golf**, golf
la **gymnastique**, gymnastics
l'**haltérophilie** *f*, weight-lifting
le **handball**, handball
le **hockey (sur glace** *f***)**, (ice)hockey
le **jogging**, jogging
le **judo**, judo
le **karaté**, karate
la **luge**, tobogganing
la **lutte**, wrestling (**le catch**, all-in wrestling)
la **marche**, walking (***faire une promenade**, to go for a
  walk; **la randonnée**, long-distance walk)
le **motonautisme**, wet-biking
la **natation**, swimming (**le crawl**, crawl; **la brasse**,
  breast-stroke; **le plongeon**, dive)
le **netball**, netball
le **parachute / le parachutisme**, parachuting (**le
  parachute ascensionnel**, parascending)
le **patinage**, skating (**le patinage à roulettes** *f pl*, roller-
  skating)
la **pêche (à la ligne)**, fishing
la **planche à roulettes**, skateboard(ing) (**la roulette**, skate)

la planche à voile, sailboard(ing) (**la voile,** sail)
la plongée (sous-marine), (skin) diving
le rafting, river-rafting
la régate, regatta
le rugby, rugby (**à treize,** League; **à quinze,** Union)
le ski (de piste *f* **/ de fond / nautique),** (downhill / cross-country / water) skiing (**le fond,** bottom)
la spéléologie, pot-holing
le squash, squash
le surf, surfboard(ing)
le tennis, tennis (**le tennis de table** *f* **/ le ping-pong,** table tennis)
le tir, shooting (**le tir à l'arc,** archery; **l'arc** *m,* bow)
la voile / le yachting / le nautisme, sailing
le vol à voile, gliding (**la voile,** sail)
le volley(-ball), volley-ball

Les Sportifs Sportspeople

l'alpiniste *m / f,* mountaineer
l'athlète *m / f,* athlete
le boxeur, boxer
le canotier, oarsman
le cavalier *f* **-ière,** rider (**le jockey,** jockey)
le chasseur, shooter / hunter
le coureur *f* **-euse,** runner
le / la cycliste, cyclist (**le coureur (** *f* **-euse) cycliste,** cycle racer)
l'escrimeur *f* **-euse,** fencer
le footballeur, footballer
le golfeur *f* **-euse,** golfer
le grimpeur, climber
le / la gymnaste, gymnast
l'haltérophile *m,* weight-lifter
le joggeur *f* **-euse,** jogger
le lugeur *f* **-euse,** tobaganner
le lutteur / le catcheur, wrestler

le nageur f **-euse**, swimmer
le / la parachutiste, parachutist
le patineur f **-euse**, skater
le pêcheur f **-euse**, angler
le plongeur f **-euse**, diver
le promeneur f **-euse**, walker
le rameur f **-euse**, rower
le rugbyman pl **-men**, rugby player
le skieur f **-euse**, skier
le / la spéléologue, potholer
le tennisman pl **-men**, tennis player
le tireur f **-euse**, shooter / shot

Ce qu'ils font What they do

boxer, to box
*courir, to run
grimper / escalader, to climb
lancer, to throw
luger, to toboggan
lutter / catcher, to wrestle
marcher, to walk
*monter à cheval m; pl **-aux / à bicyclette** f, to ride (horse / bike)
nager, to swim (***faire la planche**, to float)
patiner (à roulettes f), to (roller-)skate
pêcher, to fish
plonger, to dive
ramer, to row
sauter, to jump
skier, to ski
soulever, to lift
tirer, to shoot
trotter, to trot

Le matériel The equipment

la balle, ball / bullet
le ballon, [larger, inflated] ball
la barque, small boat
la batte (de cricket *m*), (cricket) bat
la bicyclette / le vélo, bicycle (**la bécane** *colloq*, bike)
la bombe, riding-helmet
la boule, bowl / [small, hard] ball (**la boule de hockey** *m* / **de croquet** *m*, hockey / croquet ball; **le cochonnet,** jack)
la canne à pêche *f*, fishing-rod (**la ligne,** line; **l'appât** *m*, bait)
le canoë, canoe
le champ de course(s) *f*, race-course
le chronomètre, stop-watch
la combinaison de plongée, wetsuit
le court (de tennis *m*), (tennis)-court
la crosse, hockey-stick / golf club
la flèche, arrow
le maillot, costume [swimming] / jersey [football / cycling, etc.]
les palmes *f*, flippers
le patin (à roulettes *f*), (roller-)skate
la patinoire, ice-rink
la piscine (chauffée), (heated) swimming-pool (**le plongeoir,** diving-board)
la piste, racecourse / running-track / ski-slope (**la piste cyclable,** cycle-track)
la planche (à voile *f* **/ de surf** *m*), sailboard / surfboard
le poteau *pl* **-x de départ** *m* / **d'arrivée** *f*, starting- / finishing- post
la raquette, racket / table-tennis bat
la selle, saddle (**les rênes** *f*, reins)
le ski, ski (**le bâton,** stick; **le remonte-pente** *pl* **- -s / le télésiège,** ski-lift)
le stade, stadium (**la tribune,** stand; **le vestiaire,** dressing-room)
le terrain, pitch / ground (**le terrain de golf** *m*, golf-course; **le terrain de jeux,** playing-field; **le jeu** *pl* **-x,** game)

le tuba, snorkel
le voilier, sailing-boat (**le dinghy** *pl* **-ies / le canot,**
  dinghy)

Les jeux Games

le babyfoot, table football
le billard, billiards (**la bille,** billiard ball)
les cartes *f,* cards
les dames *f,* draughts
les dominos *m,* dominoes
les échecs *m,* chess (**l'échiquier** *m,* chessboard; **la pièce,**
  chess-man)
le flipper, pinball machine
le jeu *pl* **-x,** game / ground / set / pack (**la table de jeu,**
  card-table / board; **le dé,** die / dice; **une case,** a square)
le jeu d'adresse *f* **/ de hasard** *m,* game of skill / chance
le jeu de quilles *f,* skittles
le jeu de société *f,* party game / parlour game
le jeu des sept familles, happy families
le loto, bingo
les mots croisés *always pl,* crossword
le puzzle, jigsaw

SEE ALSO: **Leisure and Hobbies; Nature**

49. Theatre Le Théâtre

l'affiche *f*, poster / playbill
les applaudissements *m*, applause
l'aria *f*, aria
le billet, ticket
la critique, review (**le critique**, critic / reviewer)
l'entracte *m*, interval
les jumelles *f* (**de théâtre** *m*), opera-glasses
la location, (advance) booking
la matinée, matinee
le numéro, number / turn
une œuvre, a work
le programme, programme
la représentation, performance
le rôle principal, lead(ing role)
le spectacle, show
en tournée *f*, on tour
le trac, stage fright
les trois coups *m*, three knocks [in French theatre,
  traditional way to silence audience before curtain rises]

applaudir, to applaud (**applaudir à tout rompre**, to
  raise the roof; **rompre**, to break)
baisser / *tomber, to fall [curtain] (**les lumières
  baissent**, the house-lights go down)
*battre des mains, to clap
danser, to dance
*entrer en scène / *sortir de scène, to come on / go off
  [stage]
se *faire acteur *m* / **actrice** *f*, to go on the stage
*faire salle comble, to sell out (**la salle**, auditorium;
  comble, full to overflowing)
s'incliner, to bow
jouer le rôle de, to play [a character]
jouer / monter une pièce, to put on a play
huer, to boo
se lever, to rise [curtain]

louer / réserver, to book
rembourser, to give the audience their money back
répéter, to rehearse
représenter, to perform
siffler, to hiss
(tout est) complet, house full
relâche, closed; no performance

Les spectacles Shows

le ballet, ballet
le cirque, circus
la comédie, comedy
la comédie musicale, musical
la danse, dance / dancing
le drame, drama
la farce, farce
le guignol, puppet-show
le mélodrame, melodrama
le music-hall *pl* **- -s**, variety / variety theatre
l'opéra *m*, opera
l'opérette *f*, operetta
la pièce (en trois actes *m***)**, (three-act) play
la pièce à sensation *f*, thriller
la tragédie, tragedy

Les gens du théâtre Theatre people

l'acteur *m* **/ l'actrice** *f*, actor / actress
l'auditoire *m* **/ les spectateurs** *m*, audience
l'auteur *m*, author
le danseur *f* **-euse**, dancer
le décorateur *f* **-trice**, designer
la distribution, cast
la doublure, understudy
le dramaturge, playwright
l'habitué *m*; *f* **-é du théâtre**, theatre-goer

le machiniste, scene-shifter
le metteur en scène *f*, director
l'ouvreuse *f*, usherette
le public, audience
le régisseur, stage-manager
le souffleur *f* **-euse**, prompter
la troupe, company
la vedette *always f*, star

Le théâtre (le bâtiment)
The theatre building

le balcon / la corbeille, (dress) circle
la caisse / le guichet / la vente de billets, box-office (**la vente**, sale; **le billet**, ticket)
la coulisse, wing (**dans les coulisses**, behind the scenes)
le dernier balcon, gallery
l'éclairage *m*, lighting
le fauteuil de balcon *m*, circle seat
le fauteuil d'orchestre *m* / **un orchestre**, stalls seat
la fosse d'orchestre *m*, orchestra pit
le foyer, foyer
la loge, box
le parterre, stalls
la place, seat
le poulailler, gallery / gods
le projecteur, spotlight
la rampe, footlights
le rang, row
le rideau *pl* **-x (de fer)**, (safety) curtain (**le fer**, iron)
la salle, auditorium
la scène, stage / scene
la sortie (de secours), (emergency) exit (**le secours**, help)
le strapontin, folding seat at end of row
le vestiaire, cloakroom

La Pièce The play

les accessoires *m*, properties
l'acte *m*, act
l'action *f* / **l'intrigue** *f*, plot
le costume, costume
le décor, set (**les décors**, scenery)
l'entrée *f* (**en scène** *f*), entrance [of actor]
le jeu dramatique / tragique / comique, dramatic /
  tragic / comic acting
le lever du rideau *pl* **-x**, curtain-up
le maquillage, make-up
la mise en scène *f*, production
le personnage, character
la première, first night
la répétition (générale), (dress) rehearsal
la représentation, performance
le rôle, part
le texte, text / lines

SEE ALSO: **Adornment; Cinema and Photography;
  Leisure and Hobbies; The Media; Music**

50. Time Le Temps

l'anniversaire *m*, birthday
le calendrier, calendar
le centenaire, centenary
le délai, delay
la durée, duration
l'éternité *f*, eternity
la fête, saint's day (**un jour de fête**, holiday)
l'heure *f*, (clock) time (**l'heure d'été** *m*, summer time)
la période, period
le temps, time (**perdre du temps**, to waste time;
  employer / passer / gaspiller son temps, to use / spend /
  fritter away one's time; **tuer le temps**, to kill time)

L'horloge The clock

l'aiguille *f*, hand (**la petite / grande aiguille**, little / big
  hand; **la trotteuse**, second hand; **trotteur** *f* **-euse**,
  trotting)
le cadran, dial (**le cadran solaire**, sundial)
le chronomètre, stop-watch
l'horloge *f*, [large, often public] clock (**avancer /
  retarder**, to be fast / slow; **sonner**, to strike)
la minuterie, timer [on stairs, cooker, etc.]
la montre, watch (**à ma montre**, by my watch;
  remonter, to wind up)
la pendule, [small domestic] clock (**la pendule à coucou**
  m, cuckoo clock)
le pendule, pendulum
le réveil (de voyage *m*), (travelling) alarm clock
  (***mettre**, to set)
le sablier, hourglass / egg-timer

L'heure Clock time

quelle heure est-il? / avez-vous l'heure?, what time is it?

il est . . .

  une heure, one o'clock

  deux heures, two o'clock

  trois heures cinq, five past three

  quatre heures et quart, quarter past four

  cinq heures et demie, half past five

  six heures moins vingt-cinq, twenty-five to six

    (**moins,** less)

  sept heures moins le quart, quarter to seven

  midi, (twelve) noon

  midi une, a minute past twelve

  midi / minuit et demi, half past twelve

  minuit, midnight

  douze heures (12 h 00), 12.00 / 12 noon

  treize heures dix (13 h 10), 13.10 / 1.10 pm

  quatorze heures quinze (14 h 15), 14.15 / 2.15 pm

  quinze heures trente (15 h 30), 15.30 / 3.30 pm

  seize heures quarante-cinq (16 h 45), 16.45 / 4.45

    pm

  vingt-quatre heures (24 h 00), 24.00 / 12 midnight

  zéro heure une (00 h 01), 00.01 / 12.01 am

après, after

avant, before

environ / vers, about

pile / exactement, exactly

du matin, in the morning / am

de l'après-midi *m or f,* in the afternoon / pm

du soir, in the evening / pm

à la tombée de la nuit, at nightfall

à l'aurore *f,* at dawn

à midi, at noon

à trois heures, at three o'clock

au crépuscule, at dusk

au lever du jour / au point du jour / à l'aube *f,* at
daybreak

au lever / au coucher du soleil, at sunrise / at sunset

Les mesures du temps Units of time

l'an *m* **/ l'année** *f* [†], year (**l'année bissextile / scolaire**, leap / school year)

l'après-midi *m or f*; *pl inv*, afternoon

la décennie, decade

une demi-heure *pl* **- -s**, half an hour

le fuseau *pl* **-x horaire**, time zone (**le décalage**, time difference)

l'heure *f*, hour (**une heure et quart / demie**, an hour and a quarter / half)

l'instant *m*, instant

le jour / la journée [†], day (**le jour férié**, holiday; **le jour ouvrable**, working day; **le jour de congé**, day off; **le congé**, leave)

le matin / la matinée [†], morning

un millénaire, a thousand years

le millésime, year [on coin; of a wine]

la minute, minute

le mois, month

le moment, moment

la nuit, night (**cette nuit**, tonight / last night)

un quart d'heure *f*, quarter of an hour (**trois quarts d'heure**, three-quarters of an hour)

la quinzaine / quinze jours *m*, fortnight

la saison, season

la seconde, second

la semaine / huit jours *m* **/ la huitaine**, week

le siècle, century

le soir / la soirée [†], evening

le trimestre, term

le week-end, weekend

annuel *f* **-elle**, yearly

hebdomadaire, weekly

mensuel *f* **-elle**, monthly (**bimensuel**, fortnightly)

quotidien *f* **-enne / journalier** *f* **-ière**, daily

[†] The masculine form is used for a countable unit; the feminine form is used when what happened during the course of the year, day, etc. is stressed

La date The date

quelle est la date / le combien sommes-nous?, what is the date?

nous sommes . . .
  le premier janvier, the first of January
  le deux février, the second of February
  le trois mars, the third of March
  le vingt et un avril, the twenty-first of April
  le vingt-neuf mai, the twenty-ninth of May

  . . . mil neuf cent quatre-vingts / . . . dix-neuf cent quatre-vingts, 1980

Les jours de la semaine The days of the week

quel jour sommes-nous?, what day is it?

nous sommes . . .
  dimanche *m*, Sunday
  lundi *m*, Monday
  mardi *m*, Tuesday
  mercredi *m*, Wednesday
  jeudi *m*, Thursday
  vendredi *m*, Friday
  samedi *m*, Saturday

lundi, on Monday (**le lundi**, on Mondays; **tous les lundis**, every Monday)
lundi dernier / passé, last Monday
lundi en huit / en quinze, a week / fortnight on Monday
lundi matin / après-midi / soir, on Monday morning / afternoon / evening
lundi prochain, next Monday
le lundi suivant, the following Monday

Les saisons Seasons

le printemps, spring (**au printemps**, in spring)
l'été *m*, summer (**en été**, in summer)

l'automne *m*, autumn (**en automne**, in autumn)
l'hiver *m*, winter (**en hiver**, in winter)

Les mois Months

janvier *m*, January
février *m*, February
mars *m*, March
avril *m*, April
mai *m*, May
juin *m*, June
juillet *m*, July
août *m*, August
septembre *m*, September
octobre *m*, October
novembre *m*, November
décembre *m*, December

à la mi-janvier, in mid-January
au vingtième siècle, in the twentieth century
dans les années quatre-vingt, in the eighties
de mon temps, in my day
en janvier / au mois de janvier, in January
en (l'an) 2000, in (the year) 2000
(en) fin *f* / **début** *m* **1999**, at the end / beginning of 1999

Quand? When does it happen?

à chaque minute *f* / **seconde** *f*, every minute / second
à la fin, in the end
à l'avenir *m*, in future
à l'heure *f* / **à temps** *m*, on time
alors, then
après-demain, the day after tomorrow
à présent *m* / **à l'instant** *m*, at present
à tout moment, any time
aujourd'hui, today (**aujourd'hui en huit / en quinze**,
   today week / fortnight)
autrefois, formerly

avant-hier, the day before yesterday

bientôt, soon

ce matin, this morning

ce soir, this evening

cet(te) après-midi, this afternoon

d'abord, first

dans deux jours, in two days

déjà, already

demain, tomorrow (**demain matin / après-midi / soir,**
tomorrow morning / afternoon / night)

de nos jours, nowadays (**le jour,** day)

depuis, since (then)

dès maintenant, right away [literally, *with effect from now*]

désormais, from now on / henceforth

de temps à autre, now and then (**autre,** other)

de temps en temps, from time to time (**de seconde [etc.]
en seconde [etc.],** from second [etc.] to second [etc.])

du matin au soir, from morning to night

en avance / tôt / de bonne heure, early

en ce moment / actuellement, at the moment / now (**à ce
moment-là,** then / in those days)

encore, still / again

enfin / finalement / à la longue, finally

en même temps, at the same time

en retard / tard, late (*****être en retard,** to be late [for
something]; *****avoir du retard,** to be late [= be
behindhand]; **il est tard,** it's late)

ensuite, then / next

entre-temps, meanwhile

hier, yesterday (**hier matin / après-midi,** yesterday
morning / afternoon; **hier soir,** last night)

il y a / voilà (une semaine etc.), (a week etc.) ago

immédiatement / tout de suite, immediately (**la suite,**
continuation)

jadis, in the past

jamais, never

l'avant-veille *f,* two days before

la veille, the day before (**la veille au soir,** the evening /
night before)

le lendemain, the day after (**le lendemain soir**, the
  following evening / night)
le surlendemain, two days later
longtemps, for a long time
maintenant, now
parfois / quelquefois, sometimes
puis, then
rarement, seldom / rarely
récemment, recently
soudain, suddenly
sous peu, shortly (**peu** *m*, little)
souvent, often
tard, late (**en retard**, late [= behindhand])
tôt, early (**de bonne heure**, early [= in good time]; **tôt ou
  tard**, sooner or later)
toujours, always
tous les jours [etc.] / chaque jour [etc.], every day [etc.]
tout à l'heure, in a moment, just now
tout d'un coup, all at once [literally, *all at a blow*]
toutes les heures, hourly

après que, after
avant que [+ subjunctive], before
au moment où, just as / at the moment when
aussitôt que / dès que, as soon as
depuis que, since
pendant que, whilst
quand / lorsque, when
un jour que, one day when (**le jour où**, the day when)

Les jours de fête   Public holidays

célébrer, to celebrate
l'Ascension *f*, Ascension day
la Chandeleur, Candlemas [February 2]
la fête de la Libération / de la Victoire, Victory day [May 8]
la fête des Morts, All Souls' day [November 2] (**les morts**
  m, the dead)
la fête des Rameaux, Palm Sunday (**le rameau** *pl* **-x**,
  branch)

la fête des Rois, Twelfth Night [January 6] (**le roi,** king)

le jour de l'an *m*, New Year's day (**bonne anné!,** happy New Year)

le mardi gras, Shrove Tuesday (**gras,** fat)

la (fête de) Noël [m in **joyeux Noël,** *happy Christmas*, etc.], Christmas (**la veille de Noël,** Christmas Eve; **la carte / l'arbre** *m* **/ le cadeau** *pl* **-x de Noël,** Christmas card / tree / present; **le Père Noël,** Father Christmas)

Pâques *f pl,* Easter

la Pentecôte, Whitsun (**le dimanche de Pentecôte,** Whit Sunday)

le premier mai / la fête du Travail, Labour Day [May 1]

le quatorze juillet / la fête Nationale, Bastille Day [French national day; July 14]

le quinze août / la fête de la Sainte Vierge, Assumption / feast of the Blessed Virgin Mary [August 15]

la Saint-Sylvestre, New Year's Eve (**le réveillon,** New Year's Eve party)

la Toussaint, All Saints' day [November 1]

le vendredi saint, Good Friday (**saint,** holy)

SEE ALSO: **Birth, Marriage, and Death; History; Numbers and Quantities**

51. Tobacco and Drugs
Le Tabac et la drogue

Le tabac Tobacco

l'allumette *f*, match (**une boîte d'allumettes**, a box of matches)

le briquet, lighter (**la pierre**, flint; **la mèche**, wick; **la recharge**, refill)

le cancer du poumon, cancer of the lung

le cendrier, ashtray

le cigare, cigar

la cigarette (mentholée / longue), (menthol / king-size) cigarette (**le bout filtre**, filter-tip; **le paquet**, packet; **le papier à cigarettes**, cigarette paper)

le cure-pipe *pl* - -s, pipe-cleaner

le fume-cigarette *pl inv*, cigarette-holder

le (non-)fumeur *f* **-euse**, (non-)smoker

l'interdiction *f*, ban (**défense de fumer**, no smoking)

le mégot, cigarette-end

la pipe, pipe (**bourrer**, to fill)

le tabac, tobacco / tobacconist's (**la blague**, pouch; **le tabac blond / brun**, light / dark tobacco; **le tabac à priser**, snuff; **priser**, to take snuff)

allumer, to light (up)

arrêter de (+ INF) / **renoncer à** (+ INF), to give up . . . ing (***reprendre**, to start again)

*avoir / donner du feu, to have / give sb. a light (**le feu**, fire)

enfumer, to fill with smoke

*éteindre, to put out

fumer, to smoke

La drogue Drugs

la cocaïne, cocaine

la dépendance, addiction

la drogue *usually sing*, drugs
la guérison, cure
le haschi(s)ch, hashish (**le hasch**, hash / dope)
l'héroïne *f*, heroin
le joint, joint
la manie, obsession
la marijuana, marijuana / pot
l'overdose *f*, overdose
la réinsertion, rehabilitation
la seringue, needle
les stupéfiants *m*, narcotics
le / la toxico(mane) / le / la drogué(e), addict
la toxicomanie, drug addiction
le trafic de la drogue *f*, drug-trafficking
le trafiquant, dealer

confisquer, to confiscate
se droguer, to take drugs (**se droguer à la cocaïne**, to take cocaine)
*prendre, take

SEE ALSO: **Crimes and Criminals; Drinks; Health and Sickness**

52. Tools Les Outils

L'outil et ce qu'on en fait
The tool and what you do with it

l'aiguille *f*, needle (**le fil**, thread; **le dé**, thimble)
   *coudre, to sew

l'aiguille à tricoter, knitting-needle (**la pelote de laine** *f*,
   ball of wool; **la maille**, stitch [in knitting])   **tricoter**, to
   knit

l'arrosoir *m*, watering-can   **arroser**, to water

le balai, broom   **balayer**, to sweep

la bêche, spade   **bêcher**, to dig

le boulon, bolt (**l'écrou**, nut)   **boulonner**, to bolt
   (down)

la brosse, brush   **brosser**, to brush

le ciseau *pl* **-x**, chisel   **ciseler**, to chisel

les ciseaux, scissors   **couper**, to cut

la clé, spanner (**la clé anglaise**, wrench)   **dévisser**, to
   unscrew

le cric, jack   **soulever**, to raise

le déplantoir, garden trowel   **déplanter**, to transplant

l'échelle *f*, ladder (**l'escabeau** *pl* **-x**, step-ladder)
   *monter (à), to go up

l'entonnoir *m*, funnel   **verser**, to pour

l'étau *m*; *pl* **-x**, vice   ***tenir**, to hold

la faux, scythe (**la faucille**, sickle)   **faucher**, to mow

le fer à repasser, iron   **repasser**, to iron

le fer à souder, soldering-iron   **souder**, to solder

le foret, drill   **forer**, to drill

la forge, forge (**une enclume**, anvil)   **forger**, to forge

la fourche, garden fork   **fourcher**, to fork

la houe / la binette, hoe   **sarcler**, to hoe

la lime, file   **limer**, to file

la machine à coudre, sewing-machine (**le point**, stitch
   [in sewing])   **piquer**, to stitch

le maillet, mallet   **enfoncer**, to knock in

le marteau *pl* **-x**, hammer (**le clou**, nail)   **clouer**, to nail

le marteau-piqueur *pl* **-x-**, pneumatic drill   **creuser**, to dig

le métier à tisser, loom   **tisser**, to weave

le niveau *pl* **-x à bulle**, spirit-level (**la bulle**, bubble)   **niveler**, to level off

le papier de verre, sandpaper (**le verre**, glass)   **poncer**, to sand

la pelle, shovel   **ramasser**, to pick up

la perceuse, drill   **percer un trou**, to drill a hole

le pic / la pioche, pickaxe   **piocher**, to dig [with a pick]

la pince *often pl*, pliers   **plier**, to bend

le pinceau *pl* **-x**, brush (**la couleur**, paint)   ***peindre**, to paint

la punaise, drawing-pin   **punaiser**, to pin up

le rabot, plane   **raboter**, to plane

le râteau *pl* **-x**, rake   **ratisser**, to rake

le scie, saw   **scier**, to saw

les tenailles, pincers   **arracher un clou,** to pull out a nail

le tour, lathe   **tourner**, to turn

le tournevis, screwdriver (**la vis**, screw)   **visser**, to screw

SEE ALSO: **Cooking and Eating (for kitchen equipment); Health and Sickness (for medical equipment); The Home (for household equipment); Jobs; Materials**

53. **Towns** Les Villes

Les agglomérations Settlements

l'agglomération *f*, built-up area / settlement
l'arrondissement *m*, district [in large towns]
la banlieue / les faubourgs *m*, suburbs (**un faubourg**, a suburb)
le bourg, market town
la capitale, capital city (**la province**, the provinces)
le chef-lieu *pl* **-s -x** (**de département** *m*), [France] principal town of department [= county town]
le hameau *pl* **-x**, hamlet
le lieu *pl* **-x / un endroit** *m*, place / locality / spot
la métropole, metropolis
le port, port
le quartier, district / quarter [of town]
le village, village
la ville, town (**en ville**, in / into town)
la zone (industrielle), (industrial) zone

En ville In town

l'abri-bus *m*; *pl* **-s -**, bus-shelter
l'aéroport *m*, airport
l'ambassade *f*, embassy
l'arrêt *m* (**d'autobus** *m*), bus-stop
l'avenue *f*, avenue
le bassin, pool
la bouche de métro, underground entrance (**la bouche**, mouth; **le métro**, underground)
le boulevard, boulevard / avenue
le caniveau *pl* **-x**, gutter
le carrefour, crossroads
le centre commercial *pl* **-aux**, shopping area / shopping mall
le centre-ville, town centre

le cimetière, cemetery / churchyard (**la tombe**, grave; **le tombeau** *pl* **-x**, tomb)

la circulation, traffic

la cité, city / old town [also *housing estate*] (**la cité universitaire**, university halls of residence)

le coin de la rue, street corner

la chaussée, roadway / carriageway

le défilé, procession

l'égout *m*, sewer

l'embouteillage *m*, traffic jam

les environs *m*, surroundings

les feux *m*, traffic-lights

la fontaine / le jet d'eau, fountain (**l'eau** *f*; *pl* **-x**, water)

la galerie, arcade

la gare (SNCF / routière), (railway / bus) station (**SNCF = Société nationale des chemins de fer français**)

la grand-rue *pl* **- -s**, high street

le gratte-ciel *pl inv*, skyscraper

l'HLM *m or f* (**habitation à loyer modéré**), council flat (**le loyer**, rent)

l'impasse *f* / **la voie sans issue** *f*, cul-de-sac

le jardin des plantes *f* / **botanique**, botanical gardens

le jardin public, (public) gardens

le kiosque (à journaux), (newspaper) kiosk (**le journal** *pl* **-aux**, newspaper)

le lac / le plan d'eau, lake (**le plan**, sheet / stretch; **l'eau** *f*; *pl* **-x**, water)

le marché (aux puces *f* / **aux antiquités** *f*), (flea / antiques) market (**la halle / le marché couvert**, covered market)

le parc, park

le parc d'attractions *f*, amusement park (**la foire**, fair)

le parking (souterrain), (underground) car-park

le passage clouté, pedestrian crossing (**clouté**, studded)

le pavé, paving stone / cobble-stone / highway

le (boulevard) périphérique, ring road

la piste cyclable, cycle-track

la place (principale), (main) square

le pont, bridge

la porte, (town) gate

le quai, embankment
le quartier des artistes *m* **/ des affaires** *f*,
  artists' / business quarter
le refuge, traffic island
le rempart, rampart
la rocade, orbital road
la route, road
la rue, street / road
la rue commerçante / piétonne / à sens *m* **unique**,
  shopping / pedestrian / one-way street
la ruelle, alley / lane
le square, square [with public garden]
la station de taxis *m*, taxi rank
le stationnement *no pl*, parking
les toilettes *f* **publiques**, public conveniences
la tour d'habitation, tower block
le trottoir, pavement
la zone bleue, restricted parking area
le zoo, zoo

Les édifices de la ville Town buildings

l'abattoir *m*, abattoir
l'abbaye *f*, abbey
l'arc *m* **de triomphe** *m*, triumphal arch
le bâtiment, building
la bibliothèque, library (**emprunter un livre**, to borrow
  a book)
le boulodrome, bowling-alley
la bourse, stock exchange
la caserne des pompiers *m*, fire station (**la caserne**,
  barracks)
la cathédrale, cathedral
la chapelle, chapel
le château *pl* **-x**, castle / great house (**la forteresse / le
  château fort**, castle / fortress)
le cinéma, cinema (**le film**, film)
le consulat, consulate
le couvent, convent (**la religieuse / la nonne**, nun)

l'**église** *f* (**catholique**), (catholic) church

la **galerie d'art** *m* / le **musée d'art**, art gallery (**la peinture**, painting; **la sculpture**, sculpture)

l'**hôpital** *m*; *pl* **-aux**, hospital

l'**hôtel** *m* **de ville** *f*, town hall [in city / large town] (**l'hôtel**, hotel / large town-house)

l'**immeuble** *m*, block of flats

la **mairie**, town hall [in small town / village] (**le conseil municipal** *pl* **-s -aux**, town council)

la **maison des jeunes** *m* (**et de la culture**), community youth centre

le **monastère**, monastery (**le religieux** / **le moine**, monk)

le **monument**, monument / public building / historic building (**le monument aux morts**, war memorial; **les morts** *m*, the dead)

la **mosquée**, mosque

le **musée**, museum (**l'exposition** *f*, exhibition)

l'**office** *m* **du tourisme** / le **syndicat d'initiative** *f*, tourist office

l'**opéra** *m*, opera-house (**un opéra**, an opera)

le **palais**, palace

le **palais de Justice** *f*, law courts

la **piscine**, swimming-pool

le **planétarium**, planetarium

la **poste** / le **bureau** *pl* **-x de poste** / les **P et T** (= **Postes** *f* **et télécommunications** *f*), post office

le **poste de police** *f* / le **commissariat**, police station [in cities] (**la gendarmerie**, police station [outside cities])

la **prison**, prison

le **réverbère**, street lamp

les **ruines** *f*, ruins

la **salle de concert** *m*, concert hall

le **stade**, stadium

la **statue**, statue

la **synagogue**, synagogue

le **temple** (**protestant**), protestant church

le **théâtre**, theatre (**la pièce de théâtre**, play)

la **tour**, tower (***monter à la tour**, to go up the tower)

l'**usine** *f* / la **fabrique**, factory

Les habitants The inhabitants

l'automobiliste *m*/*f*, car driver
le / la banlieusard(e), suburbanite
le / la bourgeois(e), middle-class man/woman
le / la citadin(e), city dweller
le / la concierge, caretaker [of block of flats]
l'habitant *m*; *f* **-te**, inhabitant / resident / occupant
le maire / la mairesse, mayor(ess)
le / la Parisien(ne), Parisian
le / la passant(e), passer-by
le / la piéton(ne), pedestrian
la population, population
le / la provincial(e) *pl* **-aux, -ales**, provincial / small-town
  dweller
le / la touriste, tourist
le / la villageois(e), villager

Ce qu'on y fait What you do there

s'égarer / perdre son chemin, to get lost
*faire visiter les endroits intéressants à qn., to show
  sb. the sights
flâner, to stroll / saunter around
habiter (+ PLACE), to live in
impressionner, to impress
montrer, to show
*parcourir, to wander through
passer devant, to go past
*servir de guide *m*/*f*, to act as a guide
traverser, to cross
visiter, to visit [a town, a monument]

SEE ALSO: **Art and Architecture; Cooking and Eating;
  Places and Languages; Post and Telephone; Shops
  and Shopping; Transport**

54. **Transport** Les Transports

Les transports routiers Road transport

LES VOITURES CARS

la bagnole / **la guimbarde** / **le tacot**, banger
le camping-car *pl* --s, camper
la caravane, caravan (**la roulotte**, horse-drawn caravan)
la conduite intérieure *pl inv*, saloon (**la conduite à gauche** /
à droite, left-hand / right-hand drive)
la décapotable, convertible
la deux-portes *pl inv*, two-door car
la familiale / **le break**, estate car
la marque, make
la remorque, trailer
la traction avant *pl inv*, front-wheel-drive car
la voiture / **l'auto(mobile)** *f*, car (**en voiture**, by car;
l'automobiliste *m* / *f*, motorist)
la voiture de course *f* / **de location** *f* / **de sport** *m* /
d'occasion *f* / **à quatre roues** *f* **motrices**, racing / rented /
sports / second-hand / four-wheel-drive car

LES MOTOS, LES BICYCLETTES
MOTOR BIKES, BICYCLES

la bicyclette, bicycle (**le vélo** / **la bécane**, bike; **à bicyclette**
/ à vélo / en vélo, by bike; **le** / **la cycliste**, cyclist)
la mobylette® / **le vélomoteur** / **le cyclomoteur**, moped
la moto, motor bike (**le** / **la motocycliste**, motor-cyclist; **à** /
en moto, by motor-bike)
le scooter, scooter

LES CAMIONS LORRIES

le camion, lorry (**le camionneur**, lorry driver)
le camion-citerne *pl* -s -s, tanker
la camionnette, van

la dépanneuse, breakdown lorry
le poids lourd *pl inv*, HGV / heavy lorry
le semi-remorque *pl --s*, articulated lorry

LES PARTIES D'UN VÉHICULE
THE PARTS OF A VEHICLE

l'accélérateur *m*, accelerator
l'aile *f*, wing
l'allumage *m*, ignition
l'alternateur *m*, alternator
l'amortisseur *m*, shock-absorber
l'autoradio *f*, car radio
l'avertisseur *m* **lumineux**, headlamp flasher
la barre, crossbar [bicycle]
la batterie, battery
le bidon, petrol can
le bouchon (de réservoir *m*), petrol cap
la bougie, spark-plug
le cadre, frame [bicycle]
le capot, bonnet
le carburateur, carburettor
la carrosserie, bodywork
la ceinture de sécurité *f*, safety-belt
la chaîne, chain [bicycle]
la chambre à air *m*, inner tube
le châssis, chassis
le chauffage, heating
la clé de contact *m*, ignition key (**la serrure**, lock)
le clignotant, indicator
le coffre, boot
le compteur kilométrique / de vitesse *f*, milometer /
  speedometer
la courroie, (fan) belt
le cric, jack
la cylindrée, cubic capacity / cc (**de grosse / petite
  cylindrée**, with a large / small engine)
le distributeur, distributor
la dynamo, dynamo

l'embrayage *m*, clutch

l'enjoliveur *m*, hub-cap

l'essuie-glace *m*; *pl inv*, windscreen wiper

l'extincteur *m*, fire-extinguisher

les feux *m* **de route** *f* **/ de croisement** *m* **/ arrière** *inv* **/ de stationnement** *m*, head / dipped head / rear / parking lights (**l'ampoule** *f*, bulb)

le frein (à main *f*), (hand)brake (**lâcher**, to fail; **le câble du frein**, brake cable)

le fusible, fuse (**fondre**, to blow)

la galerie, roof-rack

le garde-boue *pl inv*, mudguard

le guidon, handlebars

la jauge d'essence *f*, petrol gauge

le klaxon, horn

la lampe témoin, warning light

le lave-glace *pl* **- -s**, windscreen washer

le moteur (à deux temps *m*), (two-stroke) engine

le moyeu *pl* **-x**, hub

le pare-boue *pl inv*, mud-flap

le pare-brise *pl inv*, windscreen

le pare-choc(s) *pl inv*, bumper

la pédale, pedal

le phare, headlight (**le phare (en) code**, dipped headlight; **le phare anti-brouillard**, fog-light; **le phare de recul** *m*, reversing-light)

la pièce de rechange, replacement / spare part

la plaque minéralogique / d'immatriculation *f*, number-plate [originally distributed by the *service des Mines*]

le pneu, tyre (**la crevaison / le pneu crevé**, puncture; ***être à plat**, to be flat; **gonfler**, to blow up)

la pompe, pump

la porte / la portière, door (**la poignée**, handle)

le porte-bagages *pl inv*, luggage rack [on bicycle]

le pot d'échappement *m*, exhaust

la première / seconde vitesse, first / second gear (**le point mort**, neutral; **la marche arrière**, reverse; **la boîte de vitesses**, gearbox; **le levier de vitesses**, gear lever; **engager**, to engage)

le radiateur, radiator (**le volet**, grill)
le rayon, spoke
le réflecteur / le catadioptre, reflector
la réglette-jauge *pl* **-s -s**, dip-stick
le rétroviseur, rear mirror
la roue, wheel (**la roue de rechange** *m* **/ de secours**,
  spare wheel; **le secours**, help)
la selle, saddle (**la sacoche**, saddle-bag)
la serrure, lock
le siège (avant / arrière / pliant), (front / back / folding)
  seat
le silencieux, silencer
le starter (automatique), (automatic) choke
la suspension, suspension
le tableau *pl* **-x de bord**, dashboard
le timbre / la sonnette, [bicycle] bell
le toit ouvrant, sliding roof (**ouvrant**, opening)
le train avant / arrière, front / back axle
la transmission (automatique), (automatic) transmission
le triangle avertisseur, warning triangle
la valve, tyre valve (**la soupape**, engine valve)
la vitre / la glace, window
le volant, steering-wheel

SUR LA ROUTE ON THE ROAD

l'accotement *m* **(stabilisé / non-stabilisé)**, (hard / soft)
  shoulder
l'aire *f* **de repos** *m* **/ de service** *m*, rest / service area
l'assurance *f*, insurance
l'auto-école *f*; *pl* **- -s**, driving school
l'autoroute *f*, motorway
la bande médiane, central reservation
le bas-côté *pl* **- -s**, verge
une bonne / mauvaise route, a good / bad road (**la
  bonne / mauvaise route**, the right / wrong road)
la bretelle de raccordement *m*, access road / slip road
le carrefour, crossroads / road junction
la carte routière, road-map (**la carte verte**, green

[foreign insurance] card; **la carte grise**, registration document; **gris**, grey)

la chaussée (déformée / glissante), uneven / slippery) road surface

la circulation, traffic

le code de la route, highway code

une contravention, a parking ticket / fine

la crevaison, puncture

le croisement, crossroads / intersection

la déviation, diversion

l'échangeur *m*, motorway junction / intersection

l'embouteillage *m*, traffic jam

l'embranchement *m*, fork / slip-road

l'entretien *m*, maintenance

l'essence *f* / **le carburant**, petrol (**le super**, super; **le sans-plomb**, unleaded; **le gazole / le gas-oil**, diesel fuel; **le diesel**, diesel engine; **l'huile** *f*, oil; **l'antigel** *m*, antifreeze; **la pompe**, pump; **le / la pompiste**, attendant)

les feux *m*, traffic-lights (**le feu rouge / orange / vert**, red / amber / green light)

la file (de droite / de gauche), (right-hand / left-hand) lane

la fuite, leak

le garage, garage

les heures *f* **de pointe / creuses**, peak / off-peak period (**la pointe**, peak; **creux** *f* **creuse**, hollow)

le lave-auto(s) *pl inv*, car wash

la limitation de vitesse *f*, speed limit (**respecter**, to respect; ***enfreindre**, to break)

le mécanicien, mechanic

le nid de poule, pot-hole (**le nid**, nest; **la poule**, chicken)

la panne, breakdown (**la panne d'essence**, empty tank; **l'essence** *f*, petrol)

le panneau *pl* **-x**, road sign

le parc(o)mètre, parking-meter

le parking, car-park

le passage clouté / à niveau *m*; *pl* **-x**, pedestrian / level crossing (**clouté**, studded)

le péage, toll

le permis de conduire, driving-licence

la pression des pneus *m*, tyre pressure
la priorité, right of way
le rappel, reminder
le rond-point *pl* **-s -s** / **le sens giratoire**, roundabout
la route (nationale / départementale), (trunk / minor) road
 (**route barrée**, road closed)
un sens unique, a one-way street (**sens interdit**, no entry)
le stationnement, parking (**un stationnement interdit**, a
 no-parking sign)
la station-service *pl* **-s -**, service station (**l'huile** *f*, oil;
 l'eau *f* **distillée**, distilled water)
le stop, stop sign
le tournant, turning
toutes directions, through traffic
les transports *m* **en commun**, public transport
les travaux *m*; *sing* **travail**, roadworks
le trottoir, pavement
le verglas, black ice
la vidange, oil change
la vignette, road-tax disc
le virage, bend
la visibilité, visibility
la vitesse, speed (**un excès de vitesse**, speeding)
la zone bleue, restricted parking zone (**disque** *f* **obligatoire**,
 parking disc required)

LES GENS QU'ON RENCONTRE
THE PEOPLE YOU MEET

l'automobiliste *m / f*, motorist
l'auto-stoppeur *m*; *f* **-euse**, hitch-hiker
le chauffard, road-hog
le chauffeur du dimanche, weekend driver (**le dimanche**,
 Sunday)
le conducteur *f* **-trice**, driver
le contractuel *f* **-elle**, traffic warden
le / la cycliste, cyclist
le motard, motor-cycle cop / [sometimes] motor-cyclist
le / la motocycliste, motor-cyclist

le passager *f* -gère, passenger
le piéton *f* -onne, pedestrian
le routier / le camionneur, lorry driver

CE QU'ON FAIT WHAT YOU DO

accélérer, to accelerate
allumer / *éteindre les phares, to switch headlights on / off
s'arrêter, to stop
*avoir / céder la priorité, to have right of way / give way
bifurquer, to turn off (a road)
brûler un feu / un stop, to ignore a red light / a stop sign
caler, to stall
changer (une roue), to change (a wheel)
circuler, to move around [vehicle]
*conduire, to drive
couper le moteur, to switch off the engine
démarrer, to start
dépanner, to fix [a breakdown]
déraper, to skid
*descendre en roue *f* libre, to free-wheel down
doubler / dépasser, to overtake
*faire de la bicyclette / de l'auto *f*, to go cycling / motoring
*faire demi-tour *m*; *pl* --s, to do a U-turn / turn round
*faire du stop, to hitch-hike
*faire le plein, to fill up
freiner, to brake
garer la voiture / se garer / stationner, to park
klaxonner, to hoot
louer, to hire
ralentir, to slow down
se ranger, to get in lane
reculer / *faire marche *f* arrière, to reverse
remorquer, to tow
réparer, to repair
réviser, to service
rouler (au pas), to drive (at walking pace) (le pas, footstep / pace)
*tomber en panne, to break down (la panne, breakdown)

tourner, to turn
traverser, to cross
vérifier, to check
voyager, to travel

Les autres moyens de transport
Other means of transport

LES CHEMINS DE FER RAILWAYS

à destination *f* **de**, departing for
en provenance *f* **de**, arriving from

l'arrêt *m*, stop
l'arrivée *f*, arrival
les bagages *m*, luggage
la barrière, barrier
le billet, ticket (**un aller simple**, a single; **un aller-retour**, a
  return; **de première / seconde (classe)**, first / second class;
  valable / non-valable, valid / not valid; **demi-tarif** *m*, half
  price)
le buffet / la buvette, buffet
le chariot, trolley
le chef de gare *m*, station-master / supervisor
le chef de train *m*, guard
le cheminot, railway linesman
les chemins de fer, railways (**le chemin**, way; **le fer**, iron)
la consigne, left-luggage office
la consigne automatique, left-luggage lockers
le contrôleur, ticket-collector
la correspondance, connection
le coup de sifflet, whistle [the sound] (**le sifflet**, whistle [the
  object])
le départ, departure
le distributeur (de billets *m***)**, ticket machine
la gare, station (**la gare d'embranchement** *m*, junction)
les grandes lignes, main lines (**les banlieues** *f*, suburban
  services)

le guichet, ticket window
le hall (de gare *f*), (station) concourse
l'horaire *m*, timetable
l'indicateur *m* / **le panneau** *pl* **-x d'affichage** *m*, train indicator (**afficher**, to post up)
le passage à niveau *m*; *pl* **-x**, level crossing
le pont, bridge
le porteur, porter
le quai, platform
les rails *m* / **la voie ferrée**, track (**ferré**, iron *adj*; **la traverse**, sleeper; **l'aiguille** *f sing*, points)
le remblai, embankment
les renseignements *m*, information
le réseau *pl* **-x**, network
la réservation, reservation
la salle d'attente *f*, waiting-room
le signal *pl* **-aux**, signal
le (passage) souterrain, subway
le trajet, journey
la tranchée, cutting
le tunnel, tunnel
le viaduc, viaduct
le voyageur *f* **-euse**, passenger

*arriver, to arrive
changer, to change
composter, to validate
*descendre, to get out
*desservir, to stop at
enregistrer, to register [luggage]
*entrer en gare *f*, to enter the station
manquer, to miss
*monter, to get on
*partir pour, to leave for
poinçonner, to punch
*prendre le train, to take the train
réserver, to reserve

LES LOCOMOTIVES ET LES TRAINS
ENGINES AND TRAINS

l'autorail *m*, railcar

le funiculaire, funicular railway

la loco(motive), engine

la locomotive à vapeur *f* **/ électrique / diesel,** steam /
electric / diesel locomotive (**le mécanicien,** driver)

le (train) rapide / l'express *m*, express

le RER (Réseau express régional), express local
network

le TEE (Trans-Europe express), international express

le téléphérique / la télécabine, cable-car

le TGV (Train à grande vitesse), super high-speed train

le train (de voyageurs *m* **/ de marchandises** *f*)**,**
(passenger / goods) train

le train direct / omnibus / de banlieue *f*, through /
stopping / local train

le tramway, tram

DANS LE TRAIN IN THE TRAIN

le compartiment (fumeurs / non-fumeurs), (smoking /
non-smoking) compartment (**le couloir,** corridor)

la couchette, couchette / berth (**installer,** to make up)

le fourgon, luggage-van (**le chef de train,** guard)

la place (fenêtre / réservée), (window / reserved)
seat / place (**la banquette,** seat [the physical object])

le porte-bagages *pl inv* **/ le filet,** luggage rack

la portière, door

le signal *pl* **-aux d'alarme** *f*, alarm

le supplément, extra charge

la tête du train, front of the train (**en tête,** at the front; **en
queue,** at the back; **la queue,** tail)

les toilettes *f*, toilet (**occupé,** engaged; **libre,** free)

la voiture / le wagon, carriage (**la voiture directe,**
through carriage)

le wagon-lit *pl* **-s -s,** sleeper (**la voiture-couchettes**
pl **-s -,** couchette sleeper)

le wagon-restaurant *pl* **-s -s / la voiture de restauration** *f*, restaurant car

LES AVIONS PLANES

l'aéroport *m*, airport
l'aiguilleur *m* **de l'air** *m*, air-traffic controller
l'aile *f*, wing
l'altitude *f*, altitude
l'atterrissage *m* **(forcé)**, (forced / emergency) landing
l'avion *m* **/ l'appareil** *m*, aircraft (**en avion**, by plane)
les bagages *m* **(à main** *f* **/ en excédent** *m*), (hand / excess) luggage
le billet (open), (open) ticket (**le prix du billet**, fare)
la boutique hors-taxe, duty-free shop
la cabine, cabin
la ceinture (de sécurité *f*), seat-belt (**attacher**, to fasten; **détacher**, to undo)
le charter, charter flight
les commandes *f* **(de vol)**, controls (**le vol**, flight)
la compagnie / la ligne aérienne, airline
le décollage, take-off
la descente, descent
le dirigeable, airship
la douane, customs (**le douanier** *f* **-ière**, customs officer; **fouiller**, to search; **les droits** *m*, duty; **le passeport**, passport)
l'embarquement *m*, boarding (**la salle / la carte d'embarquement**, departure lounge / boarding pass)
l'enregistrement *m* **des bagages** *m*, check-in
l'équipage *m*, crew
l'escale *f*, stop-over
le fuselage, fuselage
l'hélice *f*, propeller
l'hélicoptère *m*, helicopter
l'hôtesse *f* **de l'air** *m*, air hostess / stewardess
le hublot, window
l'hydravion *m*, seaplane

l'issue *f* **/ la sortie de secours**, emergency exit (**le secours**, help)
le (jumbo-)jet, (jumbo-)jet
la navette, airport bus
le passager *f* **-gère**, passenger
le pilote, pilot
le pirate de l'air *m*, hijacker
la piste, runway (**les balises** *f*, runway lights)
la porte, gate
le radar, radar
le réacteur, (jet) engine
le retrait des bagages *m*, baggage collection
le steward, steward
le tableau *pl* **-x des départs** *m* **/ des arrivées** *f*, departures / arrivals board
le terminal *pl* **-aux**, terminal
la tour de contrôle *m*, control tower
le train d'atterrissage *m*, landing-gear
le trou d'air *m*, air pocket
la turbulence, turbulence
le vol (régulier / direct / intérieur / international *pl* **-aux)**, (scheduled / direct / domestic / international) flight (**la durée de vol**, flying time)

amerrir, to ditch / land on the sea
atterrir, to land
décoller, to take off
*descendre en piqué *m*, to nose-dive
*faire enregistrer, to register
*faire escale *f*, to stop over
*prendre / perdre de l'altitude *f*, to gain / lose height
survoler, to fly over
virer, to turn
voler, to fly (**voyager / *aller en avion** *m*, to fly [of people])

LES BATEAUX BOATS

l'aéroglisseur *m* **/ le hovercraft**, hovercraft
le bâbord, port (side)

le bac, river ferry

le bastingage, rail / railings

le bateau *pl* **-x (à voiles** *f* **/ à moteur** *m***)**, sailing- /
motor)boat; **(le bateau / le canot de sauvetage** *m*,
lifeboat)

le bateau-mouche *pl* **-x -s**, water-bus

le bateau-pilote *pl* **-x -s**, pilot boat

la bouée, buoy

le bureau *pl* **-x du commissaire**, purser's office

la cabine, cabin

le canot (automobile), (motor) launch

le capitaine, captain

le cargo, freighter

la ceinture de sauvetage *m*, lifebelt

la cheminée, funnel

la croisière, cruise

l'embarcation *f* **(de sauvetage** *m***)**, (ship's) lifeboat
(le pont des embarcations, boat-deck)

le (car)ferry, (car) ferry

le gilet de sauvetage *m*, life-jacket

le gouvernail, rudder / helm

l'hydroptère *m* **/ l'hydrofoil** *m*, hydrofoil

la jetée, jetty / pier

le (grand) large, the open sea **(au large de . . .**, off . . .)

le littoral *pl* **-aux**, coast(line)

la marée (basse / haute), (low / high) tide

le marin / le matelot, sailor

le mât, mast

le médecin de bord, ship's doctor

la mer, sea

le navire / le paquebot, liner

la passerelle, gangway **(la passerelle de
commandement** *m*, bridge)

le pavillon, flag [on boat]

le pont, deck

le port, port

la poupe, stern

la proue, bow(s)

le quai, quay

le radeau *pl* -**x**, raft
le remorqueur, tug
la traversée, crossing
le tribord, starboard (side)
le vaisseau *pl* -**x** / le bâtiment, vessel
le vapeur, steamer
le voilier, sailing-ship

accoster, to dock
*aller / voyager en bateau *m*, to sail
s'embarquer, to go on board (**embarquer**, to embark / take on board)
débarquer, to go ashore / put ashore
décharger, to unload
jeter / lever l'ancre *f*, to drop / raise the anchor
passer en bac *m*, to ferry across
*prendre le large, to put to sea

LES BUS ET LES CARS BUSES AND COACHES

l'abri-bus *m*; *pl* -**s** -, bus-shelter
l'arrêt *m* de bus *m* / de car *m*, bus- / coach-stop (**fixe**, compulsory; **facultatif**, request)
le bus / l'autobus *m*, bus
le car / l'autocar *m*, coach
la carte d'abonnement *m* / la carte orange, season ticket
la carte hebdomadaire, weekly season
le conducteur, driver
le contrôleur, inspector
la fréquence, frequency
la gare routière / l'autogare *f*, coach station
la section, stage
le terminus, terminus
le ticket, ticket
le voyageur *f* -**euse** / le passager *f* -**gère**, pasenger

LE MÉTRO THE UNDERGROUND

la bouche de métro, entrance [to underground] (**la bouche**, mouth)

le carnet, book of tickets
la correspondance, connection
la direction, direction
l'escalier *m* **roulant**, escalator
la ligne, line
la place assise / debout, seat / standing-place
le plan du réseau *pl* **-x**, network map
la rame, train
le resquilleur *f* **-euse**, fare dodger
la station, station
le ticket / le titre de transport *m*, ticket (**valable**, valid)
le tunnel, tunnel

LES TAXIS TAXIS

le chauffeur, driver
le fiacre, horse-drawn cab
le pourboire, tip
le prix de la course, fare (**payer la course**, to pay the fare)
le taxi, taxi (**appeler / *prendre un taxi**, to call / take a taxi; ***aller en taxi**, to go by taxi; **libre**, free; **occupé**, taken)
le taximètre, taximeter

SEE ALSO: **Accidents; Directions; Holidays; Towns; War, Peace, and the Armed Services**

55. War, Peace, and the Armed Services
La Guerre, la paix, et les militaires

La guerre War

l'**abri** *m* (**antiaérien** *f* **-enne** / **antiatomique**), (air-raid / nuclear) shelter

l'**allié** *m*; *f* **-ée**, ally

l'**approvisionnement** *m* / les **vivres** *m*, supplies

l'**attaque** *f*, attack (**lancer une attaque**, to launch an attack; la **contre-attaque**, counter-attack)

la **bataille**, battle (**livrer bataille**, to give battle; le **champ de bataille**, battlefield)

la **blessure**, wound

le **blocus**, blockade

le **bombardement**, bombardment

le **camouflage**, camouflage

la **campagne**, campaign

la **capitulation**, capitulation

le **château** *pl* **-x** (**fort**), (fortified) castle (le **créneau** *pl* **-x**, battlement)

les **civils** *m*, civilians

le **combat**, combat / fight

la **conquête**, conquest

la **cruauté**, cruelty

la **défaite**, defeat

le **déserteur**, deserter

l'**échec** *m*, failure

l'**engagement** *m*, enlistment

l'**ennemi** *m*; *f* **-ie**, enemy

l'**espion** *m*; *f* **-onne**, spy

l'**évacuation** *f*, evacuation

l'**exploit** *m*, feat / exploit

le **feu** *pl* **-x**, fire / firing

la forteresse, fortress

le front, the front (**l'arrière** *m*, the rear)

le gaz (lacrymogène / toxique), (tear- / poison) gas (**le masque à gaz,** gas-mark)

la gloire, glory

la guerre (mondiale), (world) war (**la guerre aérienne,** air warfare)

le héros *m*; *f* **l'héroïne,** hero / heroine (**l'héroïsme** *m*, heroism)

l'interrogatoire *m*, interrogation

l'invasion *f*, invasion

la marche (forcée), forced march

le massacre, massacre

la mobilisation, mobilization

le moral, morale

la mort, death

les munitions *f*, munitions / ammunition

les mutilés *m* **de guerre,** war wounded

l'occupation *f*, occupation

l'offensive *f*, offensive

l'otage *always m*, hostage (**la rançon,** ransom)

l'OTAN *f* **(organisation du traité de l'Atlantique nord),** NATO (North Atlantic Treaty Organisation)

le pillage, pillage (**le butin,** booty)

le prisonnier *f* **-ière,** prisoner (**la captivité,** capitivity)

le raid, raid (**le raid de bombardement** *m*, bombing raid)

la reconnaissance, reconnaissance

le rempart, rampart

les renforts *m*, reinforcements

la résistance, resistance

les retombées *f* **radioactives,** radioactive fall-out

la retraite, retreat

le service militaire, military service

le siège, siege

la stratégie, strategy

la tactique, tactics

la torture, torture

le traître *f* **-tresse,** traitor / traitress (**le peloton d'exécution** *f*, firing-squad)

la tranchée, trench
la victime *always f*, victim
la victoire, victory (**le vainqueur**, conqueror **les vaincus** *m*, the conquered)

*abattre, to shoot down
armer, to arm
attaquer, to attack
*battre, to beat (***battre en retraite** *f*, to beat a retreat)
se *battre, to fight
brûler, to burn
camoufler, to camouflage
capturer, to capture
charger, to load
cribler de, to riddle with
déclarer/*faire la guerre, to declare/make war
défendre, to defend
dévaster, to lay waste
entourer, to surround
envahir, to invade
*être à portée *f* (**de**)/**hors de portée**, to be within range (of)/out of range
*être de service *m*/**de garde** *f*, to be on duty/on guard
exploser, to explode
*faire sauter, to blow up
fortifier, to fortify
fusiller qn., to shoot sb.
gagner/perdre du terrain, to gain/lose ground
lutter, to struggle
marcher, to march
mobiliser, to mobilize
munir de, to provide with
pointer, to aim
*poursuivre, to pursue
protéger, to protect
raser, to raze
reculer, to fall back
se rendre, to surrender
renforcer, to reinforce
résister à, to resist

*souffrir, to suffer
suffoquer, to suffocate
tirer, to shoot / fire
torpiller, to torpedo
viser, to aim

blessé, wounded
disparu, missing
guerrier *f* **-ière**, warlike
héroïque, heroic
indemne, unscathed
meurtrier *f* **-ière**, deadly
sanglant, bloody
sans défense *f*, defenceless
tué, killed

La paix   Peace

l'armistice *m*, armistice
la conférence, conference
le désarmement (nucléaire), (nuclear) disarmament
les droits *m* **de l'homme**, human rights (**l'homme** *m*, man)
la liberté, freedom
la mise en vigueur *f*, enforcement [literally, *putting into force*]
la négociation, negotiation
la neutralité, neutrality
le pacifisme, pacifism
le pacte, pact
la paix, peace (**en paix**, at peace; ***faire la paix avec**, to make peace with)
les réparations *f*, reparations
la trêve, truce
le traité, treaty

accorder, to grant
*convenir, to agree
dédommager, to compensate
garantir, to guarantee
ratifier, to ratify
signer, to sign

L'armée et l'armée de l'air
The army and the air force

l'armée *f* **(de terre)**, army (**la terre**, land; **l'armée
permanente**, regular army; **l'armée de l'air** *m*, air force)
l'artillerie *f*, artillery
l'avancement *m*, promotion (***être promu . . .**, to be
promoted to the rank of . . .)
la base aérienne, air-force base
le camp, camp
la cantine, canteen
la caserne, barracks
la cavalerie, cavalry
le champ de manœuvre *f*, parade-ground
le commandement, command
le congé / la permission, leave
le conseil de guerre *f*, court martial
le corps de garde *f*, guardroom
le défilé, march-past
la discipline, discipline (**se *mettre au garde-à-vous**, to
stand to attention)
les effectifs *m*, the total strength
le génie *sing*, engineers (**un soldat du génie**, an engineer)
le grade, rank
l'infanterie *f*, infantry
les manœuvres *f*, manœuvres
le mess, mess
la musique militaire, military band
l'ordre *m*, order
la patrouille, patrol
le quartier général *pl* **-aux**, headquarters
le réveil, reveille
la troupe, troop / body of soldiers (**les troupes**, troops)
l'unité *f*, unit

LE PERSONNEL PERSONNEL

l'ancien combattant *m*, ex-serviceman
l'aumônier *m* **militaire**, chaplain

le brancardier, stretcher-bearer (**le brancard**, stretcher)
le capitaine, captain / flight-lieutenant
le caporal *pl* **-aux**, corporal
le chasseur, light-infantryman
le colonel, colonel / group-captain
le commandant, commander / major / squadron-leader
le conscrit, conscript
le dragon, dragoon
le général *pl* **-aux d'armée** *f*, general / air chief-marshal
le général *pl* **-aux de brigade** *f*, brigadier / air commodore
le général pl **-aux de corps** *m* **d'armée** *f*, lieutenant-general / air marshal
le grenadier, grenadier
le lieutenant-colonel *pl* **-s -s**, lieutenant-colonel / wing commander
le maréchal *pl* **-aux (de France)**, field-marshal (**le maréchal de l'air** *m*, marshal of the air force)
l'officier *m*, officer
la recrue *always f*, recruit
la sentinelle *always f*, sentry
le sergent, sergeant
le soldat, soldier / private / airman (**le Soldat Inconnu**, the Unknown Warrior)
le sous-lieutenant *pl* **- -s**, second lieutenant / pilot officer
le sous-officier *pl* **- -s**, NCO

LES UNITÉS UNITS

le bataillon, battalion
la brigade, brigade
la compagnie, company
le corps, corps
la division, division
l'escadrille *f*, flight
l'escadron *m*, squadron
l'escouade *f*, squad
le régiment, regiment
la section, section

LES ARMES ARMAMENTS

l'avion *m* **de combat** *m* **/ de reconnaissance** *f* **/ à réaction** *f*, combat / reconnaissance / jet aircraft

la baïonnette, bayonet (***mettre / *remettre**, to fix / unfix)

la balle, bullet (**la cartouche**, cartridge)

le blindé, armoured vehicle

le bombardier, bomber [aircraft] / bomb-aimer

la bombe (atomique / au napalm / incendiaire / lacrymogène), (atomic / napalm / incendiary / tear-gas) bomb (**jeter / lancer une bombe**, to drop a bomb)

le canon, gun / cannon

la carabine, rifle

le char (d'assaut *m*) **/ le tank**, tank

le chasseur, fighter (aircraft) (**le chasseur-bombardier** *pl* **-s -s**, fighter-bomber)

la cible, target (**le coup au but**, hit; **le coup manqué**, miss)

la défense antiaérienne / la défense contre avions *m* **/ la DCA**, anti-aircraft defence (**le canon contre avions**, anti-aircraft gun)

l'épée *f*, sword (**tirer**, to draw; **le fourreau** *pl* **-x** scabbard)

la fusée, rocket

le fusil, gun (**le fusil-mitrailleur** *pl* **-s -s**, automatic rifle)

la grenade (à main *f*), hand-grenade

l'intercepteur *m*, interceptor aircraft

la mine, mine

le missile, missile

la mitrailleuse, machine-gun (**la mitraillette**, sub-machine-gun)

le mortier, mortar

l'obus *m*, shell (**l'obusier** *m*, howitzer)

le pistolet, pistol

le radar, radar

le revolver, revolver

La Marine The navy

l'arsenal *m* (**maritime**), naval dockyard
le bateau *pl* **-x**, boat
la boussole, compass
le carré, wardroom
la flotte, fleet
le hamac, hammock
la marine, navy
la mine, mine
le navire de guerre, warship
le pont de batterie *f*, gun deck
le quart, watch (***prendre le quart**, go on watch)
la torpille, torpedo
la tourelle, gun turret

LE PERSONNEL PERSONNEL

l'amiral *m*; *pl* **-aux**, admiral (**le vice-/contre-amiral**
pls **--aux**, vice-/rear-admiral)
l'aspirant *m*, midshipman/cadet
le capitaine de vaisseau *m*; *pl* **-x**, captain (**le capitaine de
frégate** *f*/**de corvette** *f*, lieutenant/lieutenant-
commander)
l'enseigne *m*, sub-lieutenant
le lieutenant de vaisseau *m*; *pl* **-x**, lieutenant
le (premier) maître, (chief) petty officer
le maître mécanicien, chief engineer
le marin/le matelot, sailor/able seaman
le mousse, cabin-boy

LES NAVIRES SHIPS

la corvette, corvette
le croiseur, cruiser
le cuirassé, battleship
la frégate, frigate
le mouilleur/dragueur de mines, minelayer/sweeper
le sous-marin *pl* **--s**, submarine

le torpilleur, destroyer
le vaisseau-amiral *pl* **-x -aux,** flagship

SEE ALSO: **Accidents; History; Politics; Science;
Transport**

56. The Weather Le Temps

Le temps qu'il fait The weather

l'air *m*, air (le courant d'air, draught; en plein air, in the open air)

l'amélioration *f*, improvement

l'atmosphère *f*, atmosphere (la pression atmosphérique, atmospheric pressure)

le baromètre, barometer (*monter / *descendre, to go up / down; au variable, changeable; au beau fixe, set fair)

la chaleur, heat

le changement, change

le ciel, sky

le climat, climate

le froid, cold

l'humidité *f*, humidity

la météo / les prévisions *f* météorologiques, weather forecast (le bulletin, report)

les précipitations *f*, precipitation

la sécheresse, dryness / drought

la température, temperature

le (beau / mauvais) temps, (fine / bad) weather (le temps est à l'orage / à la pluie, there's thunder / rain about; l'orage *m*, storm)

le thermomètre, thermometer (le degré, degree)

la visibilité, visibility

Quel temps fait-il? What's the weather like?

il fait . . ., it's . . .

  beau, fine

  chaud, hot (j'ai chaud, I'm hot)

  de l'orage *m*, stormy

  doux, mild

  du brouillard, foggy

du soleil, sunny
du vent, windy
frais, cool
froid, cold (**j'ai froid**, I'm cold)
humide, damp
jour, daylight
lourd, close / muggy
mauvais, bad
nuit, dark

le temps est / il fait un temps . . ., the weather is . . .
le ciel est . . ., the sky is . . .
agréable, pleasant
brumeux, foggy / misty
couvert, overcast
dégagé, clear
ensoleillé, sunny
épouvantable, dreadful
étouffant, stifling
glacial, icy
humide, damp
infect, foul
nuageux / ennuagé, cloudy
orageux, stormy
pluvieux, rainy
variable, changeable

s'améliorer, to get better
s'apaiser, to die down
briller, to shine
cesser, to stop
changer, to change
crépiter, to patter / rattle
se dissiper, to lift / blow over
s'éclaircir, to clear up
empirer, to get worse
fondre, to melt
geler, to freeze (**il gèle**, it is freezing; **je gèle / je suis gelé(e)**, I'm freezing; **la glace**, ice; **le glaçon**, icicle)
grêler, to hail

menacer, to threaten
neiger, to snow (**il neige**, it is snowing)
*pleuvoir, to rain (**il pleut**, it is raining; **il pleut à verse**, it's pouring)
*prévoir, to forecast
se *remettre au beau, to turn fine again
souffler, to blow
tonner, to thunder

à l'ombre *f*, in the shade
au chaud, in a warm place
au soleil, in the sun
par beau temps, in good weather
sous la pluie / la neige, in the rain / snow

Les phénomènes météorologiques
Weather phenomena

l'arc-en-ciel *m*; *pl* -s - -, rainbow
l'avalanche *f*, avalanche
l'averse *f* / **l'ondée** *f*, shower
la bise, north wind
la bourrasque, squall
la brise, breeze
le brouillard, fog (**il y a du brouillard**, it's foggy)
la brume, mist
la canicule / la vague de chaleur *f*, heat wave (**les jours** *m* **caniculaires**, dog-days)
le crachin / la bruine, drizzle
le cyclone, cyclone
le dégel, thaw
le déluge, downpour of rain / flood
l'éclaircie *f*, bright interval
la foudre, lightning (**l'éclair** *m*, flash of lightning)
le froid, cold (**un coup de froid**, a cold snap; **le froid rude**, bitter cold)
la gelée / le gel, frost (**une forte gelée**, a hard frost; **la gelée blanche / le givre**, hoar frost)

la giboulée (de mars), (April) shower

la grêle, hail (**le grêlon**, hailstone)

le grésil, sleet

l'inondation *f*, flood

la neige, snow (**la neige fondue**, slush; **le flocon de neige**, snowflake; **la chute de neige**, snowfall; **la boule de neige**, snowball; **le bonhomme de neige**, snowman; **la congère**, snowdrift)

le nuage, cloud (**la couche de nuages**, cloud layer)

l'orage *m*, thunderstorm

l'ouragan *m*, hurricane

la pluie, rain (**les gouttes** *f* **de pluie**, raindrops)

la rafale, gust of wind (**la rafale de neige** *f*, snow flurry)

la rosée, dew

le soleil, sun (**le rayon de soleil**, sunbeam; **il y a du soleil**, it's sunny)

la tempête (de neige), (snow)storm

le tonnerre, thunder (**le coup de tonnerre**, thunderclap; **le paratonnerre**, lightning-conductor)

la tornade, tornado

le tourbillon, whirlwind

la vague de chaleur *f*, heat wave

le vent (du sud), (south) wind (**le coup / la bouffée de vent**, gust / puff of wind)

le verglas, black ice

SEE ALSO: **Accidents; Clothing; Disasters; Holidays; Nature**